Making Systems Safer

T0137750

Related titles:

Towards System Safety
Proceedings of the Seventh Safety-critical Systems Symposium, Huntingdon, UK, 1999
Redmill and Anderson (Eds)
1-85233-064-3

Lessons in System Safety
Proceedings of the Eighth Safety-critical Systems Symposium, Southampton, UK, 2000
Redmill and Anderson (Eds)
1-85233-249-2

Aspects of Safety Management
Proceedings of the Ninth Safety-critical Systems Symposium, Bristol, UK, 2001
Redmill and Anderson (Eds)
1-85233-411-8

Components of System Safety
Proceedings of the Tenth Safety-critical Systems Symposium, Southampton, UK, 2002
Redmill and Anderson (Eds)
1-85233-561-0

Current Issues in Safety-critical Systems
Proceedings of the Eleventh Safety-critical Systems Symposium, Bristol, UK, 2003
Redmill and Anderson (Eds)
1-85233-696-X

Practical Elements of Safety
Proceedings of the Twelfth Safety-critical Systems Symposium, Birmingham, UK, 2004
Redmill and Anderson (Eds)
1-85233-800-8

Constituents of Modern System-safety Thinking
Proceedings of the Thirteenth Safety-critical Systems Symposium, Southampton, UK, 2005
Redmill and Anderson (Eds)
1-85233-952-7

Developments in Risk-based Approaches to Safety
Proceedings of the Fourteenth Safety-critical Systems Symposium, Bristol, UK, 2006
Redmill and Anderson (Eds)
1-84628-333-7

The Safety of Systems
Proceedings of the Fifteenth Safety-critical Systems Symposium, Bristol, UK, 2007
Redmill and Anderson (Eds)
978-1-84628-805-0

Improvements in System Safety
Proceedings of the Sixteenth Safety-critical Systems Symposium, Bristol, UK, 2008
Redmill and Anderson (Eds)
978-1-84800-099-5

Safety-Critical Systems: Problems, Process and Practice
Proceedings of the Seventeenth Safety-Critical Systems Symposium, Brighton, UK, 2009
Dale and Anderson (Eds)
978-1-84882-348-8

Chris Dale · Tom Anderson
Editors

Making Systems Safer

Proceedings of the Eighteenth Safety-Critical
Systems Symposium, Bristol, UK,
9–11th February 2010

Safety-Critical
Systems Club

The publication of these proceedings is
sponsored by BAE Systems plc

BAE SYSTEMS

 Springer

Editors
Chris Dale
Dale Research Ltd
33 North Street
Martock
United Kingdom TA12 6DH
chris.dale@scsc.org.uk

Prof. Tom Anderson
Centre for Software Reliability
Newcastle University
Newcastle upon Tyne
United Kingdom NE1 7RU

ISBN 978-1-84996-085-4   e-ISBN 978-1-84996-086-1
DOI 10.1007/978-1-84996-086-1
Springer London Heidelberg Dordrecht New York

British Library Cataloguing in Publication Data
A catalogue record for this book is available from the British Library

Library of Congress Control Number: 2009942251

© Springer-Verlag London Limited 2010
Apart from any fair dealing for the purposes of research or private study, or criticism or review, as permitted under the Copyright, Designs and Patents Act 1988, this publication may only be reproduced, stored or transmitted, in any form or by any means, with the prior permission in writing of the publishers, or in the case of reprographic reproduction in accordance with the terms of licenses issued by the Copyright Licensing Agency. Enquiries concerning reproduction outside those terms should be sent to the publishers.
The use of registered names, trademarks, etc., in this publication does not imply, even in the absence of a specific statement, that such names are exempt from the relevant laws and regulations and therefore free for general use.
The publisher makes no representation, express or implied, with regard to the accuracy of the information contained in this book and cannot accept any legal responsibility or liability for any errors or omissions that may be made.

Printed on acid-free paper

Springer is part of Springer Science+Business Media (www.springer.com)

Preface

The Safety-critical Systems Symposium (SSS), held each February for eighteen consecutive years, offers a full-day tutorial followed by two days of presentations of papers. This book of Proceedings contains all the papers presented at SSS 2010.

The first paper accompanies the tutorial, which focuses on modern developments in formal methods and automated verification and their application to safety assurance in both standards-driven and argument-based safety cases.

The Symposium is for engineers, managers, and academics in the field of systems safety, across all industry sectors, so its papers always cover a range of topics. The eighteen years the Symposium has been running have seen a steady maturing of the discipline, but there is still room for heated debate in areas of controversy, for research into new methods and processes, and for critical examination of past work to identify improvements that are needed – as is clear from the three papers in the opening session of the event.

The management of projects developing safety-critical systems poses particular challenges. Two papers report research and experience in this important area.

Transport safety has been a perennial theme at the Symposium over the years. This time, there are papers on safety in the air and on the roads.

Another recurring theme is that of safety standards, a very active field in its own right. Papers at this year's Symposium consider standards in a number of sectors, including air traffic management, defence and healthcare.

Clearly, competence plays an important role in ensuring systems safety. People from many disciplines come together in the development of safety-critical systems. But how can their collective competences be properly managed? What guidelines are needed to define these competences? And what about the competence of the safety assessors? These issues are discussed in three papers grouped together under the safety competences heading.

The final section addresses developments in safety methods, looking in particular at the challenges posed by the increasing use of COTS (Commercial Off The Shelf) components in safety-critical systems, and at hazard management.

This year's authors have, as usual, delivered informative material touching on many of the topics that are of current concern to the safety-critical systems community, and we are grateful to them for their contributions. We also thank our sponsors for their valuable support, and the exhibitors at the Symposium's tools and services fair for their participation. And we thank Joan Atkinson and her team for laying the event's foundation through their exemplary planning and organisation.

CD & TA
October 2009

THE SAFETY-CRITICAL SYSTEMS CLUB

organiser of the

Safety-critical Systems Symposium

What is the Safety-Critical Systems Club?

This 'Community' Club exists to support developers and operators of systems that may have an impact on safety, across all industry sectors. It is an independent, non-profit organisation that co-operates with all bodies involved with safety-critical systems.

Objectives

The Club's two principal objectives are to raise awareness of safety issues in the field of safety-critical systems and to facilitate the transfer of safety technology from wherever it exists.

History

The Club was inaugurated in 1991 under the sponsorship of the UK's Department of Trade and Industry (DTI) and the Engineering and Physical Sciences Research Council (EPSRC). Its secretariat is in the Centre for Software Reliability (CSR) at Newcastle University, and its Meetings Coordinator is Chris Dale of Dale Research Ltd. Felix Redmill of Redmill Consultancy is the Newsletter Editor.

Since 1994 the Club has been self-sufficient, but it retains the active support of the EPSRC, as well as that of the Health and Safety Executive, the Institution of Engineering and Technology, and the British Computer Society. All of these bodies are represented on the Club's Steering Group.

The Club's activities

The Club achieves its goals of awareness-raising and technology transfer by focusing on current and emerging practices in safety engineering, software engineering, and standards that relate to safety in processes and products. Its activities include:

- Running the annual Safety-critical Systems Symposium each February (the first was in 1993), with Proceedings published by Springer-Verlag;

- Organising a number of full day seminars each year;
- Providing tutorials on relevant subjects;
- Publishing a newsletter, *Safety Systems*, three times annually (since 1991), in January, May and September; and
- A web-site http://www.scsc.org.uk providing member services, including a safety tools directory.

Education and communication

The Club brings together technical and managerial personnel within all sectors of the safety-critical-systems community. Its events provide education and training in principles and techniques, and it facilitates the dissemination of lessons within and between industry sectors. It promotes an inter-disciplinary approach to the engineering and management of safety, and it provides a forum for experienced practitioners to meet each other and for the exposure of newcomers to the safety-critical systems industry.

Influence on research

The Club facilitates communication among researchers, the transfer of technology from researchers to users, feedback from users, and the communication of experience between users. It provides a meeting point for industry and academia, a forum for the presentation of the results of relevant projects, and a means of learning and keeping up-to-date in the field.

The Club thus helps to achieve more effective research, a more rapid and effective transfer and use of technology, the identification of best practice, the definition of requirements for education and training, and the dissemination of information. Importantly, it does this within a 'club' atmosphere rather than a commercial environment.

Membership

Members pay a reduced fee (well below the commercial level) for events and receive the newsletter and other mailed information. Not being sponsored, the Club depends on members' subscriptions: these can be paid at the first meeting attended, and are almost always paid by the individual's employer.

To join, please contact Mrs Joan Atkinson at: The Centre for Software Reliability, Newcastle University, Newcastle upon Tyne, NE1 7RU, UK; Telephone: +44 191 221 2222; Fax: +44 191 222 7995; Email: csr@newcastle.ac.uk.

Contents

Safety Standards

Safety Competencies

Safety Methods

Tutorial Paper

Formalism in Safety Cases

John Rushby

Computer Science Laboratory, SRI International

Menlo Park, California, USA

Abstract Suitable formalisms could allow the arguments of a safety case to be checked mechanically. We examine some of the issues in doing so.

1 Introduction

A safety case provides an *argument* that a system is safe to deploy; the notion of 'safe' is made precise in suitable *claims* about the system and its context of deployment, and the argument is intended to substantiate these claims, based on *evidence* concerning the system and its design and construction. The approach can be applied recursively, so that substantiated claims about a subsystem can be used as evidence in a parent case. Evaluators examine the case and may certify the system if they are persuaded that the claims are appropriate, the evidence is valid, and the argument is correct.

The safety case approach to safety certification may be contrasted with the standards-based approach, where the applicant is recommended or required to follow certain guidelines and standards. These generally specify the development and assurance processes that should be used, the intermediate artifacts to be produced (requirements, specifications, test plans etc.), the kinds of reviews, tests, and analyses that should be performed, and the documentation that should record all of these.

The intellectual foundations for the two approaches are fundamentally very similar: we can think of the social process that generates guidelines and standards as constructing a generic safety case; documentation of the required processes and products for a particular system then constitutes the evidence for an instantiation of this case. The main difference is that the argument (and often the claims, too) are *implicit* in the standards-based approach: they presumably inform the internal debate that decides what evidence the standard should require, but are not formulated explicitly, nor recorded.

Although fundamentally similar, the two approaches do have their own advantages and disadvantages. Standards-based approaches generally incorporate much accumulated experience and community wisdom, and they establish a solid 'floor'

C. Dale, T. Anderson (eds.), *Making Systems Safer*, DOI 10.1007/978-1-84996-086-1_1,
© Springer-Verlag London Limited 2010

so that systems developed and assured according to their prescriptions are very likely to be adequately safe. On the other hand, standards tend to be slow-moving and conservative, and can be a barrier to innovation in both system design and in methods for assurance. Furthermore, a generic standard may not be well-tuned to the specifics of any given system – so that its application may be excessively onerous in some areas, yet provide insufficient scrutiny in others.

An explicit safety case can be customized very precisely for the specific characteristics of the system concerned, and therefore has the potential to provide stronger assurance for safety than a standards-based approach, and at lower cost (by eliminating unnecessary effort). Safety cases can also be more agile, allowing greater innovation than standards-based methods.

However, some observers express concern over the reliability of judgements about the quality of a safety case, particularly if some of its elements are novel. One experienced practitioner told me that he feared that regimes lacking a strong safety culture would accept almost any safety case, after demonstrating diligence by probing minor details. Of course, true diligence and competence and a strong safety ethic are required in the performance and evaluation of standards-based approaches as well as safety cases, but the social process that generates standards, and the infrastructure and skill base that develops around them, may provide a stronger support base than is available for a solitary safety case. On the other hand, the motivation for introducing safety cases in the first place came from investigations into a number of disasters where traditional approaches were deemed to have failed (Kelly 1998). Perusal of recent aircraft accident and incident reports (e.g., ATSB 2007, AAIB 2007) certainly erodes complacency about the standards-based approach employed for airborne software (RTCA 1992).

We may conclude that safety cases seem to be the better approach in principle, but that it could be worthwhile to enquire if there might be some systematic processes that could help increase confidence in the soundness of a given case. Now, a safety case is an argument, and the branch of intellectual inquiry that focuses on arguments is *logic*, with *formal* logic allowing the checking – or generation – of certain kinds of arguments to be reduced to calculation, and thereby automated. So, this paper will explore some of the opportunities and challenges in applying formalism to safety cases. It is written from my personal perspective – which is as a practitioner of formal methods – and may not coincide with the views of those with more experience in safety cases. My hope is that it will help develop a dialogue between these two bodies of knowledge and experience.

The next section considers the top-level argument of a safety case; this is followed by consideration of lower-level arguments, and then probabilistic arguments. The paper concludes with a summary and suggestions for further research.

2 The Top-Level Argument

The concepts, notations, and tools that have been developed for representing, managing, and inspecting safety cases (e.g., Kelly and Weaver 2004, Bishop et al. 2004) provide strong support for structuring the argument of a safety case. Nonetheless, the safety case for a real system is a very large object and one wonders how reliably a human reviewer can evaluate such an argument: consider the thought experiment of slightly perturbing a sound case so that it becomes unsound and ask how confident can we be that a human reviewer would detect the flaws in the perturbed case. These concerns are not merely speculative: Greenwell and colleagues found flaws in several cases that they examined (Greenwell et al. 2006).

Although a safety case is an argument, it will generally contain elements that are not simple logical deductions: some elements of the argument will be probabilistic, some will enumerate over a set that is imperfectly known (e.g., '*all* hazards are adequately handled'), and others will appeal to expert judgement or historical experience. All of these are likely to require human review. While suggesting that there may be benefits in formalizing elements of a safety case, I do not propose that we should eliminate or replace those elements that may be difficult to formalize. Rather, my proposal is that by formalizing the elements that do lend themselves to this process, we may be able to reduce some of the analysis to mechanized calculation, thereby preserving the precious resource of expert human review for those elements that truly do require it. Furthermore, formalization of some elements may allow the context for human reviews (e.g., assumptions) to be more precisely articulated and checked.

By formalization and calculation, I mean representing elements of the argument in a formal notation that is supported by strong and automated methods of deduction – that is, theorem proving. I do not see good prospects for adoption of formalization in safety cases, nor much value in doing so, unless it is supported by pushbutton automation. Fortunately, I believe the prospects for achieving this are good: the arguments in a safety case are not intricate ones that tax a theorem prover – they are large, but simple.

An important choice is the logical system in which to formalize safety case arguments. Experiments and experience will be needed to make a well-informed decision, but I can suggest some considerations. On the one hand, we should choose a logic and theories that are supported by pushbutton automation, and on the other, we need a choice that is able to express the kinds of arguments used in a safety case. To make this concrete, here is the top level of an argument examined by Holloway (Holloway 2008):

'The control system is acceptably safe, given a definition of acceptably safe, because all identified hazards have been eliminated or sufficiently mitigated and the software has been developed to the integrity levels appropriate to the hazards involved.'

We can decompose and slightly restructure this into the following elements.

1. We have a `system` in an `environment`, and a safety `claim` about these, and the claim is appropriate for that system in that environment.
2. There is a set `hset` of hazards, and the members of this set are all the hazards relevant to the claim for the system in its environment.
3. The system `handles` all members of the set `hset` of hazards.

   Note: I have restructured the prose argument here: my notion of 'handles' includes either elimination or mitigation of each hazard and, for the latter, assurance that the software has been developed to a suitable integrity level. The decomposition into elimination and mitigation-plus-integrity will be performed at a later stage of the argument.
4. Satisfaction of the preceding items is sufficient to ensure that the system is safe in its environment.

We can formalize item 1 as

```
appropriate(claim, system, env)
```

where `claim`, `system`, and `env` are uninterpreted constants, and `appropriate` is an uninterpreted predicate. *Uninterpreted* means that no properties are known about these entities (other than that they are distinct from each other), apart from what we might introduce through axioms; this is in contrast to *interpreted* types and predicates (such as `integer`, or `iszero`) whose meaning is built-in to the theories of the logical system concerned. We can informally attach interpretations to the symbols (e.g., `system` means 'the system under consideration'), or we can do so formally by supplying axioms or formal *theory interpretations*. If the formal elaborations are done correctly (and part of what a theorem prover does is check that we do do it correctly), then anything we can prove about the uninterpreted constants remains true of their interpretations.

Here, the justification that the particular claim is appropriate presumably rests on precedent, legislation, experience, and judgement, and will be documented suitably. We can introduce an uninterpreted constant `approp_claim_doc` to represent existence of this documentation, and the documentation itself can be attached to the constant. Attachments are used quite widely in AI and in formal verification (e.g., Crow et al. 2001), usually to provide a computational interpretation to some term, in which case they are called 'semantic attachments'. Here, we have 'documentation attachments' and a theorem prover could easily be augmented to assemble or cite the documentation that supports a particular chain of deduction. Mere existence of documentation is insufficient, however: the developers, reviewers, or evaluators of the safety case need to record their judgement that it is adequate. We can allow for this by an uninterpreted predicate `good_doc` and the following axiom.

```
good_doc(approp_claim_doc)
  IMPLIES appropriate(claim, system, env)
```

The reviewers can indicate their assent by adding `good_doc(approp_claim_doc)` as an axiom; the theorem prover will then derive `appropriate(claim, system, env)` by forward chaining. The triviality of the deduction here does not negate its value: it provides a computationally effective way to record the existence of documentation, the evidence that it supports, and a judgement about its adequacy. By introducing variants to `good_doc`, we can distinguish the developers' judgement from those of the reviewers or evaluators.

We can formalize item 2 in a similar way as

```
hset = allhazards(claim, system, env)
```

where `allhazards` is an uninterpreted function whose informal interpretation is that its value is the set of all hazards to the claim about the system in its environment.

Then item 3 becomes

```
FORALL h IN hset: handles(system, h)
```

where `handles` is an uninterpreted predicate whose informal interpretation is that the system successfully eliminates or mitigates the hazard `h`, and `FORALL...IN...` is universal quantification (a concept from logic).

Item 4 can be expressed as

```
safe(claim, env, system)
```

where `safe` is an uninterpreted predicate whose informal interpretation is that the system is acceptably safe.

The structure of the top-level argument is then expressed in the following axiom.

```
LET hset = allhazards(claim, system, env) IN
   appropriate(claim, system, env)
      AND FORALL h IN hset: handles(system, h)
   IMPLIES safe(claim, env, system)
```

where `AND` and `IMPLIES` are the logical symbols for conjunction and material implication, respectively, and are written in upper case simply to distinguish them from what logicians call the 'nonlogical' symbols. The `LET...IN` construction is syntactic sugar that can be eliminated by simply replacing all instances of the left hand side by the right.

This axiom actually expresses one of several general tactics for constructing a safety case: namely, enumerating the hazards and showing that each is handled effectively. This general tactic could be expressed by replacing the constants claim, system, and env by variables (free variables are assumed to be universally quantified). The axiom shown above would then be an instantiation of the general tactic.

The next step in this example is to record the process of hazard identification. This is one of the most important elements of a safety case, and one that depends crucially on human judgement. Although formalization cannot and should not aim to replace this judgement and its supporting processes, it should record them, and lend calculational assistance where feasible. Human judgement in identification of hazards is usually supported by systematic but manual processes such as checklists, HAZOP/guidewords, or functional hazard analysis (FHA). Evidence that all hazards have been identified is generally by reference to documentation describing conformance with an accepted process or standard for performing hazard analysis.

In our example, we could express this in the following axiom.

```
good_doc(hazard_doc) IMPLIES
    allhazards(goal, system, env) = {: H1, H2, H3 :}
```

where H1, H2, and H3, are the (otherwise undescribed) hazards named by Holloway, {: ... :} is the extensional set constructor, and hazard_doc is an uninterpreted constant associated with the documentation of the hazard analysis performed. As before, the predicate good_doc is used to indicate that human review, and other processes that might be required, concur that the documentation attached to hazard_doc does indeed establish that the hazards are just the three identified. We indicate that this 'signoff' has been achieved by asserting good_doc(hazard_doc) as an axiom.

Observe that we have chosen to use the function allhazards, which returns the set of hazards. An alternative would be to quantify over all possible hazards and have a predicate ishazard that identifies those that are true hazards. These seem almost equivalent from a logical point of view, but reflect a different balance between formalism and judgement. As mentioned previously, identification of hazards is one of the most delicate and important judgements required in a safety case, and formalization should be done in a way that respects that judgement. Quantifying over all potential hazards and picking those that are true hazards carries the implication that there is some objective, external set of potential hazards – which is not so. In the formalization used here, the 'mystery' of hazard identification is hidden inside the allhazards function, where it will be described and justified – as it should be – as the application of human judgement, aided by a systematic, but informal process.

We will take this example just one step further. Holloway's description states that hazard analysis determines that hazard H2 has potentially catastrophic consequences, and that the acceptable probability of such hazards is 1×10^{-6} per year. These can be recorded in the following axioms.

```
good_doc(hazard_doc) IMPLIES
  severity(H2) = catastrophic

max_prob(catastrophic) = 1/1000000
```

We can then state that a general tactic for mitigating hazards is to use fault tree analysis to show that their maximum probability of occurrence does not exceed that established for their severity level, and that the *integrity level* of the system software is at least that required for the given severity level. We can state this as a generalized axiom (with variables) as follows.

```
mitigate(s, h) =
  fta(s, h) <= max_prob(severity(h))
    AND integrity(s, h) >= sil(severity(h))

mitigate(s, h) IMPLIES handles(s, h)
```

Here, s and h are variables representing a system and a hazard; fta is an uninterpreted function whose value is informally understood to be the probability of hazard h in system s, integrity is an uninterpreted function whose value is the integrity level of the software in s with respect to hazard h, and max_prob and sil give the required maximum probability and minimum integrity level for the severity level of h. Furthermore, we assert that mitigation is an acceptable way to handle a hazard.

We will then instantiate these general axioms for the case of our system and hazard H2, and assert axioms such as the following.

```
sil(catastrophic) = 5

good_doc(H2_fta_doc) IMPLIES
  fta(system, H2) <= 1/1000000

good_doc(H2_integrity_doc) IMPLIES
  integrity(system, H2) = 5
```

Here, H2_fta_doc is documentation that describes the fault tree analysis performed and justifies the claim that this establishes the given probability; similarly, H2_integrity_doc is documentation that justifies the claim that the software satisfies the requirements for integrity level 5 (in some scale).

My purpose in sketching this formalization is simply to identify suitable logics and theories in which to frame it. What is used in this example so far is first order logic (with set theory), which is undecidable and so cannot be automated in its full generality. However, various fragments of this logic are decidable and have been found to be pragmatically adequate for most purposes. In particular, the unquantified fragment with uninterpreted symbols and equality is decidable. The example does use quantification, but only in elementary ways that are easily automated.

Thus, my conclusion is that to describe safety case arguments, we need a formalism that includes quantification, uninterpreted predicates and constants, set theory, and arithmetic – but the theorem proving needs pushbutton automation only for the unquantified case. These capabilities are (a subset of) the capabilities of formalisms built on, or employing, SMT solvers (i.e., solvers for the problem of Satisfiability Modulo Theories) (Rushby 2006). Modern SMT solvers are very effective, often able to solve problems with hundreds of variables and thousands of constraints in seconds. They are the subject of an annual competition, and this has driven very rapid improvement in both their performance and the range of theories over which they operate.

Many specification and modeling formalisms are able to use SMT solvers to provide pushbutton automation. One example is the PVS verification system, which uses the Yices SMT solver (both of these are from my institution (SRI 2009)). The formalization of the example safety case shown above can be typed into PVS almost verbatim and checked in seconds. PVS is actually a higher order logic, and this allows a particularly straightforward mechanization of the simple set theory used in the example (sets are predicates). PVS is able to report the axioms actually used in the construction of a proof: for a fuller version of Holloway's example, PVS reports that it uses the top-level tactic of enumeration over hazards (shown above), and the lower-level tactics of eliminating and mitigating hazards (the latter also shown above), plus the axioms associating probabilities and integrity levels with hazard severities (also shown above). PVS also enumerates the good_doc axioms required to discharge the claims made in the case: these must justify the appropriateness of the claim, the identification of hazards and their severity, the elimination of the hazard H1 (by formal verification), the probability of occurrence (by fault tree analysis) of hazards H2 and H3, and the integrity level of associated software.

3 Lower-Level Arguments

Our formalization of Holloway's example safety case involves only the most abstract treatment of the system itself. Lower levels of the case, however, will be very much concerned with details of its design and implementation, and the assumptions underlying these. Formal verification is a very well-understood application of formal methods to those concerns. In formal verification, we develop detailed formal models of algorithms, designs, or programs, and use theorem proving, model checking, or other methods of automated deduction to show that these have desired properties. Verification systems such as PVS have been used to verify important properties of significant designs (e.g., Miner et al. 2004). However, PVS and its like are general purpose – that is why they can model abstract safety cases – and greater automation in verification of software systems and their designs can be achieved using notations and techniques specialized to these tasks. Tools employing these are generally referred to as 'model checkers', even though most are not model checkers in the strict sense used by logicians. A particularly interesting type of tool in this class is an 'infinite bounded model checker', such as the one in the SAL suite developed in my institution (SRI 2009). Infinite bounded model checkers make very effective use of SMT solvers and thereby provide very powerful automation.

The models verified by model checkers are usually very detailed and explicit – equivalent to executable programs. However, and this is not widely understood, infinite bounded model checkers can be applied to rather abstract descriptions that use uninterpreted functions to hide detail. This is feasible because the underlying SMT solvers provide effective automation for this theory. Properties can be attached to the uninterpreted functions by means of axioms supplied directly to the SMT solver or, indirectly, by synchronous observers attached to the model supplied to the model checker (Rushby 2009a).

The value in applying formal verification to very abstract designs is that this can be used to automate, or provide automated assistance for, some kinds of safety analyses traditionally performed informally. Many of these analyses can be thought of as informal ways to examine all the possible states of a system, to see if any are unsafe or otherwise undesirable. The reachable states of any interesting system are vast, if not infinite, in number. To examine the reachable states in reasonable time using unaided informal reasoning, we group many similar states together (that is abstraction), and consider only those states encountered on paths that are considered likely to throw up interesting cases. For example, Failure Modes and Effects Analysis (FMEA) explores only those paths that start from a state in which some component has failed; Fault Tree Analysis (FTA) explores paths backwards from an undesired state to see if there is some combination of events (usually failures) that render it reachable. These analyses are typically applied to very abstract models; this is because they are often performed early in design exploration, before detailed designs have been developed, and because abstraction reduces the search space. The benefit in applying automation to these activities is that, unlike informal analyses, they can examine *all* possible states and scenarios. Infinite bounded model checkers are particularly suitable for this purpose because they can operate on abstract models (using uninterpreted functions); however, because of the power of the automation available, they may be able to operate on more realistic abstractions than those used informally. Furthermore, like all model checkers, they not only verify true properties, but also provide explicit counterexamples to false ones (cf. a cut set in FTA). The counterexample capability can be exploited for other purposes, such as the generation of test cases (Hamon et al. 2004).

Holloway's example states that hazard H1 is eliminated by formal verification, and that the probabilities of hazards H2 and H3 are established by FTA. The formalized top-level safety case simply makes reference to the documentation for these, but we can imagine that they could themselves be partially or fully formalized and automated. For example, infinite bounded model checking on a detailed formal model of the system design could verify that H1 is unreachable, and similar model checking on more abstract models could identify the precipitating events for H2 and H3; separate, informal analysis could then estimate their probability. The following section considers probabilistic arguments in more detail.

4 Probabilistic Arguments

Probability plays an important part in safety cases, quite apart from its use in FTA. Safety is about controlling *risk*, which is the product of the severity of an outcome and its probability, so a good part of most safety cases is concerned with assessment of probabilities. Estimating the probability of system failure given probabilities for component failures is a well-understood task, with its own methods and tools. The task is more challenging, however, where software is concerned. Software contributes to system failures through faults in its requirements, design, or implementation, and these, in the language of safety analysis, produce 'systematic failures', meaning they are not random but are *certain* to occur whenever circumstances activate the fault concerned. But although the failure is certain, given circumstances that activate the fault, those circumstances have a probability of occurrence: some faults are activated by almost any input, others require very specific, and unusual combinations of inputs. Hence, failure probabilities can be associated with software and are determined by the likelihood of encountering circumstances that activate its faults.

For modest values, say down to about 1×10^{-4} probability of failure on demand, it is feasible to measure software failure probabilities by statistically valid random testing (Butler and Finelli 1993), where 'statistically valid' means that the test case selection probabilities are exactly the same as those that are encountered in real operation. When the required probabilities are smaller than can be verified by direct measurement, the general recourse is to show that the software has been developed to some Software Integrity Level (SIL), as in Holloway's example. However, the practices recommended for most high-level SILs (e.g., DO-178B Level A), such as elaborate documentation of requirements, specifications, and designs, traceability among these, and extensive reviews and testing, are really about ensuring *correctness*, and there is no clear justification for determining a correspondence between SILs and failure probabilities.

In contrast, Littlewood (Littlewood 2000) introduced the idea that software may be *possibly perfect* and that we can contemplate its *probability of perfection*. This is attractive because probability of perfection can be interpreted as a subjective assessment of confidence in the verification activities performed on the software. Furthermore, a probability of perfection can be related to reliability, and this has particularly great utility in fault-tolerant systems, where the possible perfection of one 'channel' can be shown to be conditionally independent of the reliability of the other; hence, the probability of system failure is the product of these individual probabilities (Littlewood and Rushby 2009).

Using the idea of possible perfection has two ramifications on a safety case. One is that the upper level assessment of the probability of system failure will employ probabilities of software perfection; the other is that the subcase concerned with software must consider the possibility (and probabilities) of its own imperfections. These are likely to be smaller when parts of the case, particularly any verifications and analyses, are formalized and subject to mechanical checking. I suggest considerations for the assessment of these probabilities in a recent paper (Rushby 2009b).

Another area where formalization intersects with probability is in assurance for fault-tolerant systems. Many system failures are due to flaws in fault tolerance: the very mechanisms that are intended to prevent failure become the dominant source of failure! Formal verification of these mechanisms produces two very valuable results: first, it requires precise specification of assumed component failure modes, the number of these to be tolerated, and their assumed probabilities; second, it provides convincing evidence (i.e., a proof) that the mechanisms work, provided the number and modes of component failure are consistent with those specified. This bipartite division separates assurance for the correctness of the mechanisms from calculation of system reliability.

The reason that many fault-tolerant systems fail is that their components fail in ways different than assumed in the design of the mechanism for fault tolerance. When the fault-tolerance aspects of the safety case are informal, the failure assumptions may be imprecise, and their probabilities assessed optimistically (Johnson and Holloway 2006). Formal verification forces precision in the statement of failure mode assumptions and, thereby, explicit recognition of the cases not tolerated – and realistic assessment of their probability. The latter should drive the design of fault-tolerant mechanisms toward those that make minimal assumptions and are uniformly effective (e.g., Byzantine-resilient algorithms) and away from the special-case treatments that are prevalent in homespun designs.

Even principled designs can benefit from this type of consideration; for example, it is well-known that Byzantine-resilient algorithms that use 'signed messages' can tolerate more faults than those that use 'oral messages'; but if signatures are flawed for some reason, the signed messages algorithms will fail. Given this information, a developer or assessor can perform principled analysis of the tradeoff between a design that makes fewer assumptions vs one that tolerates more faults at the cost of more assumptions – or they can be motivated to explore algorithms that combine the best of both choices (Gong et al. 1995).

Analysis of fault-tolerant systems is one example where appropriate formalization allows the case for correctness to be separated from the case for reliability: formal verification provides assurance that the system does not fail, given assumptions about the failures of components; separately, we estimate the probability of the assumptions, and thereby calculate the reliability of the system. There can be other circumstances in a safety case where logic assures a conclusion, given certain premises, but we are not completely confident in the premises. Our (lack of) confidence in the premises can be represented by attaching a probability to them.

For fault tolerance, calculation of the probability of the conclusion given the probabilities of the premises is very straightforward, but the general case is more difficult – largely because the probabilities on the premises may not be independent. In its general form, this topic enters the domains of probabilistic logic and methods for probabilistic and evidential reasoning, such as Bayesian Belief Nets (BBNs) and Dempster-Shafer theory.

Since safety is about risk, which involves probability, it is quite likely that some of the argument at or near the top level of a safety case will involve probabilistic reasoning of these kinds. For example, we may have evidence for software based on testing and on its integrity level, and we will wish to combine these two 'legs' to yield a 'multi-legged' case, perhaps using BBNs (Littlewood and Wright 2007). A question is whether these probabilistic calculations should be opaque to the formalization, in the way that hazard analysis is, or at least partially, represented in the formalization – e.g., by attaching probabilities to formal statements representing uncertain evidence or deductions. There are techniques that combine formal methods with probabilistic calculations, such as probabilistic model checkers, and there are also techniques that use formal methods to estimate probabilities, such as Monte Carlo model counting using SAT solvers. Experimentation is needed to understand how best to meld the logical and probabilistic elements of a safety case, but my own belief is that no matter how it is done, both kinds of analysis must be driven from the same representation of the structure of the case.

5 Summary, and Suggestions for Future Work

I have adumbrated some of the issues in using formalization to represent arguments in a safety case. One benefit of formalization is that it allows use of automated tools to check the logical soundness of the case. Whether this is worthwhile or not depends on whether unsoundness is a significant hazard to real safety cases. My own experience in formal verification is that I have repeatedly been humbled as the theorem prover finds flaws in arguments that I considered either cast iron, or obvious. And in reading even tutorial examples of safety cases, I have been unsettled by the size and diverse tactics of the arguments. Other small examples have been found to employ flawed reasoning (Greenwell et al. 2006), but I do not know whether this is a threat in real cases.

Formalization and automation bring another benefit: by assuring us that the overall argument is sound, they allow us to focus on the evidence and assumptions that support the argument. Being able to concentrate on each such item in isolation seems a valuable benefit to me. In addition, some new opportunities become available: for example, the validity of certain kinds of assumptions can be assured by checking or monitoring them at runtime. If the assumptions are formalized, then construction of monitors can be automated by methods developed in the field of *runtime verification* (Rushby 2008). Reliability of monitored architectures with formal (and possibly perfect) monitors is an interesting topic (Littlewood and Rushby 2009).

Yet another benefit of formalization is that it could allow development of canonical representations for various tactics of argument, and of 'metacases' (cases about cases). I think this could be of value in its own right, as it would allow a social process of community review and thereby reduce the vulnerability of intellectually isolated 'one-off' cases. Current work at Adelard is exploring these topics.

Using a simple example (Holloway 2008), I illustrated one way to formalize the top-level argument of a simple case in classical logic (I actually used the higher order logic PVS). Basir and colleagues (Basir et al. 2009) have undertaken a similar exercise using pure first order logic. The example illustrates only one tactic for safety argumentation: namely, enumeration over hazards. The work at Adelard has identified eight different tactics and it remains to be seen whether each of these can be formalized effectively.

Some proponents of safety cases look to Toulmin (Toulmin 2003) rather than classical logic in framing cases (Bishop et al. 2004); Toulmin stresses justification rather than inference. My opinion is that Toulmin's approach has merit in arguing topics such as aesthetics or morality, where reasonable people can hold different views; but a safety case should be based on agreed evidence about a designed artifact, and here the expectation is that reasonable people must concur on the concluding claim if the argument is sound. Thus, I remain of the opinion that classical logic is adequate for formalizing safety cases, but I do agree that it is worth seeking ways to represent Toulmin's 'warrant', 'backing', and 'rebuttal' within the formalization. The predicate good_doc that I used in the example can be seen as a way to link to an extralogical 'warrant' for certain steps in the argument.

At the upper levels of a safety case, the system is represented very abstractly, or even indirectly (e.g., by its hazards); at lower levels, there is generally an explicit model of the system and the reasoning is closer to traditional formal verification, or its variants (such as mechanized FMEA). There is obvious benefit if the formalization and reasoning at these levels can be connected in some way. Similarly, we would like a connection between the logical and probabilistic modes of formalization and reasoning. It is not at all clear how to do this, but a *tool bus* may be one way forward, as it does not require all tools to share a common representation (Rushby 2006).

A tool bus or other integration for the different modes and kinds of formalization and reasoning used in safety cases is a good topic for future investigation. Another is the identification, formalization, and analysis of canonical tactics for safety case argumentation. Techniques for developing safety cases in a modular or *compositional* manner would be a breakthrough; the topic of *emergent properties* is particularly interesting in that context (Black and Koopman 2008). The most important tasks for the future, however, are experiments to determine whether formalization does deliver benefit in the development and assessment of safety cases.

Acknowledgments   My research was supported by NASA cooperative agreements NNX08AC64A and NNX08AY53A, and by National Science Foundation grant CNS-0720908. I am grateful to Robin Bloomfield and his colleagues at Adelard and City University for exposing me to some of these topics and sharing their own ongoing investigations. However, the views expressed here are mine alone and do not represent those of my sponsors or collaborators.

References

AAIB (2007) Report on the incident to Airbus A340-642, registration G-VATL en-route from Hong Kong to London Heathrow on 8 February 2005. UK Air Investigations Branch. http://www.aaib.gov.uk/publications/formal_reports/4_2007_g_vatl.cfm. Accessed 19 October 2009

ATSB (2007) In-flight upset event, 240 km north-west of Perth, WA, Boeing Company 777200, 9M-MRG, 1 August 2005. Australian Transport Safety Bureau. Reference number Mar2007/DOTARS 50165. http://www.atsb.gov.au/publications/investigation_reports/2005/AAIR/aair200503722.aspx. Accessed 19 October 2009

Basir N, Denney E, Fischer B (2009) Deriving safety cases from automatically constructed proofs. In: 4th IET International Conference on System Safety, London, UK. The Institutions of Engineering and Technology

Bishop P, Bloomfield R, Guerra S (2004) The future of goal-based assurance cases. In DSN Workshop on Assurance Cases: Best Practices, Possible Obstacles, and Future Opportunities, Florence, Italy

Black J, Koopman P (2008) System safety as an emergent property in composite systems. In: International Conference on Dependable Systems and Networks, Estoril, Portugal. IEEE Computer Society

Butler RW, Finelli GB (1993) The infeasibility of experimental quantification of life-critical software reliability. IEEE Trans Softw Eng 19:3–12

Crow J, Owre S, Rushby J et al (2001) Evaluating, testing, and animating PVS specifications. Technical report, Computer Science Laboratory, SRI International, Menlo Park, CA. http://www.csl.sri.com/users/rushby/abstracts/attachments. Accessed 19 October 2009

Gong L, Lincoln P, Rushby J (1995) Byzantine agreement with authentication: observations and applications in tolerating hybrid and link faults. In: Iyer RK et el (eds) Dependable Computing for Critical Applications 5, Champaign, IL. Volume 10 of Dependable Computing and Fault Tolerant Systems. IEEE Computer Society

Greenwell WS, Knight JC, Holloway CM, Pease JJ (2006) A taxonomy of fallacies in system safety arguments. In Proc 24th International System Safety Conference, Albuquerque, NM

Hamon G, de Moura L, Rushby J (2004) Generating efficient test sets with a model checker. In: 2nd International Conference on Software Engineering and Formal Methods (SEFM), Beijing, China. IEEE Computer Society

Holloway CM (2008) Safety case notations: alternatives for the non-graphically inclined? In 3rd IET International Conference on System Safety, Birmingham, UK. The Institution of Engineering and Technology

Johnson CW, Holloway CM (2006) Why system safety professionals should read accident reports. In 1st IET International Conference on System Safety, London, UK. The Institutions of Engineering and Technology

Kelly T (1998) Arguing safety – a systematic approach to safety case management. PhD thesis, Department of Computer Science, University of York, UK

Kelly TP, Weaver RA (2004) The goal structuring notation – a safety argument notation. In: DSN Workshop on Assurance Cases: Best Practices, Possible Obstacles, and Future Opportunities, Florence, Italy

Littlewood B (2000) The use of proof in diversity arguments. IEEE Trans Softw Eng 26:1022–1023

Littlewood B, Rushby J (2009) Reasoning about the reliability of fault-tolerant systems in which one component is 'possibly perfect'. City University UK and SRI International USA. In preparation

Littlewood B, Wright D (2007) The use of multi-legged arguments to increase confidence in safety claims for software-based systems: a study based on a BBN analysis of an idealised example. IEEE Trans Softw Eng 33:347–365

Miner P, Geser A, Pike L, Maddalon J (2004) A unified fault-tolerance protocol. In: Formal Techniques in Real-Time and Fault-Tolerant Systems, volume 3253 of Lecture Notes in Computer Science, Grenoble, France. Springer-Verlag.

RTCA (1992) DO-178B: Software considerations in airborne systems and equipment certification. Requirements and Technical Concepts for Aviation, Washington, DC. This document is known as EUROCAE ED-12B in Europe.

Rushby J (2006) Harnessing disruptive innovation in formal verification. In: Hung DV, Pandya P (eds) Fourth International Conference on Software Engineering and Formal Methods (SEFM), Pune, India. IEEE Computer Society

Rushby J (2008) Runtime certification. In: Leucker, M (ed) Eighth Workshop on Runtime Verification: RV08, Budapest, Hungary. Volume 5289 of Lecture Notes in Computer Science. Springer-Verlag

Rushby J (2009a) A safety-case approach for certifying adaptive systems. In: AIAA Infotech@Aerospace Conference, Seattle, WA. American Institute of Aeronautics and Astronautics

Rushby J (2009b) Software verification and system assurance. In: Seventh International Conference on Software Engineering and Formal Methods (SEFM), Hanoi, Vietnam. IEEE Computer Society

SRI (2009) SRI International Formal Methods Program, home page. http://fm.csl.sri.com/. Accessed 19 October 2009

Toulmin SE (2003) The uses of argument. Cambridge University Press. Updated edition (the original is dated 1958)

Perspectives on Systems Safety

Bureaucracy, Safety and Software: a Potentially Lethal Cocktail

Les Hatton

CISM, University of Kingston

London, UK

Abstract This position paper identifies a potential problem with the evolution of software controlled safety critical systems. It observes that the rapid growth of bureaucracy in society quickly spills over into rules for behaviour. Whether the need for the rules comes first or there is simple anticipation of the need for a rule by a bureaucrat is unclear in many cases. Many such rules lead to draconian restrictions and often make the existing situation worse due to the presence of unintended consequences as will be shown with a number of examples.

In science and engineering, the effects of such bureaucracy are generally mitigated because the rules naturally devolve from the exercise of the scientific method whereby evidence leads to policy and lasting benefit. In the absence of the scientific method (which is usually the case in software systems development), policy flourishes like weeds without the constraints of reality. In software controlled systems, any consequent unintended side-effects could be lethal.

1 Overview

Complex systems often exhibit unintended behaviour as a result of well-intentioned change. Some examples follow under a number of general headings.

1.1 Division of Responsibility

Dividing safety amongst separate bodies is known to be problematic. China's response to the melamine scandal that sickened over 53,000 infants who drank toxic milk formula in 2007-2008 is a perfect example. As (Lelyveld 2008) points out, the World Health Organisation specifically criticised China's division of responsibility for the part it played in this sad incident. In particular, China has separate ministries for health, agriculture, and commerce, as well as the State Food and

C. Dale, T. Anderson (eds.), *Making Systems Safer*, DOI 10.1007/978-1-84996-086-1_2,
© Springer-Verlag London Limited 2010

Drug Administration (SFDA), the State Administration of Industry and Commerce (SAIC), and the General Administration of Quality Supervision, Inspection and Quarantine (GAQSIQ). Poor communication amongst such a diverse set of agencies is inevitable. This has considerable relevance to the corresponding position for safety-related software development as will be discussed further below.

The Chinese government has responded in the classic bureaucratic tradition by drafting new laws intended to prevent this happening again. Regrettably the new law is decidedly underwhelming. First the draft law bans all substances even those known to be harmless unless they have been officially approved as additives. Second, the draft law only,

> 'asks the departments, especially those at the grassroots level, to improve communication, cooperate closely with each other and faithfully fulfill their legal responsibilities'

However, this does nothing to solve one of the major problems, which is conflict of interest. As one commentator in this article noted about the departments intended to carry out these directives,

> 'They have an incentive to keep the local economy growing and vibrant. But on the other hand, at the ministry level, they're supposed to be taking care of food safety.'

In other words, it is a classic bureaucratic fix whereby a law is made which may well make things worse (it is impossible to say), whereas one of the real problems is completely ignored.

1.2 Naming Confusion

There is of course a related problem to confusion over responsibility with no clear division of authority, that of nomenclature. A perfect example of this occurs with the naming of drugs. Since Celebrex (generic name celecoxib) made its debut in January 1999, there have been 53 reports of errors due to name confusion (Eustice and Eustice 1999).

The confusion arises because there are two other similarly-named drugs, Cerebyx and Celexa, with very different application.

- Celebrex (celecoxib) is the new COX-2 selective inhibitor used for the treatment of arthritis.
- Cerebyx (fosphenytoin) is an intravenous drug used to treat epilepsy.
- Celexa (citalopram) is a medication used to treat depression and symptoms of fibromyalgia.

The similarity among the names has caused confusion and mistakes, but no serious injuries or fatalities at the time of reporting in the reference. In 10 of the 53 reported cases, the patient actually received the wrong drug. In 19 of the cases, the wrong drug was prescribed but the error was caught before the patient was dispensed the wrong drug. In the remaining 24 cases, doctors and pharmacists reported the name Celebrex to be confusing. The reported number of errors is the most the Food and Drug Administration (FDA) had ever received for any drug that had only been available to consumers for four months and it is typically only around 5% of all cases which get reported anyway. In this case, drug marketing and wider implications of naming are not controlled by the same authority, although the FDA does indeed have an Office of Post-marketing to attempt to address this.

1.3 Interference based on Well-intentioned Meddling

Well-intentioned meddling is normally the result of an inadequate grasp of number and specifically, probability. This is exceedingly widespread and essentially disables a large section of the population from making rational life decisions (Paulos 2001). In essence, somebody or possibly a group of people get a collective bee in their bonnet that something is important and then do something about it without any attempt to assess objectively whether it is important or not. Some examples follow.

1.3.1 HM Coastguard bans flares

This extraordinary piece of meddling occurred in November 2008 when the MCA (Maritime and Coastguard Agency), a U.K. government organisation which coordinates search and rescue missions decided to stop HM Coastguard from using flares after discovering that they hadn't been used much recently. This is in spite of an MCA spokesman admitting that he was unaware of any incidents in which coastguard personnel had been injured using flares, and that the few times they had been used, they were apparently successful in saving lives which might not have been saved if the ban had been in place earlier. The suggestion by the way is that torches are used instead. Anybody who has been at sea in a boat at night will probably share the following quoted (Britten 2008) view from a crewman:

'This is the most stupid, ignorant thing I've heard of. Flares have been used for a century and, until now, have been a vital bit of kit.'

I could easily suggest a corollary to this to be erected next to a lifebelt.

'Do not use if the ship is sinking. You may drop it on your toe causing injury.'

As a warm-up to this piece of bureaucracy, the MCA had two months earlier disciplined a coastguard crew after they saved a girl with an inshore boat which was alleged to be structurally unsound (Daily Mail 2008). The boat had been repaired out of the crew's own funds because of the slow response of the MCA and was awaiting inspection (also by the MCA). As a result of this incident, the boat was then locked up to prevent the crew having a 'moral dilemma' in future. You really couldn't make this kind of thing up.

1.3.2 Yellowstone National Park

Yellowstone National Park is a wonderful example of sustained well-intentioned meddling based on things which taken individually might sound reasonable, as described so eloquently by Michael Crichton (Crichton 2005). This quotation paints the background well.

> 'What, then, happened in Yellowstone? I would argue, people thought they understood
> the system. They thought they understood how nature worked. And they were wrong.'

They were not only wrong, they were lamentably and persistently wrong. Yellowstone National Park was set up in 1872 as the first formal nature reserve in the world. (Note that I am paraphrasing here – Michael Crichton's version is far more eloquent.) In 1903 President Theodore Roosevelt visited it for a dedication ceremony and noted with pleasure the abundant wild life – a thousand antelope, plentiful cougar, mountain sheep, deer, coyote, and many thousands of elk. Yet only thirty years later, the park service acknowledged that 'white-tailed deer, cougar, lynx, wolf, and possibly wolverine and fisher are gone from the Yellowstone'. What they didn't say was that they had actually caused this by well-intentioned muddled interference roughly as follows.

1. In the 1890s, it was believed off no evidence that elk were becoming extinct, and so these animals were fed and encouraged. Over the next few years the numbers of elk in the park exploded.
2. From 1914 antelope and deer began to decline, overgrazing changed the flora, aspen and willows were being eaten heavily and did not regenerate. In an effort to stem the loss of animals, the park rangers began to kill predators, which they did without public knowledge. They eliminated the wolf and cougar and were well on their way to getting rid of the coyote when the public realised and there was a national scandal. Independent studies showed that it was the elk explosion and the resultant over-grazing which were the problem. This was denied.
3. Aspen disappeared because of the over-grazing taking the beaver with them. Without beaver there was no water management.
4. By 1930, the small predators had disappeared. Those not finished by the park service needed a diet of beaver and other small animals and they had gone.

The whole charade continued in a similar vein into the 1980s until a devastating fire occurred by which time it had become abundantly obvious that when it comes to managing 2.2 million acres of wilderness, nobody since the Indians has had the faintest idea how to do it. (The Indians had regular controlled fires and otherwise left the park alone.)

The essential feature of all this was the problem of trying to manage a highly complex interconnected system by locally linear small changes, but more of this particular hallucination later.

1.3.3 CRB and the Independent Safeguarding Authority

The CRB is the Criminal Records Bureau in the UK. It is a Home Office Agency and was set up in March 2002 with the laudable goal of vetting those working with children and young people. It checks for criminal convictions and cautions but more insidiously an enhanced check also examines any other relevant and proportionate information held by the police, whatever that means. It was set up originally with the excellent intention to protect children from paedophiles and rapidly expanded to cover 1.5 million adults largely driven by the failure to stop Ian Huntley being given a job as a school caretaker in Soham, with tragic consequences. (It turns out that this was simply a failure in police communications but again the bureaucratic response is taking unintended directions (Hope 2009).

From 2010 (it has been delayed twice), this is being supplemented by the Independent Safeguarding Authority (ISA), a new agency intended to greatly increase the reach of the CRB. The ISA will use the enhanced checks to check anybody having any access to children, however remote. This even includes spectators taking photographs at sports competitions, officials, coaches, drivers and so on and includes the whole of the voluntary sector.

The bottom line for this is that by 2015, a staggering 11 million people are planned to be in the register. In other words, the UK is intending to screen about one third of its adult population for anti-paedophile tests, an example of a disproportionate response which simply beggars belief.

So what are the unintended consequences here? By far the worst is that the public at large will no longer help a child in distress for fear of being considered a paedophile. (Beckford 2008) describes an ITV program which set up two child actors in apparent distress in a shopping mall, observed by hidden cameras. 1,817 people walked past them but only five offered to help and even those who stopped to help all admitted they had been worried their actions would be seen as suspicious.

In addition to this worrying trend, sadly, the UK Government has a dismal record of looking after its sensitive data. Even the best database management systems make mistakes, and in 2008 as reported in (Hope 2009), some 1,570 people were wrongly accused of criminal behaviour (False Positive) or not identified as having criminal records (False Negative), up from 690 the previous year. Even worse, most of these were towards the end of the year, (almost 1,000 in December 2008 alone). The appeals procedure is of course bureaucratic with only 90% being cleared up in 21 days, during which time a great deal of anguish was created, due to the extreme sensitivity of the subject area. When the system is operating at its full level, this is likely to wrongly accuse around 5,000 people a year, with a bad month being around 2,000, assuming of course that it doesn't become overloaded and the error rate grows correspondingly.

A likely consequence of this, as can be seen from the ITV experiment, will be that volunteers simply stop volunteering and that children will not benefit from their skills and time. Many sports in the UK depend entirely on the voluntary sector to function at all. If these sports suffer as a result, the children suffer directly. This does not appear to have been considered. Last but not least, another unintended consequence of this is caused by the incompetence and oversight of the agencies themselves in soliciting data. As of the time of writing (early September 2009), the ISA web-site was still encouraging people to submit potentially highly sensitive whistle-blowing information by e-mail, in spite of it being completely insecure and some six weeks after I warned them of this.

1.3.4 Black-outs and the Battle of the River Plate

The great Black-out in Britain at the start of the Second World War is a classic example of wildly inaccurate expert advice, over-reaction and bureaucratic meddling. It was argued by experts from the Air Ministry (Isaacs 1973, episode 2, for example), that 'millions' of people would die in air attacks. To prevent this, all the lights would be extinguished during the hours of darkness so that such attacks could not take place. This black-out came into force on 1 September 1939, two days before the outbreak of the war. It was absolute (even a lit cigarette was considered a breach) and any breaches were harshly punished with big fines or court appearances.

The side-effect was that road traffic and other accidents such as drowning skyrocketed. Between September and November, there were 3,000 deaths. Some attempts to ameliorate this horrific toll were made. Torches were allowed from mid-September 1939 onwards but they had to be pointed down and covered with tissue, rendering them almost useless. From 3 November, the black-out was shortened by one hour but it remained in place until September 1944 with many more casualties.

To put this into context, in the Battle of the River Plate, the first major sea battle of the Second World War and very widely published, the German pocket battleship Admiral Graf Spee fought a bloody battle with three Allied cruisers, the Achilles, Ajax and Exeter over three days in December 1939. The total casualties in this engagement, German and British were 109. Indeed for the first three months of the Second World War, more civilians were killed in the UK through black-out accidents than service personnel died on active service.

This observation is echoed by Michael Crichton (Crichton 2005), who when intending to write a novel about Chernobyl and its reported 15,000-30,000 deaths with estimates of 500,000 more delayed deaths, discovered that the real figures were 56 dead and around 4,000 delayed deaths. Nobody wishes to undervalue this tragedy but the meal the media make of everything for their own ends can seriously distort the policy which then follows.

This is echoed yet again in the current scares about swine flu. The UK is reporting far more cases than other comparable population centres causing considerable panic, again amply swollen by media intervention. As of the time of writing it is unclear why, but a major contributing factor appears to be the practice of attempting to diagnose it over the phone to avoid spreading it. Unfortunately, there are significant concerns over this practice (Campbell 2009). An unintended consequence is that people have been given the anti-viral drug Tamiflu without actually having flu, including patients with a knee infection and even tonsillitis. This drug has caused unpleasant side-effects in a significant number of patients and would be ineffective for potentially serious conditions such as meningitis which has similar symptoms. The drug was also dished out to young people in whom it caused significant side-effects.

In the absence of good, reliable data, media-driven distortion will always prevail. Even when there is good reliable data, media-driven distortion may still prevail if there is a good enough story as will be seen shortly.

1.3.5 Documentation Proliferation and Information Overload

Although it is impossible to quantify its effect on safety yet, the gradual proliferation in road signs may be causing problems of information overload for drivers (AA 2009), with some junctions having more than sixteen signs. This sometimes has a humorous side as (Johnson 2009) notes about a major road sign displayed in Swansea. The English version said that this was a residential area and there was no entry for heavy goods vehicles. The Welsh translation was in a different league altogether. It read:

'Nid wyf yn y swyddfa ar hyn o bryd. Anfonwch unrhyw waith i'w gyfielthu.'

A little while passed before someone had the nerve to point out that this gnomic message meant:

'I am not in the office at the moment. Send any work to be translated.'

1.4 Interference based on Political Meddling and/or Selectionism

Even when there is considerable scientific evidence available, the nature of political will coupled with a generally out of control and digitally lubricated media with its own agenda and needs can lead to important evidence being ignored with outrageous selectionism to give a highly distorted result.

1.4.1 Seat Belt and Other Road Safety Legislation

(Adams 1995) gives convincing arguments from detailed empirical studies that a number of road safety initiatives do not in fact reduce the total number of accidents. In fact for certain kinds of legislation (e.g. mandatory safety belt legislation), he argues that the total number of injuries has gone up due to the phenomenon of risk compensation. In short, drivers when given safety aids, just drive faster. The effect is to transfer some of the risk to other more vulnerable road users, such as cyclists and pedestrians.

1.4.2 MMR and Autism

This woeful piece of appalling science stoked up by a rapacious media is a perfect example of selectionism at its worst. It is described in detail by (Goldacre 2008). Little more need be said here apart from the fact that the media in essence selected one particular discredited study which claimed a relationship between MMR and autism. In spite of all continuing evidence to the contrary, this has led to a significant percentage of children failing to be vaccinated against Measles, Mumps and Rubella, each a particularly nasty disease. As a consequence, there is now a measles epidemic (Smith 2009), for which the media can collectively claim the majority of the responsibility.

1.4.3 Risk Assessment

In consort with the generally declining public awareness of number, there has been a rapid growth to the point of obsession with risk assessments and risk registers. Whilst thinking about risk has some value, assigning a level of risk is rather more difficult. Indeed, according to (Adams 1995), risk is when you don't really know what will happen but you do know the odds. Uncertainty is when you don't know either. Most of the attempts at risk assessment I have seen are in fact uncertainty assessments and are usually devoid of any numeracy.

As a public service, here is how to do risk assessments so you don't get asked again.

- Write the risk equation at the top, $R = F \times C$ (Risk is Frequency times Consequence). This will immediately panic Human Resources as people join Human Resources to avoid nasty things like multiplication.
- Write the principal risk as 'End of Universe', for which F is very tiny according to the Large Hadron Collider website (the end of the universe is one of the risks), but not zero. Since the Consequence is infinite, then the Risk is infinite.
- Include no other risks as they are finite and therefore compared with the end of the universe, can be neglected.

- Forward to Human Resources. They will say something like, 'You are not taking this seriously', to which you can answer, 'I take the end of the universe very seriously.' At this point, they will give up.

2 Safety Standards and Software Development

So what has all the above to do with software development in safety-critical environments?

2.1 Software Development as a Measurement Free Zone

The first thing I will note is that software development is a highly vulnerable activity in the sense that it is unusually prone to well-intentioned meddling because there has been insufficient attention paid to laying down a measurement basis from which to make reasoned conclusions about the reliability and potential safety of any system of which software plays a part. Indeed, one of the reasons why there are so many software project failures is the generally abysmal understanding of what it takes to build a successful software system (REng 2004). There is a touching but misguided belief in some quarters that this is because engineers need more management skills. Unfortunately, the reverse is true. Managers need more engineering skills to be able to assess what is happening as their latest software project crashes silently around their ears.

It has long been known that software development inhabits a measurement-free zone. Walter Tichy made this point more than ten years ago in an excellent review (Tichy 1998). As far as I can see, little has changed. We have even more technologies but experimental verification of them using the tried and trusty scientific method has simply not kept up.

As we have seen from the numerous examples above, bureaucracy and poor advice proliferates in areas devoid of the scientific method. Even when there is good quality data available, it can be seen that the media in pursuit of manufacturing a good story or some kind of political agenda can distort the evidence to lead to false conclusions. If there is almost no data to begin with, there is simply nothing with which to fight it.

2.2 Proliferation of Software Standards

I have just been sent a safety flier exhorting me to 'Start Your Safety Library' with:

1. MIL-STD-882C
2. MIL-STD-882B 300 Series Tasks
3. SAE ARP4754, ARP4761
4. IEC 61508
5. SAE ARP5580
6. MIL-STD-1629A (it continues to be used)
7. DEF STAN 00-56
8. NRC Fault Tree Handbook

Note the use of the word 'Start' here. I don't know how much more I am intended to acquire but this is one of the reasons that I refuse to work on safety-related systems any more (the other being that it is a legal minefield with lawyers just waiting for a juicy test case – and no wonder, given that we don't even know what constitutes best practice (Hatton 1999)).

The first and most important lesson to be learnt is that software standards are a nice little earner. The general idea is to get together a team of willing volunteers to produce some sort of draft document for nothing. Then their free contributions are exploited, it is publicised as much as possible, and released at a handsome price with a set of copyright conditions which will make you wince. Having been released, nothing ever happens again and the standard rapidly becomes obsolete if it wasn't already when it was first released. I have sat on such committees pro bono publico and will not do so again.

A perfect example of this is the safety standard IEC 61508. This is a mighty tome of seven parts, matched only by its mighty price. Since I couldn't get hold of it any other way, I actually bought a copy of part 3, which purports to be about software, solely for the purposes of writing this paper. I regret it deeply. It cost 193 Swiss Francs and for that I got the same standard twice, once in English and once in French, fifty pages of each and not updated since 1998. It comes with an alarming set of conditions which apparently even forbid me from backing it up. I have backed it up to protect my investment and challenge them to sue me. I will enlarge upon this standard shortly but in my view it is so vague that it is almost completely useless.

There are others. DO-178B comes in at 162.50 US dollars and ISO 26262-1 at 66 Swiss Francs. The MISRA-C standard is 40 UK pounds and its C++ twin is 45 UK pounds at the time of writing, although you can download them more cheaply.

The one thing that all of these standards have in common is that they are primarily based on guesswork. They give lots of little titbits of advice which sound sort of reasonable but much of it is either out of date, never supported in the first place, maddeningly ill-defined or shamelessly imported from some other standard (Hatton 2004). For example, Table A.3 of IEC 61508-3 tells us that a certificated translator is highly recommended at Safety Integrity Level (SIL) 2-4 but only recommended at SIL 1. SIL 1 has safety implications so why wouldn't it be highly recommended that the program translator, compiler or whatever had some form of quality control? As it happens, and far more seriously, it doesn't really matter anyway because you can't get one any more – the certification of compilers disappeared in April 2000 without apparently a murmur from the software safety community.

We are also told that a suitable programming language is highly recommended at all SILs. This begs the question as to how we determine which language is suitable. What does suitable even mean? There are no guidelines on what such a language might look like or how you would choose it although much of the technology it specifically mentions has disappeared anyway. What I think it really means is that the contributors to this document couldn't agree on anything, because choice of programming language is emotive and highly subjective, so they simply pass the buck on to the user. Of course the practical problems of finding engineers who are sufficiently fluent in a particular language are not considered; neither are there any references to enable further research.

How about testing? In Table A.5, we are told that Dynamic Analysis and Testing is recommended at SIL 1 but highly recommended at SIL 2-4. With respect, this is just mumbo-jumbo. It is word-spinning with no quantifiable merit whatsoever.

There is of course a long history of inscrutability about belief systems and their rules. Take the following two quotations for example.

'These ye may eat of all that are in the waters: whatsoever hath fins and scales may ye eat; and whatsoever hath not fins and scales ye shall not eat; it is unclean unto you.'
Deuteronomy 14:9-10

This sensible advice probably reflected the fact that it is harder to keep shellfish fresh, but this does not exactly shine through the wording and the original justification is lost. Modern people who strictly adhere to these rules will continue to apply this in spite of massive advances in food handling hygiene and the fact that the people who wrote this very likely thought the earth was flat.

'Star Alchemy, or Sealing of the Five Senses. This unifies the five shen, the five streams of personal consciousness that operate through our senses, with the five forces of the collective Stellar Self. The body of our stellar mind can be viewed in the four quadrants of fixed stars in the night sky, originally symbolized by heraldic animals (Black Turtle, Red Phoenix, Green Dragon, White Tiger).' 5th formula of inner alchemy, The Seven Dao Alchemy Formulas of the Immortal Self (Winn 2009)

Is this supposed to mean anything? It certainly doesn't to me. I don't have a collective Stellar Self, have only one stream of personal consciousness as far as I am aware unless I am missing out, the stars aren't fixed and their names differ both with culture and time. For example, I have always thought of the Red Phoenix more as a Concussed Lobster. No doubt, its supporters would consider me a callow scientist but I'm sure those supporters would be equally happy to have access to MRI scanners if necessary, neglecting the fact that they are a natural development of the scientific method, the antithesis of their own sphere.

So is IEC 61508 really the cutting edge of safety-related software standards? Well, it isn't going to change unless another group of public-spirited individuals volunteers. Instead we will have other standards. A glance through the IEC, ISO and RTCA web-sites reveals that there is certainly no shortage of standards to adopt. Which ones do we choose? It probably doesn't matter anyway. If I showed my copy of IEC 61508 to my students (which I am specifically forbidden to do by its terms and conditions, in the best traditions of intellectual dissemination), I doubt if they would even agree on what the words meant.

Of course, what these standards really fall down on is that the individual engineers have to be competent. The activity known as Dynamic Analysis and Testing can cover almost anything from one useless test to an expensive, concerted, highly sophisticated but ultimately unsuccessful attempt to break the system somehow by people who really know what they are doing. The whole thing has been dehumanised into a box-ticking process as if engineer quality was a given. In my view, we would be far better off giving engineers a copy of The Mythical Man Month (Brooks 1975) and breaking fingers for lapses of concentration. Only kidding.

2.2.1 The Human Interface

If anything, this is even worse with an astonishing array of standards, ISO or ISO/IEC 9126 (various parts), 9241 (various parts), 20282, 10741 (various parts), 11581, 11064, 13406, 14915, 14754, 61997, 18021, 18789, 18019, 15910, 13407, 14598, 16982, 18529, 10075 (various parts), 16071 and there may be more (Bevan 2006), but I was beginning to lose consciousness in my search.

In spite of all this energy, the quality of human computer interfaces in many devices, safety and non safety-related, remains appalling. A perfect example is afforded by the McDonnell Douglas MD-11, which in spite of an obvious enormous amount of money spent on its avionics software, attracted this comment from its test pilot:

> 'The airplane [computer system] manuals were written as though by creatures from another planet.'

He noted this after being presented with the wonderfully inscrutable 'Button push ignored' by the Flight Management system (Drury 1997).

I list a few more examples of this kind of thing in (Hatton 2007). There is no shortage.

2.3 Growth of Software Standards

Another important thing to note about software standards is that they must always grow. Shrinkage is considered unthinkable. Most ISO language standards grow substantially in size at each standards cycle until they collapse into obscurity rather like stars which exceed the Chandrasekhar limit and collapse into a white dwarf. For example the ISO C standard increased from 190 pages in ISO C 9899:1990 to around 400 pages in ISO C 9899:1999. This is a natural implication of the fact that it is much easier under ISO rules to introduce new things that might work than to take out old things that don't work (on the principle of maintaining backwards compatibility, a supremely broken concept in engineering systems). Eventually language standards evolve into mind-bogglingly complex documents which defeat any individual's understanding. The ISO C++ standard is a good case in point, weighing in at over 800 pages in its 1999 incarnation and with so much undefined behaviour (implicit and explicit) that it is very difficult indeed to reason about many language constructs, let alone the intended functionality of the program of which they form a part.

2.4 Naming Confusion

Naming is historically a rich source of confusion in software development. I have recently received notification of a seminar entitled 'Providing Confidence in Safety Judgements'. This is organised by the IET/BCS ISA Working Group and advertises that it will describe an 'ISA Code of Practice' and an 'ISA Competence Framework'. I presume that ISA means Independent Software Assessment although I don't actually know and the flier does not say. This is what Google reported as of 1 September 2009:

- Google (ISA Code of Practice): A Code of Practice to minimise Infectious Salmon Anaemia.
- Google (ISA Competence Framework): Reveals various competency frameworks none of which have ISA in them.
- Google (ISA): The Independent Safeguarding Authority. A U.K. government site created to help prevent unsuitable people from working with children and vulnerable adults (of which we have already seen much above).

Perhaps this example would be considered slightly unfair, but the existence of other authorities associated with safety but nothing to do with software assurance and with much greater search engine impact (arguably the only arbiter of success in modern times), is not going to be helpful.

2.5 The Role of Gravitas, Governance, Stakeholder-Speak and Other Distractions

And so we come to the Tower of Babel. Management speak is full of nonsensical, ephemeral jargon. Because software development has no really well-agreed vocabulary (even the definitions of fault and failure differ in some standards), management can intrude with its own peculiar rapidly evolving double-speak, introducing words like gravitas, governance and stakeholders into the jargon of software projects as if this had the slightest effect on how a system actually functions, or how it should be built. Using such jargon, people who really have no idea what is going on can give the illusion of control.

3 Conclusions – What is to be done?

I am conscious of the fact that this short paper is critical but there are things which can be done if the will is there.

Perhaps the most urgent item for computer scientists to attend to is to lay down a representation independent measurement framework of quantifiable quality so that we actually know which techniques work, why and by how much. In spite of efforts to provide a forum for this by journals such as the Journal of Empirical Software Engineering, much remains to be done in the face of the seemingly endless supply of new paradigms, techniques and languages. Only by providing such a framework can the benefits of bureaucracy be gained without the well-intentioned meddling and arbitrary complexity which otherwise tends to emerge.

The standardisation process is broken. Standards need to be open source to facilitate easy updating in a highly volatile profession, and of unlimited free access. Proprietary file formats have caused enough misery without compounding it with proprietary standards. The current situation whereby standards are heavily protected, expensive and frequently outdated before they even appear is unhelpful to say the least and it is possible that Wikipedia and its like may play a substantial future role. NASA also has always been an excellent role model here, providing free access to lots of useful documents and data (e.g. Dvorak 2009). However, on a cautionary note, open source standards without measurement constraint will simply produce free words.

Finally, the belief that defined process leads automatically to good product needs to be tempered. Much of what we do in successful software development, safety-related or otherwise, requires considerable analytical skills and it has always been true that good products are built by good engineers. Yet we face real challenges in the training and supply of such engineers with continuing and in some cases worsening shortages of trained engineers in the USA, Europe and Australasia as exemplified by these quotations:-

'It was perceived that student handling of mathematics had declined significantly and continues to decline. The perceived decline is steeper with home students and should be addressed via Government policy at pre-University level.' (Browne et al. 2004).

'Analysis of public maths exam papers taken by 16-year-olds between 1951 and 2006 shows standards have declined markedly, the report for Reform argues.'

'India and China are producing four million graduates every year. The single largest area of graduate growth is mathematics, science and engineering.'

'A third of graduates in China are engineers – here [the UK] it's just 8%. Between 1994 and 2004, more than 30% of the physics departments in Britain disappeared.'

These latter three were all culled from http://news.bbc.co.uk/1/hi/education/7431840.stm on 7 September 2009.

That shortages in some parts of the world are balanced by growth in India and China will comfort only the most ardent of outsourcers and unless all of the above factors are resolved, there is a real danger that unnecessarily bureaucratic structures will overwhelm our systems development skills.

References

AA (2009) UK road sign review. The Automobile Association. http://www.theaa.com/public_affairs/aa-populus-panel/aa-populus-too-many-road-signs.html. Accessed 2 October 2009

Adams J (1995) Risk. UCL Press, London

Beckford M (2008) Esther Rantzen: Fear of paedophiles is harming children. http://www.telegraph.co.uk/news/newstopics/celebritynews/3122417/Esther-Rantzen-Fear-of-paedophiles-is-harming-children.html. Accessed 2 October 2009

Bevan N (2006) International standards for HCI and usability. http://www.usabilitynet.org/tools/r_international.htm. Accessed 2 October 2009

Britten N (2008) Coastguards banned from using flares over health and safety fears. http://www.telegraph.co.uk/news/uknews/3372215/Coastguards-banned-from-using-flares-over-health-and-safety-fears.html. Accessed 2 October 2009

Brooks FP Jr (1975) The Mythical Man Month. Addison-Wesley, Reading MA

Browne W, Gregory D, Phillips A, Unwin M (2004) Declining mathematical standards among science and engineering undergraduates: fact or fallacy? http://www.nottingham.ac.uk/pesl/browse/faculty/cross/declinin208/. Accessed 7 September 2009

Campbell D (2009) GPs fear swine flu misdiagnosis. http://www.guardian.co.uk/world/2009/aug/05/gps-fear-swine-flu-misdiagnosis. Accessed 2 October 2009

Crichton M (2005) Complexity theory and environmental management. http://www.crichton-official.com/speech-complexity.html. Accessed 2 October 2009

Daily Mail (2008) Lifeboat banned by health and safety three hours after saving drowning schoolgirl. http://www.dailymail.co.uk/news/article-1045170/Lifeboat-banned-health-safety-hours-saving-drowning-schoolgirl.html. Accessed 2 October 2009

Drury RS (1997) Flying the MD-11: one pilot's perspective. Airways Magazine, September/October 1997, pp 39–49

Dvorak DL (ed) (2009) NASA study on flight software complexity. http://oceexternal.nasa.gov/OCE_LIB/pdf/1021608main_FSWC_Final_Report.pdf. Accessed 2 October 2009

Eustice C, Eustice R (1999) Celebrex causes concern. http://arthritis.about.com/od/celebrex/a/causesconcern.htm. Accessed 2 October 2009

Goldacre B (2008) Bad science. Fourth Estate, London

Hatton L (1999) Towards a consistent legal framework for understanding software systems behaviour. LLM thesis, Strathclyde Law School

Hatton L (2004) Safer language subsets: an overview and a case history, MISRA C. Information and Software Technology 46:465–472

Hatton L (2007) The chimera of software quality. IEEE Computer 40(8):101–103

Hope C (2009) Hundreds wrongly branded criminals by agency. London Daily Telegraph, 4 August, including editorial

Isaacs J (1973) The world at war. Thames Television. http://en.wikipedia.org/wiki/The_World_At_War. Accessed 2 October 2009

Johnson B (2009) Health and safety fears are making Britain a safe place for extremely stupid people. http://www.telegraph.co.uk/comment/columnists/borisjohnson/5754533/Health-and-safety-fears-are-making-Britain-a-safe-place-for-extremely-stupid-people.html. Accessed 2 October 2009

Lelyveld M (2008) China's bureaucracy stymies food safety. http://www.rfa.org/english/energy_ watch /food-safety-11042008154540.html. Accessed 2 October 2009

Paulos JA (2001) Innumeracy: mathematical illiteracy and its consequences. Hill and Wang, New York

REng (2004) The challenge of complex IT projects. Royal Academy of Engineering, London

Smith R (2009) Measles epidemic feared after 'unprecedented rise' in cases. http://www. telegraph.co.uk/health/healthnews/4208552/Measles-epidemic-feared-after-unprecedented- rise-in-cases.html. Accessed 2 October 2009

Tichy WF (1998) Should computer scientists experiment more? IEEE Computer 31(5):32–40

Winn M (2009) The seven Dao alchemy formulas of the immortal self. http://www.healingtaousa .com/tao_alchemy_formulas.html. Accessed 6 August 2009

Cost-Efficient Methods and Processes for Safety Relevant Embedded Systems (CESAR) – An Objective Overview

Graham Jolliffe

Quintec Associates Ltd

Basingstoke, UK

Abstract For developing embedded safety critical systems, industrial companies have to face increasing complexity and variety coupled with increasing regulatory constraints, while costs, performances and time to market are constantly challenged. This has led to a profusion of enablers (new processes, methods and tools), which are neither integrated nor interoperable because they have been developed more or less independently (addressing only a part of the complexity: e.g. Safety) in the absence of internationally recognized open standards. CESAR has been established under ARTEMIS, the European Union's Joint Technology Initiative for research in embedded systems, with the aim to improve this situation and this paper will explain what CESAR's objectives are, how they are expected to be achieved and, in particular, how current best practice can ensure that safety engineering requirements can be met.

1 Introduction

The proposal for CESAR (Cost-efficient methods and processes for safety relevant embedded systems) (Affenzeller et al 2008) mentions forecasts for 2015 which show a strong global increase (around 150%) in systems/software development costs for all domains considered by CESAR related projects. This increase will be well above the market growth and almost twice the growth of general R&D expenditure. This means that systems/software development and especially safety-critical software development is a key and increasingly strategic factor for industry competitiveness overall.

CESAR is focussing on safety and cost-effectiveness to bring significant and conclusive innovations in the two most improvable systems engineering disciplines:

- Requirements engineering including through formalization of requirements,

C. Dale, T. Anderson (eds.), *Making Systems Safer*, DOI 10.1007/978-1-84996-086-1_3,
© Springer-Verlag London Limited 2010

- Component based engineering applied to design space exploration comprising multi view/multi criteria architecture trade-offs, together with development and implementation.

In addition CESAR intends to provide industrial companies with a breakthrough in system development by deploying a customizable systems engineering platform making it possible to integrate existing or emerging available technologies.

Most important European industry players are gathered in the project. It is expected that this critical mass will provide a capability, called the Reference Technology Platform (RTP). This will be a significant step forward in terms of industrial performance improvement and will allow the establishment of de-facto standards and contribution to the standardization effort from a European perspective. The participants represent the following domains:

- Aviation (on board and ground systems, not air traffic control)
- Space
- Automotive (on board systems and part of the roadside infrastructure)
- Rail (on board and interlocking systems)
- Industrial automation.

Jointly, the cross-domain and cross-supplier chain coverage of CESAR's industrial stakeholders together with academia assures a strong market impact, establishing the meta-modelling and tool-interoperability standards provided in the RTP as future standards for safety critical system design.

This paper will explain the concept and benefits of CESAR and, in particular, it will concentrate on how best practice within the safety domain can help achieve these benefits.

2 Concept and Objectives

CESAR addresses the industrial needs for embedded system development for safety relevant applications of developing ultra-reliable embedded components in an extremely competitive global market requiring drastic cost reductions. Applications developed in CESAR address these needs, and are used to demonstrate the cross-domain relevance of CESAR innovations in five application domains listed above. Though the requirements management and design practices in each domain are highly structured by specific supply chain organizations and by specific certification or qualification rules, it is recognized that:

- the scientific basis of component based design of dependable systems are common to the domains; and
- there is room in the market for technically innovative cross-domain support tools.

To maintain the European leading edge position in the transportation and automation market against competition CESAR aims at boosting cost efficiency of embedded systems development and safety and certification processes by an order of magnitude, according to the quantitative objectives shown below in Table 1.

Table 1. CESAR Quantitative Objectives

		Scope			
Area	Quantitative Objective	Aerospace	Automotive	Rail	Automation
Process	Introduce in each domain at least one significant innovation in design, integration or validation process, clearly supported by CESAR, acceptable across the supply chain and by certification authorities when appropriate, resulting in overall reduction of development time or effort, between 30% and 50%, depending on the domain	x	x	x	x
Process	Demonstrate, at least in one domain, a reduction by 50% of the effort of re-validation and re-certification after change, the process being acceptable across the supply chain if appropriate, and by certification authorities	x	n/a	x	x
Product Process	Demonstrate, at least in one domain a 100% complexity increase of the product with 20% engineering effort reduction		x		
Product	Introduce in each domain at least one major product capability improvement clearly related with CESAR, without impact on recurring cost	x	x	x	x

This will be achieved by:

- Creating the European cross-domain standard RTP providing meta-models, methods, and tools for safety-relevant hard-real-time system development;
- Supporting holistic multi-criteria end-to-end design flows from system conception and requirement capturing to system realization based on a standardized formal requirement capturing language;
- Allowing the guiding, optimization and assessment of systems/multi-systems architecture choices against business and operational criteria (cost, safety, reliability, minimization of system interfaces, response times mass, …);
- Providing complete encapsulation and full design re-use through multi-criteria rich component models; and
- A suite of multi-criteria design, analysis and validation methods supporting consistency analysis, safety analysis, verification and validation supporting the CESAR RTP.

3 Creating the RTP

3.1 Concept

CESAR is broken down into a number of Sub-Projects (SPs), one of which envisages a reference technology platform (RTP) comprising meta-models for design artefacts, engineering processes, application classes and tools allowing the automated configuration of a suite of seamless integrated fully interoperable design tools fitting the needs for dedicated application classes. This is illustrated in Figure 1 below, which shows how the RTP builds on meta-models (1) and compatible components (2) to enable construction of customized System Development Environments (3).

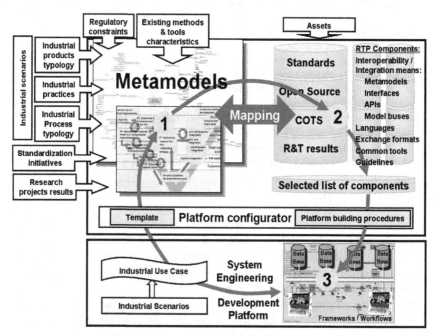

Fig. 1. The CESAR Reference Technology Platform

The current state of the art for meta-modelling is characterized by an increasing trend towards extending domain specific de-facto standard meta-models as well as modelling standards such as SysML towards meta-models completely covering all design levels of embedded system design. The number of initiatives provides ample evidence of providing extensions to enable comprehensive support for all phases of embedded systems design.

These include the development of timing and testing profiles for UML, extensions of the AUTOSAR (AUTomotive Open System ARchitecture) meta-model to increase support for timing analysis and to cover the higher phases of automotive system development.

3.2 Progress beyond the industrial state-of-the-art

The RTP would be of very limited value if it only captured the status quo. Although capturing the current state-of-the art includes best practice, it is recognised that there are still deficiencies and room for improvement with current processes, particularly with respect to new and emerging technologies. Consequently, embedded systems with high safety requirements will contribute more and more to the total costs and value creation in a large variety of equipment serving application areas such as transportation applications (automotive, aerospace, rail), industrial applications (process control and automation), and medical and energy generation applications. Many prominent stakeholders of these domains are already represented in the project.

Table 2. Snap-Shot of Current Major Weaknesses

Weaknesses	Automotive	Aerospace	Expected Benefits
Lack of requirements formalisation	Requirements are manually written and subject to interpretation.	Requirements are manually written based on internal patterns. For highly critical systems, a translation in a semi formal language is sometimes used. Most of the errors discovered before delivery to the flight tests come from the requirements, not from the development process.	Formalisation of requirements will help to avoid misinterpretation, and interference between levels. Consistency checking will force early answers to difficult questions and force detail early, reducing rework through identifying issues earlier.
Integration issues	AUTOSAR initiative already provides a potential de facto standard for system software development, integration and reuse. This needs wider discussion.	IMA already provides a potential de facto standard for system and software integration and reuse. However, there are differing definitions of Integrated Modular Avionics and to what extent is should be developed further.	Reduce the number of problem reports by 30 % at first integration at system level then 50 %. Reduce the risks of integration of new software with existing software.
A system is certified or used as a whole in a specific application.		Modular certification can be achieved by robust partitioning, but other techniques need investigating.	Modular certification reduces costs dramatically while contributing to the overall system performance.

Table 2 above is a snap-shot of some of the current major weaknesses identified regarding electronic and safety critical software development in the various domains and the expected benefits after CESAR is implemented.

A fuller table in the CESAR proposal considers all of the system engineering weaknesses for each domain. However, this paper is confined to the safety aspects of CESAR. In order to address these issues a safety and diagnosability task force has been established, whose objectives are outlined below.

4 Safety-Diagnosability Task Force

4.1 Objectives

Safety and diagnosability are core issues of the project aiming at providing efficient approaches to develop and validate critical embedded systems all along the product life cycle (development and maintenance). 'Diagnosability' is defined as the ability of a system to support the identification of information related to its potential faults. Although this paper concentrates upon the safety aspects of the task force, the industrial partners within CESAR have placed a significant emphasis on the ability of systems to support diagnosability, as this is seen as having increasing significance as systems are developed with more complexity and greater automation.

The task force will enrich the specifications by fault robustness and diagnosability requirements in order to prove lack of errors in design/architecture, to ensure proper identification and efficient processing/containment of faults and to perform upfront verifications during the design process, in compliance with relevant safety standards such as:

- SAE ARP4761 Guidelines and Methods for Conducting the Safety Assessment Process on Civil Airborne Systems and Equipment (SAE 1996b)
- CENELEC EN 50126/8/9 railway applications safety standards (CENELEC 1999, 2000, 2001)
- ECSS-Q-ST-40C safety standard for space systems (ECSS 2009)
- ISO/DIS 26262 in automotive safety projects (ISO 2009)
- IEC 61508, Functional Safety of Electrical/Electronic/Programmable Electronic Safety-Related Systems in the industrial process control and automation industry (IEC 2001)

From a safety perspective this needs to be a combination of evidence from both design process and product test results. Ideally, both should complement and reinforce each other, but product evidence will always be stronger than process evidence.

Model-based engineering and validation approaches must be exploited to efficiently support the design for safety and diagnosability approach and the rigorous assessment of these properties. There are a number of modelling techniques that safety engineers use which need to be integrated with model based engineering. Thess includes but are not limited to Fault Tree Analysis (FTA), Event Tree Analysis (ETA), Reliability, Availability and Maintainability techniques (Markov, Reliability Block Diagrams), and Goal Structured Notation. The latter is used to illustrate a safety argument within the safety case, but has many other applications which have yet to be fully exploited.

The task force will therefore provide safety and diagnosability requirements to the innovation subprojects, assess results with respect to these requirements and provide feedback and advices for the RTP versions.

The task force objectives are to:

- Analyze all use cases and scenarios of project partners so as to identify which ones are relevant to safety and diagnosability issues addressed in the project;
- Extract from those scenarios and partner user requirements the safety and diagnosability requirements for the project;
- Assure that requirements on processes and methods from pertinent safety standards are met;
- Monitor and assess the project results with respect to the safety and diagnosability requirements, and provide guidance to the technical SPs regarding innovative methods and techniques. This will be done iteratively during the project, based on the use cases and scenario experimentations as performed by domain subproject partners.

To achieve this, the task force will need to interact with bodies in control of pertinent safety standards ensuring awareness and acceptance of methods and tools included in the RTP.

4.2 Achievements To-Date

4.2.1 State of the Practice Survey

In order to establish the status quo within system safety in each domain, it was identified early that a project level global survey would be required which identified the state of the art and the state of practice on safety and diagnosability issues, and identify gaps and potentials for improvement. The focus was put especially on the links between dependability, safety and diagnosability properties and advanced engineering and validation approaches. This survey is an input for the definition of the RTP, to be taken into account by the innovation SPs and used in the application domain specific SPs to detect techniques in this area that can be used across domains, but are not yet standard beyond the application specific context.

The survey invited participants to complete a questionnaire which needed to identify why each of the safety aspects listed below were required together with their benefits and drawbacks. The safety aspects considered included:

- Applicable Standards, Norms and Regulations
- Constraints imposed by Standards, Norms and Regulations
- Requirements Engineering Process including;

  - Process Description
  - Traceability
  - Consistency and Completeness
  - Re-Use
  - Non-functional Requirements
  - Interoperability
  - Languages, Methods and Tools

- Design Process
- Implementation Process
- V&V Process
- Configuration Management Process
- Documentation Process
- Safety Process including:

  - Certification Issues
  - Process Description
  - Languages, Methods and Tools

- Diagnosability
- Product Lines

The safety-diagnosability task force then performed a synthesis (Blanquart et al 2009) focused on safety and diagnosability, from the answers to the questionnaires, which were also used by other groups of Cesar for their own objectives. In order to inform the rest of the CESAR project, this task was completed within a two month timeframe. However, it was acknowledged that the limited time available would mean that the survey would potentially be incomplete. Therefore, it is expected to update this survey as the rest of the project continues.

4.2.2 Safety and Diagnosability Subproject Requirements Elicitation

Safety and diagnosability approaches in different domains vary due to the specific requirements of the application domain. Therefore, the identification of requirements is necessary for common cross domain core safety, which includes diagnosability techniques and methods. This task provides these requirements as input to the innovation subprojects and is split into three iterative phases. In the first and current phase, the requirements are listed in each application domain and the constraints imposed by the standards are explained together with the applicable safety process in each respective domain (Machrouh et al 2009). This task also uses the results from the survey above to establish whether different approaches between domains are due to the specific safety requirements of the domain or whether they have shared properties. Care needs to be taken here, not to attempt to force fit 'common' safety methods in specialist areas. There needs to be 'buy-in' of any unfamiliar techniques. Ideally, a particular domain should clearly be able to see the benefit of using a proposed common technique. A particular area needing investigation is accreditation. This is usually embedded in legislative requirements, which may not be open to discussion. Although there is a considerable amount of experience within the group of participants, it is recognised that a lot of work has been completed by other distinguished authors. Reference has been made to a number of papers (Coombes 1999, Pygott 1999, Kelly and McDermid 1997) on related issues in order to ensure the input to the elicitation is as comprehensive as possible. The results so far provide some description of standards used in different application domains and a description about safety processes and why standards are used and needed to deal with functional safety.

It is important to understand the hierarchical relationship between different standards, as illustrated in Figure 2.

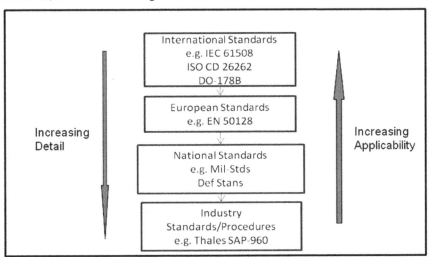

Fig. 2. Hierarchy of Standards

Usually, the higher the level (e.g. International) the less technical detail is contained, since this is likely to prevent the widespread use intended. This may be caused by differing legislative requirements at international and national levels, for example. Therefore, it is often the case that such standards contain generic principles and processes, which can be used in a variety of domains, thus increasing the standards' intended applicability. At the other end of the scale, specific standards and processes may be used by industry to cover local practices, techniques and procedures. These will often depend upon the established tools and experience within that industry and, therefore, will not be suitable or applicable outside that industry's domain or location.

There is also a relationship between standards across domains to consider. Some standards will be developed which are specific to a particular domain, whilst others are more generic and can be applied irrespective of the domain in question. Figure 3 below shows just one example of how this relationship might be considered. However, this is not intended to be comprehensive at this stage of the project and there are also examples of standards written specifically for one domain, which have since been used in other domains. This is usually because of the common good practice used. An example of this is the UK Motor Industry's MISRA C standard, which identifies a 'safer' subset of C for use in safety related software development. The widespread use of C has meant that some other (but not all) engineering domains have been keen to adopt the same standard.

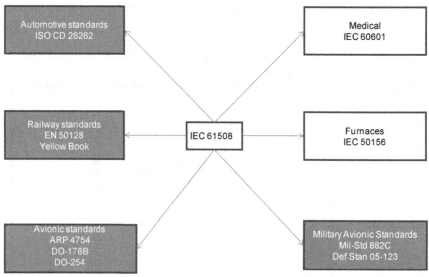

Fig. 3. Relationship of Standards between Domains

It is also important to understand that common standards are not a pre-requisite for specific domains. For example, it is not essential to comply with IEC 61508 (IEC 2001) in order to develop a safe rail, automotive or avionic system. Equally, compliance with IEC 61508 will not ensure that all of the safety considerations within a specific domain have been taken into account. The standards within those domains may well be sufficient to ensure sufficient safety of systems within those domains. The question then becomes, to what extent does compliance to IEC 61508 satisfy the domain standards, and vice versa? The answer invariably depends upon the project. The question has become increasingly relevant in recent years as systems have become more complex and utilise previously qualified components and sub-systems used in other domains.

The shaded cases in Figure 3 represent some of the application domains covered by CESAR.

The investigation has shown that, despite the difference at detailed level, the different standards describe very similar approaches to the development and assessment of safety critical systems. These commonalities can help us to extract the common requirements.

With respect to the safety processes, it has been found, perhaps not surprisingly, that the aerospace domain is the most detailed. As far as the aerospace domain is concerned CESAR has a specific sub-project addressing specific requirements in that domain. ARP 4754 (SAE 1996a) and ARP 4761 (SAE 1996b) provide the system context under which those avionics are developed and integrated. However, DO-178B (RTCA 1992) and DO-254 (RTCA 2000) are the main standards for developing qualifiable avionics as part of a commercial civil aeroplane Type Certificate (TC). Figure 4 below summarises and links the elements of avionics standards.

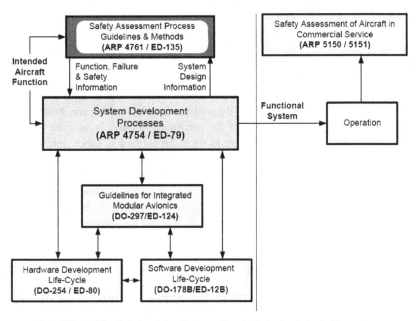

Fig. 4. The Relationships Between Standards in the Avionic Domain

The description of each safety process for each domain will allow us to extract a list of safety requirements for the RTP.

Two further iterations of this task are planned and will allow understanding of the processes used in different applications domain covered by CESAR. The major changes expected for the next iteration include:

- Standards evolution and their impact in the safety process
- Definition of common safety requirements for the CESAR tools platform
- Support tools
- Diagnosability.

5 CESAR Challenges

CESAR has very ambitious objectives and the task for the safety team is particularly challenging as it seeks to achieve commonality and consensus across a variety of engineering domains. The project also has considerable project management, communication and coordination difficulties to overcome, which is to be expected in a pan-European project. It is not intended to detail these aspects in this paper, which are being addressed by a very proficient team used to working on projects across different nations, using a very good web-based communications platform to ensure all participants have the best visibility of each others activities. Instead, this paper is focused on the safety challenges resulting from the objectives of CESAR. The safety challenges can be grouped into three areas. The first group covers the varying approaches to safety by each of the engineering domains. This is well recognised in the CESAR proposal and has been addressed by the way in which the project is planned. The initial deliverable from the Safety Task Force has already identified these differing approaches in the way in which system safety is currently achieved. However, the Task Force has yet to attempt to synthesise these approaches, or indeed, to determine if there is a common strategy for achieving best practice. For instance if the aerospace domain is deemed to have the most comprehensive processes, should these be applied to other domains, or will that make them less efficient and over-engineered from a safety perspective?

The second group of challenges covers how new developments in system safety techniques should be assessed and to what extent should they should be adopted by the individual domains. There are numerous examples here including the extent to which requirements should be specified in a formal language and whether 'goal' orientated standards should be used more widely. These issues cover all or most domains, but they may well be new concepts in some of those domains and, therefore, there will be issues and challenges of acceptance.

Finally, there are legislative considerations to take into account. Fortunately, there has been a great deal of harmonisation work in EC directives, which should limit potential areas of conflict. However, there are still variations between EU member states. The most obvious is the application of ALARP in the UK, which has not been adopted to the same extend elsewhere within the EU. There are also domain variations, where historically, system safety has taken differing approaches. The rail industry is a good example in this respect, with differences due to the historical development within each nation.

These challenges are what make the CESAR project interesting. However, the fact that these challenges are recognised does at least mean that effort will be applied to address them.

6 Conclusion

Although CESAR will need to address and overcome a number of issues from a safety perspective, the diversification and varied experience of the participants will add new dimensions and perspectives. To achieve these benefits and meet the objectives does require an open mind and the right mix of flexibility and determination.

CESAR (CESAR 2009) commenced in March 2009 and has a planned duration of three years. It is part of the ARTEMIS Joint Technology Initiative and is partially funded by the European Commission. So, at the time of writing, the progress made from a safety perspective has been limited to the production of the state of the art survey and the first iteration of safety and diagnosability requirements elicitation. Perhaps greater time should have been allowed for the survey, which will need further development to make it as comprehensive as possible. However, some initial results were needed to permit other SPs and tasks to commence and any shortcomings can be rectified if it is continually updated. The requirements elicitation has proved more successful, with substantial contributions from a large number of participants from a variety of engineering domains. These have been collated and peer reviewed to produce a fairly comprehensive document. It does acknowledge that there are areas for further work, and it is hoped that recent developments in system safety techniques, including those promoted in the UK, will be integrated into subsequent releases, ultimately to populate the RTP.

The objectives for CESAR are challenging, but achievable. It may be too soon to determine if the project will be a success, but there is no doubt that CESAR will be an important step in achieving a consistent and cost-effective approach to systems engineering of safety relevant systems.

References

Affenzeller J et al (2008) Cost-efficient methods and processes for safety relevant embedded systems. Available from info@cesarproject.eu
Blanquart J-P et al (2009) Safety-Diagnosability state-of-the-art survey D_SP1_R5.1_M1. Available from info@cesarproject.eu
CENELEC (1999) EN 50126 Railway Applications – The Specification and Demonstration of Reliability, Availability, Maintainability and Safety (RAMS). European Committee for Electrotechnical Standardization
CENELEC (2000) EN 50129 Railway Applications – Safety related Electronic Systems for Signalling. European Committee for Electrotechnical Standardization
CENELEC (2001) EN 50128 Railway Applications – Software for Railway Control and Protection Systems. European Committee for Electrotechnical Standardization
CESAR (2009) CESAR Project Website. https://cesarproject.eu/. Accessed 9 September 2009

Coombes A (1999) Comparison of Standards for Safety Related Software Development CF171/3/53. Available from CSE International Ltd, Glanford House, Bellwin Drive, Flixborough Industrial Estate, Flixborough, Scunthorpe, DN15 8SN

DoD (1993) Mil-Std 882C System Safety Program Requirements. Department of Defense

ECSS (2009) ECSS-Q-ST-40C Space Product Assurance – Safety. European Cooperation for Space Standardization

IEC (2001) IEC 61508 Functional Safety of Electrical/Electronic/Programmable Electronic Safety-Related Systems. International Electrotechnical Commission

ISO CD 26262 (2005) Road vehicles - Functional safety. International Organization for Standardization

Kelly T and McDermid J (1997) Safety Case Construction and Reuse using Patterns. Available from the authors at Department of Computer Science, University of York, York, Y01 5DD

Machrouh J et al (2009) Safety-Diagnosability Requirements Specification V1 D_SP1_R5.2_M1. Available from info@cesarproject.eu

MISRA (2004) MISRA-C Guidelines for the use of the C language in critical systems. www.misra-c2.com. Accessed 21 September 2009

MoD (2004) Def Stan 05-123 Technical Procedures for the Procurement of Aircraft, Weapons and Electronic Systems. Ministry of Defence

Pygott C (1999) A Comparison of Avionics Standards. Available from the author at QinetiQ Farnborough, Farnborough, Hampshire, GU14 0LX

RTCA (1992) DO-178B Software Considerations in Airborne Systems and Equipment Certification. RTCA Inc.

RTCA (2000) DO-254 Design Assurance Guidance for Airborne Electrical Hardware. RTCA Inc.

SAE (1996a) ARP4754 Certification Considerations for Highly-Integrated or Complex Aircraft Systems. SAE International

SAE (1996b) ARP4761 Guidelines and Methods for Conducting the Safety Assessment Process on Civil Airborne Systems and Equipment. SAE International

Safety and Assurance Cases: Past, Present and Possible Future – an Adelard Perspective

Robin Bloomfield and Peter Bishop

Adelard LLP

London, UK

Abstract This paper focuses on the approaches used in safety cases for software based systems. We outline the history of approaches for assuring the safety of software-based systems, the current uptake of safety and assurance cases and the current practice on structured safety cases. Directions for further development are discussed.

1 History of Computer System Safety and Related Standards

The nuclear industry has had a major influence on the development of approaches to safety related computer system development and assurance. From the late 1970s the European Working Group on Industrial Computer Systems (EWICS), a cross-sector pre-standardisation working group, developed a series of guidelines and books that documented best practices. The guidance was subsequently incorporated into the IEC 880 standard on software for nuclear systems (IEC 1986). The experience of EDF and Merlin-Gerin with the first generation of reactor protection systems, SPIN, was fed into the committee. The software engineering approach in the EWICS guidelines (Redmill 1988, 1989) and their book on safety techniques (Bishop 1990) represented the then state of the art.

In the UK there were a number of policy initiatives. The ACARD report (ACARD 1986) and subsequent IEE/BCS and HSE studies (IEE 1989, HSE 1987) set the scene and in 1988 the Interdepartmental Committee on Software Engineering (ICSE) established its Safety-Related Software (SRS) Working Group to coordinate the Government's approach to this important issue. Members were drawn from a wide range of departments and agencies: CAA, CEGB, DES, DoE, DTI, DoH, DoT, HSE, MoD, RSRE and SERC. The work was motivated 'not by recognition of particular present dangers; rather by a desire to anticipate and forestall hazards which may arise with the very rapid pace of technical change'.

The UK Health and Safety Executive (HSE) were active in taking the lead in ICSE and this, with support from DTI, led to a consultation document known as

C. Dale, T. Anderson (eds.), *Making Systems Safer*, DOI 10.1007/978-1-84996-086-1_4,
© Springer-Verlag London Limited 2010

SafeIT (Bloomfield 1990) and an associated standards framework (Bloomfield and Brazendale 1990). HSE also published awareness documents on the safety of programmable electronic systems (PES), including the Out of Control report (HSE 1993), and some earlier studies that looked at the feasibility of providing a validated framework for selecting software engineering techniques. SafeIT identified four main areas of activity requiring a coordinated approach: standards and certification; research and development; technology transfer; education and training.

The UK MoD were, as one might expect, pioneers in the use of critical software and the development of static analysis tools to analyse the code (Malpas) as well as forays into formally proven hardware designs. In the light of finding defects in certain operational systems, dramatic changes to the supply chain as well as reductions in MoD scientific personnel, they responded in 1989 with the publication of a new draft interim standard 00-55 (MoD 1989). This used expertise from the nuclear and aerospace industry, MoD and elsewhere to develop a market leading standard around the requirements for mathematically formally verified software and statistical testing.

It was soon realised – in part because of the attempt to classify systems as non-safety critical and outside the remit of 00-55 – that a wider system standard was needed. This led to Def Stan 00-56 (MoD 1991). There was considerable work to take into account strong industry and trade association comments (led by the DTI that developed a detailed trace from all comments to the final issue of the standard).

In parallel with the development in the defence sector, the HSE led the production of the IEC generic standards that became known as IEC 61508 (IEC 1998). Draft publications (IEC 1993) emerged in the early 1990s sharing much in common with the defence standards but addressing a wide range of systems and safety criticalities. During their prolonged drafting they developed detail, consistency and international recognition. However the technical basis of their software aspects remained fixed. The software techniques guidance in IEC 61508 and its software engineering approach was essentially just an extension and internationalisation of EWICS guidance on techniques (Bishop 1990). There are still a number of technical difficulties in IEC 61508 (e.g. how SILs are used) and it lacks a requirement for a safety case.

Around 1993 the limitations to the claims that could be justified by testing were investigated by NASA (Butler and Finelli 1993), and similar results, involving testing and other evidence, were published by Littlewood and Strigini (1993). The 10^{-4} limit was one set by pragmatics of testing technology, but did not include the assumption doubt that we might now make explicit (Bloomfield and Littlewood 2007).

In 1997 the 1991 Interim MoD Def Stan 00-55 was revised to become a full standard and became the first standard to explicitly require a software safety case. This was a radical departure from previous standards but offered some flexibility in the justification of the software, important in view of industry comments on the interim standard. The key features of the revised standard were:

- Deterministic reasoning and proof
- Statistical testing
- Importance of a range of attributes (not just correctness)
- Multi-legged arguments and associated metaphors (belt and braces rather than a wing and a prayer)
- Safety cases and reports
- Sound process to provide trustworthy evidence
- Systematic approach and clarity of roles and responsibilities and other recommendations to reduce project risks
- Evidence preferences: *deterministic* evidence is usually to be preferred to statistical; *quantitative* evidence is usually to be preferred to qualitative; *direct* evidence is usually to be preferred to indirect

The nuclear expertise was influential in Def Stan 00-55. As with many standards and guidelines 00-55 grappled with how to treat software of lower criticalities: at one extreme everything is required and at the other a minimum set of good practices. Populating the regions in between has been problematic and largely a product of the standards process rather than the scientific one. More recently 00-55 has become part of a reissued 00-56 (MoD 2004) and no longer contains software integrity levels.

Adelard had an important role in the development of the defence standards and drafted the safety case requirements. The origins of the work go back to the individuals' involvement (Bloomfield, Bishop and Froome) in the days of the Public Inquiry into the Sizewell B Primary Protection System (CEGB 1982). The work is similar to the approach used by Toulmin (1958) although developed somewhat independently. The concepts were first documented in the EU SHIP project and the work was taken up within a UK nuclear research programme. This led to the first software safety case publication and, in 1998, to ASCAD (Bloomfield et al. 1998, Bishop and Bloomfield 1998), a safety case development manual (still the only one). ASCAD provided the now customary definition of a case as 'a documented body of evidence that provides a convincing and valid argument that a system is adequately safe for a given application in a given environment'. In addition to the Adelard work there was research being done at York University (McDermid 1994) that later led to the Goal Structuring Notation described in Kelly's PhD (Kelly 1998).

The ASCAD manual incorporated, with permission, considerable work from the UK nuclear research programme:

- On long-term and safety case maintenance
- How to address specific design issues, even the work on reversible computing
- The work on worst case reliability bounds
- Field experience collected from a range of projects and also used in the SOCS report (ACSNI 1997)
- On argument architecture based on analogies and analysis of PWR pressure vessel cases (Hunns and Wainwright 1991, CEGB 1982).

It also made use of nuclear work on safety culture and work from REAIMS on organisational learning and human factors (Bloomfield et al. 1998).

In 1995 the Advisory Committee on the Safety of Nuclear Installations (ACSNI)[1] set up the Study Group on the Safety of Operational Computer Systems with the following terms of reference:

- to review the current and potential uses of computer systems in safety-critical applications;
- to consider the implications for the nuclear industry;
- in this context, to consider developments in the design and safety assessment of such computer-based systems, including other aspects of control systems; and
- to advise ACSNI where further research is necessary.

The report from this group (ACSNI 1998) addressed the broad principles upon which the evidence and reasoning of an acceptable safety case for a computer-based, safety-critical system should be based. It also discussed, but did not attempt to cover in detail, the extent to which the UK nuclear industry already accepts these principles in theory, and the extent to which they act on them in practice. It made a number of recommendations on regulatory practice, safety cases, computer system design and software engineering, standards, and research.

2 Current Practice in Software Safety and Regulation

The justification that a system is fit for purpose (and continues to be fit for purpose as the environment, use and implementation change) is a complex socio-technical process. In safety regulation in general there has been a widespread adoption of safety case regimes. The Robens Report (Robens 1972) and the Cullen Inquiry (Cullen 1990) were major drivers behind the UK regulatory agencies exploring the benefits of introducing goal-based regulations. The reports noted several shortcomings with prescriptive safety regulations: that is regulations that provide a strict definition of how to achieve the desired outcome.

Firstly, with prescriptive regulations, the service provider is required only to carry out the mandated actions to discharge his legal responsibilities. If these actions then prove to be insufficient to prevent a subsequent accident, it is the regulations and those that set them that are seen to be deficient. Thus safety can be viewed as the responsibility of the regulator and not the service provider whose responsibility, in law, it actually is.

Secondly, prescriptive regulations tend to be a distillation of past experience and, as such, can prove to be inappropriate or at worst to create unnecessary dangers in industries that are technically innovative.

Thirdly, prescriptive regulations encode the best engineering practice at the time that they were written and rapidly become deficient where best practice is

---

[1] Became the Nuclear Safety Advisory Committee (NuSAC) and then disbanded.

changing e.g. with evolving technologies. In fact it is quite probable that prescriptive regulations eventually prevent the service provider from adopting current best practice.

Another driver for adopting goal-based regulation, from a legal viewpoint, is that overly-restrictive regulation may be viewed as a barrier to open markets. Various international agreements, EC Directives and Regulations are intended to promote open markets and equivalent safety across nations. Whilst it is necessary to prescribe interoperability requirements and minimum levels of safety, prescription in other areas would defeat the aim of facilitating open markets and competition.

Finally, from a commercial viewpoint, prescriptive regulations could affect the cost and technical quality of available solutions provided by commercial suppliers. So there can be clear benefits in adopting a goal-based approach as it gives greater freedom in developing technical solutions and accommodating different standards.

A system safety case is now a requirement in many safety standards and regulations. Explicit safety cases are required for military systems, the off shore oil industry, rail transport and the nuclear industry. For example, in the UK a nuclear safety case must demonstrate, by one or other means, the achievement of ALARP. In the Health and Safety Commission's submission to the Government's 'Nuclear Review'[2] a Safety Case is defined as 'a suite of documents providing a written demonstration that risks have been reduced to ALARP. It is intended to be a living dossier which underpins every safety-related decision made by the licensee.'

The system safety case of course varies from sector to sector. The core of a nuclear system safety case is (i) a deterministic analysis of the hazards and faults which could arise and cause injury, disability or loss of life from the plant either on or off the site, and (ii) a demonstration of the sufficiency and adequacy of the provisions (engineering and procedural) for ensuring that the combined frequencies of such events will be acceptably low. Safety systems will feature amongst the risk reducing provisions comprised in this demonstration, which will thus include qualitative substantiations of compliance with appropriate safety engineering standards supplemented (where practicable) by probabilistic analyses of their reliabilities. Other techniques which may be used for structuring the safety case include fault and event tree analysis, failure mode and effects analysis (FMEA) and hazard and operability studies (HAZOPS).

The safety case, particularly for computer based systems, traditionally contains diverse arguments that support its claims. These arguments are sometimes called the 'legs' of the safety case and are based on different evidence. Just as there is defence in depth in employing diversity at system architecture level, so we see an analogous approach within the safety case itself. Another important feature of the safety case process is independent assessment. The objective of independent assessment is to ensure that more than one person or team sees the evidence so as to overcome possible conflicts of interest and blinkered views that may arise from a single assessment. The existence of an independent assessor can also motivate the

---

[2] The review of the future of nuclear power in the UK's electricity supply industry.

assessed organisation. The relationship between independent assessment and 'legs' can however be complex.

Safety cases are important not only to minimise safety risks but also to reduce commercial and project risks. In industries such as nuclear, the need to demonstrate safety to a regulator can be a major commercial risk.

So to sum up, the motivation for a safety case is to:

- provide an assurance viewpoint that demonstrates that safety properties are satisfied and risks have been satisfactorily mitigated
- provide a mechanism for efficient review and the involvement of all stakeholders
- provide a focus and rationale for safety activities
- demonstrate discharge duty to public and shareholders
- allow interworking between different standards and support innovation.

So in a safety case the emphasis should be on the behaviour of product not just the process used to develop it: a useful slogan is 'What has been achieved not how hard you have tried'.

3 Uptake and Development of the Safety Case Approach

The incorporation of software safety case requirements in the defence standards drove interest in safety cases, and other forms of assurance case. A generalisation of the safety case concept also appears in Def Stan 00-42 Part 3 (MoD 2008), on the reliability and maintainability case, and in Part 2 (MoD 1997), which deals with the software reliability case. Similar requirements appear in equivalent NATO standards. Adelard has developed and marketed a supporting tool for safety cases (ASCE) and published a supporting methodology in the ASCAD manual. The University of York was also active in developing the safety case approach, such as the use of contracts to modularise safety cases (Fan and Kelly 2004) and safety case patterns (Kelly and McDermid 1997). Much of the work on safety cases and the supporting research is not published and this is becoming increasingly an issue. By their nature safety cases are sensitive for a variety of reasons (security, confidentiality, sensitivities) and not many are available in the public domain. Some safety case work has been published by the University of York (e.g. Chinneck 2004), some anonymised cases are available from Adelard, and John Knight maintains a list of some public cases (Virginia 2009). There is also useful briefing material at (Bloomfield et al. 2002) on safety and (Lipson 2008) on assurance cases. There are also some safety case templates available for UK defence projects.

Goal-based software safety cases have seen take up and interest shown from other sectors. In 1998 the UK CAA Safety Regulation Group drafted a goal based approach to the regulation of air traffic management systems and its proposals are contained in CAP 670 SW01, *Regulatory Objectives for Software Safety Assur-*

ance in Safety Related ATS Equipment' (CAA 2009). This has gone through a number of iterations. Proposals from Eurocontrol (Eurocontrol 2003) incorporate similar top level goals to CAP 670 SW01 and there is a guidance document from Eurocontrol on safety cases along with some examples and an introduction to GSN (Eurocontrol 2006).

The idea of a case has also applied in areas outside the safety arena. In the medical domain there is considerable work on trust cases (Gorski 2004) for IT systems and there is an International Working Group on Assurance Cases (for Security) (Bloomfield et al. 2006). In terms of security, the uptake by the US DHS of Assurance Cases is significant (Lipson 2008) as is their sponsorship of the draft international standard ISO/IEC 50126. The whole issue of evidence based approaches is receiving considerable international interest as indicated by the US NAS study (Jackson et al. 2007).

There is also work in validating simulation by the use of 'cases' – that is whether one can trust the results of a simulation for a new system. This is led by SE Validation, a small UK company.

4 Current Practice in Safety Cases

Our early definition of a safety case (Bloomfield et al. 1998) was

'a documented body of evidence that provides a convincing and valid argument that a system is adequately safe for a given application in a given environment'

More recent definitions (e.g. in the revised Def Stan 00-56) make explicit the concept of structured argumentation

'A structured *argument*, supported by a body of *evidence*, that provides a compelling, comprehensible and valid case that a *system is safe* for a given application in a given environment'

Current safety case practice makes use of the basic approach that can be related to the approach developed by Toulmin (1958) where claims are supported by evidence and a 'warrant' that links the evidence to the claim. There are variants of this basic approach that present the claim structure graphically such as Goal Structuring Notation (GSN) (Kelly and Weaver 2004) or Claims-Argument-Evidence (CAE) (Bloomfield et al. 1998). GSN is the dominant approach in the UK defence sector. These notations can be supported by tools (McDermid 1994, Emmett and Cleland 2002) that can help to create and modify the claim structure and also assist in the tracking of evidence status, propagation of changes through the case, and handling of automatic links to other requirements and management tools. However the actual claim decomposition and structuring is normally very informal and argumentation is seldom explicit. In practice, the emphasis is on communication and knowledge management of the case, with little guidance on what claim or claim decomposition should be performed.

Toulmin's scheme addresses all types of reasoning whether scientific, legal, aesthetic or management. The CAE style is much more like Toulmin's where we articulate and elaborate textually and yet retain the overall structure. The philosophical approach is that context and assumptions are often rich and complicated and best captured in narrative. A purely graphical rendering would be simplistic and verbose and would certainly go against the spirit of Toulmin in that reasoning can rarely be reduced to just a flow chart or logic network.

The 'case' and associated supporting tools can be seen as having two main roles:

Reasoning and argumentation. As an over-arching argumentation framework that allows us to reason as formally as necessary about all the claims being made. Here there are two very different viewpoints: the one that sees argumentation as primarily a narrative and the other where we seek to model judgements in a formal framework. There are some hybrid approaches where the case can be seen to integrate and communicate a selection of formal analyses and evidence, e.g. it would not seek to reason formally about the timing of a component but leave that to a separate analysis. The balance between these two approaches should be part of ongoing research.

Negotiation, communication, trust. As a boundary objective between the different stakeholders who have to agree (or not) the claims being made about the system. To this end it has to be detailed and rigorous enough to effectively communicate the case and allow challenges and the subsequent deepening of the case.

4.1 Safety Case Structures

One approach that we used in Adelard is to explain safety assurance in terms of a 'triangle' comprising:

- The use of accepted standards and guidelines.
- Justification via a set of claims/goals about the system's safety behaviour.
- An investigation of known potential vulnerabilities of the system.

This is illustrated in Figure 1 below.

The first approach is based on demonstrating compliance to a known safety standard. This is a common strategy, for example the Emphasis tool (Smith and Stockham 2007) produced by the nuclear industry supports an initial assessment of compliance with IEC61508.

The second approach is goal-based – where specific safety goals for the systems are supported by arguments and evidence at progressively more detailed levels. This would typically be implemented using Claims-Argument-Evidence (CAE) or goals-structuring notation (GSN) notations.

The final approach is a vulnerability-based argument, where it is demonstrated that potential vulnerabilities within a system do not constitute a problem. This is essentially a 'bottom-up' approach as opposed to the 'top-down' approach used in goal-based methods.

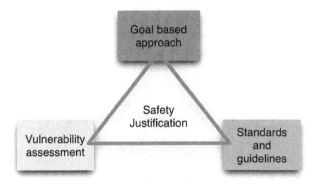

Fig. 1. The Safety Case Triangle

These approaches are not mutually exclusive, and a combination can be used to support a safety justification, especially where the system consists of both off-the-shelf (OTS) components and application-specific elements.

On behalf of the UK nuclear industry we have also been developing a more rigorous approach to claim decomposition. While the details have yet to be published this has involved an empirical study of a large number of safety cases available to Adelard (and reflecting the take up of the cases approach) allowing an informal empirical study of what is needed for a claims decomposition language.

The key technical concept behind the work is the idea that claims decomposition can be formalised in a rigorous way to demonstrate that the decomposition is complete, i.e. that the sub-claims actually do demonstrate the higher claim. This demonstration of completeness requires an extra 'side-condition' to the set of sub-claims that also need to be demonstrated to be correct. The soundness of the approach was established using the PVS proof tool. In practice a user need only choose the type of claim decomposition from the set of sound options. Demonstration of the 'side-condition' could be implemented informally via a checklist derived from the formal analysis, but in principle, it could be proved formally via a formal model of the system under consideration (e.g. to show that the timing of sub-components is additive).

An analysis of actual safety cases from a range of industries showed that only a limited number of decomposition strategies were used. The claim decompositions that we have identified empirically and then formalised are shown in Table 1 below.

Table 1. Formal Claim Decompositions (to be published)

Main types – keywords	Comment
architecture	splitting a component into several sub-components
functional	splitting a component into several sub-functions
set of attributes	splitting a property into several attributes
infinite set	inductive partitioning from a base case (e.g., over time)
complete	capturing the full set of values for risks, requirements, etc.
monotonic	the new system only improves on the old system
concretion	making informal statements less vague

4.2 Confidence, Challenge and Meta-Cases

The structured safety case, either in CAE or GSN notations, needs to be challenged and assessed if we are to be sure that it is fit for purpose. In some areas such as defence and nuclear there is a well defined process for such independent assessment.

The basic measure of efficacy of an argument in this work is the *confidence* that the argument engenders in a dependability claim. Informally here, a dependability case[3] is taken to be some *reasoning*, based upon *assumptions* and *evidence*, allowing certain *confidence* to be placed in a dependability *claim*. For a given claim (e.g. *pfd* is smaller than 10^{-3}), the confidence – and its complement, *doubt* – will depend upon confidence/doubt in the truth of assumptions, in correctness of reasoning, and in 'strength' of evidence.

A key notion here is the recognition that there is uncertainty involved in the assessment of system dependability: it is (almost) never possible to claim with certainty that a dependability claim is true. In the jargon this kind of uncertainty is called *epistemic* (Littlewood and Wright 2007). It concerns uncertainty in an expert's 'beliefs-about-the-world'. It contrasts with the more common *aleatory* uncertainty, which deals with 'uncertainty-in-the-world': e.g. uncertainty about when a software-based system will fail next. It is now widely accepted – even for software-based systems – that the latter is best measured using probabilities, such as probability of failure on demand.

In this work, probability is used to capture the epistemic uncertainty involved in the dependability case: it is the confidence in the truth of the dependability claim. An important part of the work investigates how effective multi-legged arguments are increasing such confidence (i.e. over and above the confidence that would arise from one of the legs alone). This work has been published in the open literature (Bloomfield and Littlewood 2003, Littlewood and Wright 2007).

---

[3] This is usually a *safety* case, but the ideas apply more generally to other dependability attributes such as reliability and security.

The results from this work concerning the efficacy of multi-legged arguments are, at first glance, not surprising. For example, it is shown that:

- there are benefits from the use of multi-legged arguments, compared with the single legs (the work only treats 2-legged arguments so far); and
- these benefits fall short of what could be expected if arguments 'failed' independently (e.g. if you have two argument legs, for each of which you obtain 10% doubt in the dependability claim, then you cannot expect your doubt to fall to 1% when they form the legs of a '1-out-of-2' argument).

But the work is more interesting than these bald results suggest, in two ways.

Firstly, the formal probabilistic treatment of confidence in claims is novel. It treats rigorously what is often ignored, or treated very informally, even in safety critical standards. It could be used to satisfy the recommendation arising from the SOCS report (ACSNI 1997) that an ACARP (As Confident As Reasonably Practical) principle be introduced into safety cases. So far, however, only theoretical modelling work has been done and its practicality needs to be proved on real safety cases, or realistic case studies. There also needs to be further work on how the formalism might fit into current regulatory practice (Bloomfield and Littlewood 2007).

Secondly, the detailed study of idealised safety cases, as in (Littlewood and Wright 2007), demonstrates how there can be subtle and non-intuitive interactions between the different – and usually disparate – components of a safety case. Although this example concerns a multi-legged case, the insights apply to any safety case in which confidence in a dependability claim rests upon disparate evidence (and this is, essentially, always). The BBN (Bayesian belief network) methodology used in this work – which retains a complete analytical description of the uncertainty – seems much more powerful than the usual numerical BBN treatments.

This work is not yet in a state where it could be taken up as the basis for tools to be used to help build safety cases. More work is needed in several areas – e.g. on the difficult problems of eliciting probabilistic beliefs from experts for input to the Bayesian analyses. On the other hand, it has given some novel insights and it points the way toward more rigorous ways of constructing quantitative probabilistic safety cases.

Current practice regarding confidence in often very pragmatic (e.g. 'traffic lighting' of evidence nodes in a graphical case).

4.3 Other Research

In addition to the work cited above, there has been a variety of other research into safety cases: work on modularity within the avionics sector (Bloomfield et al. 2002), work sponsored by HSE on assessing Software of Uncertain Pedigree (SOUP) (Jones et al. 2001, Bishop et al. 2002b, Bloomfield and Littlewood 2007, Bishop et al. 2002a, ACSNI 1997) and US work on fallibility and other issues

(Greenwell et al. 2006). A large amount of research has been sponsored by the nuclear industry, particularly in the UK.

Within the European nuclear industry, the Cemsis project – Cost Effective Modernisation of Systems Important to Safety (2001-4) – sought to *maximise safety* and *minimise costs* by developing common approaches within the EU to the development and approval of control and instrumentation systems that are regarded as 'systems important to safety' (SIS) that use modern commercial technology. The project had close contacts with the Task Force on Licensing Safety Critical Software of the Nuclear Regulator Working Group (NRWG) of the EU DG for Energy and Transport. The main results of the project are guidance documents on a proposed formal approach to safety justification of SIS (Courtois 2001), on requirements engineering for SIS and a qualification strategy for 'Commercial Off-The Shelf' (COTS) or 'pre-existing' software products. These were evaluated in a number of industrial-based case studies including a 'public domain' example that was used to explain and illustrate the guidance. The approach to new build in the UK specifically distinguishes claims, argument and evidence in the licensing requirements for the Generic Design Assessment for new reactors.

4.4 Specific Tool Support

Tool support for safety cases can be considered in three broad categories:

Decision Support and Elicitation Tools. These allow one to expose the thinking behind the argument, advise on how to construct a case, and assist in reading and review. The most commonly deployed tool specific to graphical safety cases is the Adelard ASCE tool. There is considerable research and development of alternative types of tool and integration with different environments. There is currently standardisation effort with the OMG on claims-argument-evidence and this should provide a good foundation for interoperability of tools and longevity of case documentation.

Tools to Generate Evidence. These provide the evidence that support the safety case argument. They include safety analysis tools (fault trees, FMECAs), tools for collecting and analysing field experience, static analysis , test and proof tools.

Safety Management System Infrastructure Support. In this category there are the tools for configuration management and traceability such as Requirements Engineering support tools and Hazard Logs.

5 Future Directions

Based on our review of past and current work on computer-based cases, we can identify a number of directions for the future development of cases.

5.1 Safety Case Methodology Enhancement

A lot of the current research has been focused on notation and structuring, but far less on how to develop a safety case and what arguments to deploy (Bishop and Bloomfield 1998, Eurocontrol 2006). We also have to recognise that safety cases are costly to develop, so we should seek more efficient means of construction. So there is scope for far more work in this area, including:

- Development of industry and sector specific argument 'templates' and linkage to sector standards and generic standards such as IEC 61508.
- Development of cases for specific classes of system for less critical and ultra critical systems (Littlewood 2000).
- Strategies for justifying COTS components within an overall safety justification.

5.2 Extension to Other Areas

Safety case concepts can be used in other areas that require assurance. There are a range of systems (e.g. for finance or communications) which are critical parts of the infrastructure where loss could have severe impacts on society. Assurance cases have been used to a limited degree, but may well be used more widely in future.

Also, as systems become more distributed and interconnected, there is an increasing need to include security and other attributes with the assurance case together with the incorporation of threat assumptions that include consideration of deliberate attacks as well as random events.

As part of this process, we need to extend our view of the 'system' we are seeking to assure. In the early days, the focus was on the technical system (hardware, software, sensor and actuators). In the future we need to think about the larger *socio-technical* system that includes the management, people and processes that interact with the technical system.

5.3 Safety Case Structuring

There is further work needed on structuring a case. This includes:

- more rigorous methods for claim decomposition
- modularisation of safety cases (so that safety arguments for subsystems can be re-used)
- the use of diverse arguments and evidence
- understanding and exploiting the relationship between the argument structure and the architecture of a system
- ensuring that the case is understandable by all stakeholders

We note that the use of diverse arguments and diverse evidence can help enhance confidence in a claim (discussed in the next section), but more work is needed on the integration of such evidence (like operational experience; statistical testing, formal proof, and process evidence) to support specific claims (such as reliability).

We also need to work on 'stopping rules', i.e. when to stop expanding claims. This is probably related to the degree of confidence the claim is correct without the need for any further supporting evidence.

5.4 Confidence and Challenge

Safety cases are open to challenge at a number of levels, such as the applicability of the arguments and the credibility of the evidence. Currently confidence is expressed in simplistic terms (e.g. using traffic lights) but it is not clear how a lack of confidence will propagate through to higher level claims. The means of expressing confidence in different aspects of the case requirements and modelling the impact on the top-level claims needs more formality and rigour.

There are also pragmatic issues of how such challenges and rebuttals are accommodated with the case. If they are included as nodes in the overall case, this can become very cluttered. It may be desirable to construct a 'meta-case' linked to the main case that includes such material, e.g. to justify the claim decomposition and the credibility of the evidence.

6 Concluding Remarks

The state of the art of safety cases for computer based systems has to be addressed within the context of regulation and system level approaches to safety. A structured approach to safety cases for computer based systems has been developed that addresses both the reasoning that safety properties are satisfied as well as providing an effective approach to communicating this reasoning. The acceptance of a case is (or should be), in the end, a social process.

The use of goal-based, structured cases is very appealing, supporting as it does innovation and flexibility but as can be seen from this review much work is needed to develop a case and put it on a convincing footing. While the basis of Toulmin's scheme is really very simple the industrialisation and application to complex systems is a significant undertaking. Our current approaches rely very heavily on the expertise and best practice of the community and the challenge and review that cases receive. The work is normally not published as there are sensitivities in most real cases and even the research that is being done is not well represented in the literature. This paper has attempted to identify public domain sources of information for those interested in the field. We hope that more will be made available during the year.

Acknowledgments The authors wish to acknowledge the support given by the UK Control and Instrumentation Nuclear Industry Forum (CINIF) research programme, the UK Health and Safety Executive research programme, the EU Environment programme (sub-theme Major Industrial Hazards) and the EU nuclear research programme who funded some of the research presented in this paper.

Disclaimer The views expressed in this paper are those of the authors and do not necessarily represent the views of the research sponsors.

References

ACARD (1986) Software: a vital key to UK competitiveness. Advisory Council on Applied Research and Development. HMSO
ACSNI (1997) The use of computers in safety-critical applications. Final Report of the Study Group on the Safety of Operational Computer Systems (SOCS) constituted by the Advisory Committee on the Safety of Nuclear Installations. HSE Books, London
Bishop PG (ed) (1990) Dependability of critical computer systems 3. Elsevier Applied Science
Bishop PG, Bloomfield RE (1995) The SHIP safety case. In: Rabe G (ed) Proc SafeComp 95, 14th IFAC Conf on Computer Safety, Reliability and Security, Belgirate, Italy
Bishop PG, Bloomfield RE (1998) A methodology for safety case development. In: Redmill F, Anderson T (eds) Industrial perspectives of safety-critical systems. Springer-Verlag
Bishop PG, Bloomfield RE, Clement TP, Guerra ASL (2002a) Software criticality analysis of COTS/SOUP. SAFECOMP 2002, Catania, Italy
Bishop PG, Bloomfield RE, Froome PKD (2002b) Justifying the use of software of uncertain pedigree (SOUP) in safety related applications. 5th Int Symp Programmable Electronic Systems in Safety Related Applications, Cologne
Bloomfield RE (1990) SafeIT, the safety of programmable electronic systems: a government consultation document on activities to promote the safety of computer-controlled systems. Department of Trade and Industry
Bloomfield RE, Brazendale J (1990) SafeIT2, standards framework. Department of Trade and Industry
Bloomfield RE, Littlewood B (2003) Multi-legged arguments: the impact of diversity upon confidence in dependability arguments. Proc DSN 2003. IEEE Computer Society
Bloomfield RE, Littlewood B (2007) Confidence: its role in dependability cases for risk assessment. Intl Conf Dependable Systems and Networks, Edinburgh, IEEE Computer Society

Bloomfield RE, Bishop PG, Jones CCM, Froome PKD (1998) ASCAD – Adelard safety case development manual. Adelard

Bloomfield RE et al (2002) Safety cases for PES. Adelard. http://www.adelard.com/web/hnav/resources/iee_pn/index.html. Accessed 17 October 2009

Bloomfield RE, Guerra S, Miller A et al (2006) International Working Group on Assurance Cases (for Security). IEEE Secur Priv 4:66-68

Butler R, Finelli G (1993) The infeasibility of quantifying the reliability of life-critical real-time software. IEEE Trans Software Engineering 19:3-12

CAA (2009) CAP 670 Air traffic services safety requirements, SW01 regulatory objectives for software safety assurance. Civil Aviation Authority Safety Regulation Group

CEGB (1982) Sizewell B preconstruction safety report. Central Electricity Generating Board

Chinneck P, Pumfrey DJ, Kelly TP (2004) Turning up the HEAT on safety case construction. In: Redmill F, Anderson T (eds) Practical elements of safety. Springer-Verlag

Courtois PJ (2001) Semantic structures and logic properties of computer-based system dependability cases. Nucl Eng Des 203:87-106

Cullen (1990) The public inquiry into the piper alpha disaster. HMSO Cm 1310

Emmet L, Cleland G (2002) Graphical notations, narratives and persuasion: a pliant systems approach to hypertext tool design. In: Proc ACM Hypertext, College Park, Maryland, USA

Eurocontrol (2003) ESARR6 Software in ATM systems.

Eurocontrol (2006) Safety Case Development Manual. http://www.eurocontrol.int/cascade/gallery/content/public/documents/safetycasedevmanual.pdf. Accessed 17 October 2009

Fan Y, Kelly T (2004) Contract-based justification for COTS component within safety-critical applications. Proc 9th Australian workshop on safety critical systems and software, Brisbane

Gorski J (2004) Trust Case – a case for trustworthiness of it infrastructures. In Proc NATO Advanced Research Workshop on Cyberspace Security and Defence: Research Issues, Gdansk, Poland

Greenwell WS, Knight JC, Holloway CM, Pease J (2006) A taxonomy of fallacies in system safety argument. 24th International System Safety Conference, Albuequerque

HSE (1987) Programmable electronic systems in safety related applications. Health and Safety Executive

HSE (1993), Out of control – a compilation of incidents involving control systems. Health and Safety Executive (draft document)

IEC (1986) IEC 880 Software for computers in the safety systems of nuclear power stations. International Electrotechnical Commission

IEC (1993) Functional safety of electrical/electronic/programmable electronic systems: generic aspects. Part 1: General requirements. Draft standard from IEC Sub-Committee 65A: System Aspects, Working Group 10. International Electrotechnical Commission

IEC (1998) Functional safety of electrical, electronic, and programmable electronic safety related systems. IEC 61508, Parts 1 to 7, 1998 to 2000. International Electrotechnical Commission

IEE (1989) Software in safety related systems. The Institution of Electrical Engineers and the British Computer Society

Jackson D, Thomas M, Millett LI (eds) (2007) Software for dependable systems: sufficient evidence? Committee on Certifiably Dependable Software Systems, National Research Council

Jones C, Bloomfield RE, Froome PKD, Bishop PG (2001) Methods for assessing the safety integrity of safety-related software of uncertain pedigree (SOUP). HSE Contract Research Report CRR 337/2001. Health and Safety Executive

Kelly TP (1998) Arguing safety: a systematic approach to managing safety cases. PhD thesis, University of York

Kelly T, McDermid J (1997) Safety case construction and reuse using patterns. Proc 16th Conf on Computer Safety, Reliability and Security (Safecomp '97)

Kelly TP, Weaver RA (2004) The goal structuring notation – a safety argument notation. Proc Dependable Systems and Networks Workshop on Assurance Cases

Lipson H (2008) Assurance cases overview. US Department of Homeland Security. https://
buildsecurityin.us-cert.gov/daisy/bsi/articles/knowledge/assurance/641-BSI.html.   Accessed
17 October 2009

Littlewood B (2000) The use of proofs in diversity arguments. IEEE Trans Softw Eng 26:1022-
1023

Littlewood B, Strigini L (1993) Assessment of ultra-high dependability for software-based systems. Comm ACM 36:69-80

Littlewood B, Wright D (2007) The use of multi-legged arguments to increase confidence in
safety claims for software-based systems: a study based on a BBN of an idealised example.
IEEE Trans Softw Eng 33:347-365

McDermid JA (1994) Support for safety cases and safety argument using SAM. Reliab Eng Syst
Saf 43:111-127

MoD (1989) Draft Interim Def-Stan 00-55, the procurement of safety critical software in defence
equipment. Ministry of Defence

MoD (1991) Interim Def-Stan 00-56, hazard analysis and safety classification of the computer
and programmable electronic system elements of defence equipment. Ministry of Defence

MoD (1997) Def Stan 00-42 Reliability and Maintainability (R&M) assurance guide, Part 2
Software. Ministry of Defence

MoD (2004) Def Stan 00-56 Safety management requirements for defence systems. Issue 3. Ministry of Defence

MoD (2008) Def Stan 00-42 Reliability and Maintainability (R&M) assurance guide, Part 3
R&M Case. Ministry of Defence

Redmill F (ed) (1988) Dependability of critical computer systems 1. Elsevier Applied Science

Redmill F (ed) (1989) Dependability of critical computer systems 2. Elsevier Applied Science

Robens (1972) Safety and health at work. Report of the committee 1970-72. HMSO Cmnd 5034

Smith PR, Stockham R (2007) EMPHASIS – An assessment tool for smart instruments,
PRfsS/Moore Industries-Europe, United Kingdom

Toulmin SE (1958) The uses of argument. Cambridge University Press

Virginia (2009) Safety cases repository. University of Virginia Dependability Research Group.
http://dependability.cs.virginia.edu/info/Safety_Cases:Repository. Accessed 17 October 2009

Managing Safety-Related Projects

An Integrated Project Management Life Cycle Supporting System Safety

Hans Tschürtz[1] and Gabriele Schedl[2]

[1]University of Applied Sciences, Vienna, Austria

[2]Frequentis AG, Vienna, Austria

Abstract System failures in safety-critical domains can lead to harmful consequences for humans, the environment and for the system itself. The field of 'system safety' provides relief and aims at identifying possible risks already during the project planning phase of the system development. This requires modern project management support. The realisation of innovative ideas in software often increases the complexity and increasingly leads to dangerous system states or even system failures that put the safety of the system at risk.

This paper addresses the development of an integrated project management approach for software development projects in safety-related domains. The core elements are project management, the process maturity model SPICE and system safety in general based on IEC 61508. The project management process sets the framework. The development life cycle and the safety life cycle are integrated into this process model. The result is an integrated project management life cycle for safety-related software development projects.

This integrated project management life cycle offers a generic approach on a high level of abstraction in order to cover a broad range of applications. It gives project managers and furthermore the whole project team the opportunity to influence quality and system safety in a preventative manner.

1 Introduction

Complexity of technical systems is on the rise and with it increases the potential risk that those systems bear for humans and the environment. The trend of implementing most of the functions in software instead of hardware poses a great challenge for the industry. Future technological developments will exacerbate the problem. The task of ensuring quality as well as of identifying hazards and reducing risks therefore gets increasingly demanding. Providing system safety is a continuously growing challenge. A methodical, process-oriented approach to the development activities has to be taken in order to meet this challenge.

C. Dale, T. Anderson (eds.), *Making Systems Safer*, DOI 10.1007/978-1-84996-086-1_5,
© Springer-Verlag London Limited 2010

People not only expect error-free operation of technical systems surrounding them but even take it for guaranteed. But for the responsible project managers and system engineers as well as their senior organisational units it is a separated science to ensure that no one is hurt by the operation of the technical systems developed.

Many failures still occur despite the existence of many technical methods for safe system design, numerous standards and norms for safety-critical systems and the immense costs that accidents impose upon the responsible parties. In fact the industry and especially small and medium-sized companies suffer a great lack of implementation knowledge when it comes to safety-related systems. Apart from that, seemingly additional costs that are induced by the development of safe systems – especially resulting from poor project management – pose a great challenge with respect to competition in the marketplace.

This paper addresses exactly those shortcomings from the project management point of view. Thereby it focuses on software project management but continuously it always shows the context of the whole system.

Software development projects in safety-related domains have to be carried out within a well-organised framework ensuring that activities are performed in a certain order.

In the subsequent sections, decisive approaches for steering safety-related projects will be shown. Thereby redundancies and the resulting expenses and costs in such projects can be reduced and the effectiveness increased. The focus is on a generic procedure model which complies with SPICE Level 2 of ISO/IEC 15504 (ISO 2004) and meets the demands of IEC 61508 (IEC 2005). The compliant project management process of the International Project Management Association (IPMA) forms the framework for this model (PMA 2007).

The following three sections provide an overview of the project management life cycle, the software engineering life cycle derived from ISO/IEC 15504 and the generic safety life cycle derived from the IEC 61508. The last section outlines the integration of those life cycles into an integrative project management life cycle.

1.1 Project Management Life Cycle

Project management is a business process in the project-oriented company. It starts with the project assignment and ends with the project approval. The project life cycle is divided into the sub-processes of project start, project control and project close-down. At the same time project coordination and project marketing are carried out continuously. Another possible sub-process is project crisis resolution, which is not discussed in this paper. At the end of each phase the project owner and the project team organize a milestone review and decide whether the next phase can be started or not. Those reviews reduce the technical risk from the management perspective.

Generally, the objectives of the project management process are to manage the project complexity and dynamics, to successfully achieve the project objectives and to manage the relationships of the project phases.

Fig. 1. Project Management Life Cycle

Project Start. The objectives of the project start process are to establish the project as a social system and to create a holistic project picture. The project start addresses the activities related to developing the project plan, involving the stakeholders appropriately and getting the commitment to the plan. The project plan covers project management and engineering activities. During the project start the engineering discipline covers the sub-processes of requirements development and design creation. In this paper the engineering process applies to the development of a system in the software development domain. The engineering life cycle is explained in more detail later on.

The project plan provides the basis for the project control and project coordination processes. Furthermore, it addresses the project owner's commitment. Since it is revised periodically, it should be viewed as a living document.

Project Control Process. Because projects are very dynamic it is necessary to perform project control. The project control process periodically compares the planned activities with the activities that are actually taking place. It is divided into several categories. The first step is to determine the project status and create a common project reality within the project team. The question, 'What is happening in the project?' has to be answered. In the second step the actual data has to be compared with the planned data. If deviations are encountered, possible solutions are discussed and integrated into the project plan. If necessary, the project objectives have to be adjusted or changed and brought in line with the project owner's point of view.

Project Coordination Process. The project coordination process continuously ensures the performance and the quality of the project. It provides the project team, the project owner and the project environment with adequate status information. Project coordination begins at project start with the project assignment and ends with the project approval. It is an ongoing task for the project manager which needs to be carried out continuously.

Project Marketing. Project marketing is a process that has to be performed by the whole project team. It ensures the acceptance of the project via different forms of communication. Moreover, it encourages the project members to identify themselves with the project.

Project Close-down. The objectives of the project close-down process are the planning of the completion of the remaining tasks, project evaluation and the dissolving of the project team. Transfer of 'lessons learned' to the permanent organization and to other projects as well as the dissolution of the project environment relationships close the project. Ultimately, the project owner's approval of the project finalizes the project close-down.

1.2 Software Engineering Life Cycle

In addition to the project management life cycle an engineering life cycle has to be defined in order to demonstrate the way of working at the development level. IEC 61508 requires the selection of a life cycle model and suggests the V-Model. The selected model has to be elaborated during the project start process and specified in the project management plan. Since this paper is concentrated on software, this section creates a V-Model at the systems level and derives the software life cycle from it.

This section gives an overview of the V-Model and its relevant engineering processes. Those processes are derived from ISO 12207 (ISO 2008) which is used as a reference-model by ISO 15504 (SPICE). The software engineering processes have to be defined preliminarily in the project management plan and have to be applied accordingly. Furthermore IEC 61508 requires that each phase of the life cycle shall be divided into elementary activities with the scope, inputs, and outputs specified for each phase. Figure 2 and the following paragraphs show an adapted V-Model according to the requirements of the respective standards. Support processes like quality assurance and configuration management are not included in this model.

Generally the V-Model can be divided into three levels: the customer, the system and the software level. The customer level describes *what* has to be done while the other two levels below describe *how* it is to be done. In the following, all three levels are considered in order to establish a better understanding of the whole system that has to be developed. However, the focus of this paper lies on the software level which will be discussed in detail below.

The V-Model describes the general steps of system development. Hereby the transitions between the particular phases are of utmost importance. The essential goal lies in the error-free, complete and traceable transfer of the individual requirements starting from the customer requirements down to the software code.

The model begins with the customer requirements on the left side. These are defined in cooperation with the customer and documented in the customer requirements specification. Here it is a crucial factor that the specification is formulated in a way that is completely comprehensible for the customer. In the next step the customer requirements are transferred to the system design. The system design describes the whole system that has to be developed. In order to reduce the complexity, large-scale systems are usually broken down into several sub-systems. Then the functional requirements derived from the sub-systems are defined and form the basis for the development of the software architecture. Next, the components defined in the software architecture are described in the component design which in turn provides the basis for the coding of the software later on.

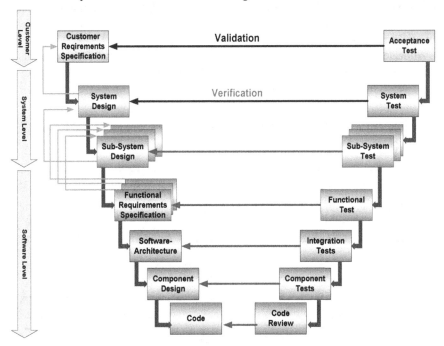

Fig. 2. Adapted V-Model according to ISO 12207

The transitions from one phase to the next are of particular importance. Reviews and inspections are performed to ensure the effective transfer of the requirements during those transitions. The participants of the reviews should be relevant personnel associated with the present phase, the phase before and the one after. For example a review of the software architecture should include the software architect as well as the software requirements engineer and the component design engineers. The requirements engineer who is responsible for the input document (e.g. functional requirements specification) has to be able to check that the functional requirements have been properly transferred into the architecture. The design engineer who is going to derive the component design from the architecture has to assess whether the described components can be realized. Only by this means can the quality and the proper transfer to the next phase be ensured. Additionally all other relevant engineers like the safety engineers, test engineers and quality managers should be included.

On the right side of Figure 2 the model depicts the individual testing phases during which the outputs of the corresponding phases on the left side are tested and respectively verified. Code reviews are carried out during the coding phase and verification tests are conducted from the component phase to the system phase. Finally, the validation of the whole system is carried out at the customer level by means of acceptance testing.

The basic prerequisites for an effective and efficient procedure are the clean definition and clear communication of the transitions between the particular phases. The quality of the transitions has to be ensured by reviews being carried out by the relevant project roles.

Allocated to the framework specified in ISO/IEC 15504 Part 5 the core and support processes depicted in Figure 3 result for the software development life cycle in accordance with the V-Model.

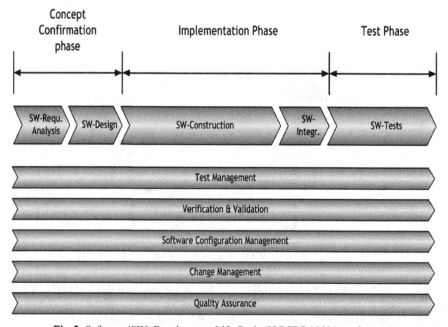

Fig. 3. Software (SW) Development Life Cycle (ISO/IEC 15504-conformant)

Figure 3 shows the software development life cycle which is divided into the three phases of concept confirmation, implementation and testing. The concept confirmation phase includes the processes of requirements development and software design. The software requirements will be derived from the system requirements and the system design. They include functional, performance and interface requirements. Inputs for the software requirements are:

• the system requirements

- the system design
- the interface specification from the system life cycle
- the applied standards that are defined in the project management plan
- the requirements which are defined by the testing group, the factory and the service and maintenance organisations.

The primary output of the design process is the software architecture. Of utmost importance is traceability to the defined high level requirements: the software requirements as well as the system design requirements and the customer requirements.

When the concept confirmation phase has been completed, all software requirements specifications and design documents need to be approved in order to enable commitment from all relevant parties to the implementation. All these documents have to ensure that an adequate safety integrity level has been achieved.

The implementation phase consists of the software construction and software integration processes. Both include adequate test activities like component tests and integration tests. The software architecture, the interface specifications and the defined coding standards are inputs for the software coding process. Some complex software projects demand for more detailed component designs from which the source code can be directly derived and implemented. This phase is completed when all relevant requirements are implemented, integrated and tested. Also here, traceability to all the previous phases is demanded.

Test Management is mentioned neither in ISO 12207 nor in ISO/IEC 15504, but is of crucial importance for large and complex projects. The test plan that includes the test strategy, test schedule and the allocated resources should already be developed during the concept confirmation phase. For small projects the test plan can be part of the overall project management plan; for large projects the test plan should be a dedicated document which must be synchronised with the overall project management plan.

The Verification activities ensure the conformance of the work products to the defined requirements. Verification methods are not only test activities but also reviews, inspections, code-analysis and assessments. The Validation activities confirm that the requirements for the intended use of the work product are fulfilled.

Software Configuration Management is a set of engineering procedures to identify, control, track and document the work products and the software throughout the software development cycle. Change Request Management ensures that all changes are recorded and controlled. Consequently, the status of current and previous versions of the software and of relevant documents is known and reproducible at all times.

The Software Quality Assurance Process is applied as defined in the project management plan and/or in the quality assurance plan. It assesses the engineering life cycle and its work products to assure that the software system and software work products comply with the defined plans.

1.3 Generic Safety Life Cycle

This section discusses a generic safety life cycle, illustrated in Figure 4, and its relationship to the system life cycle. The first row represents a generic and simplified version of the development process. The second row shows the main phases of the safety life cycle, which consists of Preliminary Hazard Identification (PHI), Functional Hazard Assessment (FHA), Preliminary System Safety Assessment (PSSA) and System Safety Assessment (SSA). The primary question to be answered during each phase is shown at the bottom of Figure 4.

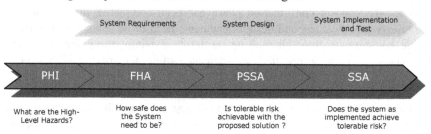

Fig. 4. Safety Life Cycle

The PHI triggers the core safety processes. During that phase high-level hazards will be identified based on a first concept of the whole system. With the help of checklists and available data such as lessons learned, accident records, known hazards in an existing hazard log or relevant review results, a group of experts performs a brainstorming session to create a preliminary hazard list. Additionally high level safety requirements will be defined as a project management input.

The preliminary hazard list and the customer requirements form the basis for the Functional Hazard Assessment (FHA). While considering the required functionality and the respective system environment the FHA shall answer the question: How safe does the system need to be? The analysis performed during the FHA provides the safety objectives and a first set of system safety requirements which are necessary in order to fulfil the safety goals and to prevent the identified hazards from occurring. The system requirements are amended by the system safety requirements. Doing this in the early project phase assures that the safety requirements are appropriately considered in the system design.

The customer, system and system safety requirements form the parent requirements. These are passed on to the sub-system requirements and subsequently to the component requirements according to the parent/child principle. Figure 5 demonstrates this transmission from the various requirements states to the design states. In addition, it shows the transition from the system level to the software level.

The Preliminary System Safety Assessment (PSSA) is performed at the design level. The PSSA shall answer the question: Is tolerable risk achievable with the proposed solution? Therefore it is verified whether the safety objectives can be satisfied with the available design. Of course, this assessment can result in the definition of additionally derived safety requirements.

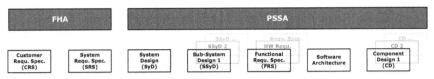

Fig. 5. Requirements Transmission

If a design modification is required due to e.g. improper implementation of safety requirements or additional identified hazards, the PSSA must be repeated for the altered design.

One important point is doing the Software Safety Analysis as part of the overall System Safety Assessment, and not as an independent task. During the FHA critical system functions and system hazards are identified and subsequently broken down to the hardware and software level. Based on the software architecture, potential software faults which might contribute to the system hazards are detected during the Software Safety Analysis. The results of the Software Safety Analysis must be considered at the system level as well. Thus, the Software Safety Analysis is an integrated element of the System Safety Assessment.

The System Safety Assessment (SSA) shall answer the question: Does the implemented system achieve tolerable risk? The system must implement all safety requirements and must provide the intended functionality such that the remaining risk is kept at an acceptable level. In order to assure this, test methods such as those proposed by IEC 61508 are applied. Thereby it is verified that the safety goals are achieved and that the safety requirements are considered accordingly in the design. SSAs are consequently performed in an iterative way over the remainder of the system life cycle. In this context the safety case report has to be regarded as a living document that must be kept up-to-date especially with regard to modifications of the system or the system environment.

2 Integrated Project Management Life Cycle

After the derivation of the project management life cycle, the software engineering life cycle and the generic safety life cycle, a common process landscape integrating those life cycles shall be outlined and the respective inter-relationship shall be explained. For the sake of comprehensibility only the core processes of the life cycles described above shall be considered in the following text.

In order to meet the process of project creation we add a project initialisation phase at the beginning of the integrated project management life cycle. Project management, safety and engineering activities are already relevant for the project creation. The different phases of the integrated project management life cycle may be mapped to dedicated spaces. The project initialisation phase maps onto the 'problem space', the project start phase onto the 'model space' and project control as well as project finalisation onto the 'solution space'.

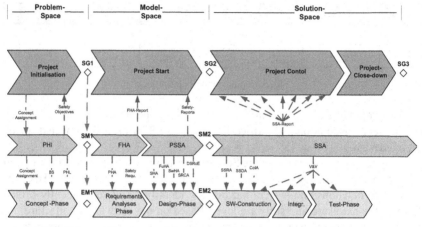

Fig. 6. Process Landscape of the Integrated Project Management Life Cycle

2.1 The 'Problem Space'

Dedicated problems, preliminary studies, customer requests, ideas, etc. are the primary triggers for system development. At first, the purpose and the target of the system must be defined. In addition, a macro concept of the respective system as well as the definition of the system boundaries and the system context must be derived. A concept assignment is issued to the safety team and the engineering team. Using the macro concept a Preliminary Hazard Identification (PHI) is done during which first safety requirements are defined and, thereof, resulting objectives of project management are determined. On this basis rough planning is possible which allows realistic estimation of the costs of system development and scheduling of milestones and deliverables. With cost estimation and schedule a business case analysis can be performed and, if the business case looks promising, the application for a project is set up.

2.2 The 'Model Space'

Stage gate SG1 symbolizes the project start which triggers the safety milestone SM1 and the engineering milestone EM1 and, therefore, starts the activities of the project start phase. The planning activities in the project start phase include project plan development and co-ordination of all involved disciplines and stakeholders. Project planning starts with the definition of the scope of work. The scope of work is defined from the scope statement and includes the requirements of ISO/IEC 15504:

- Reason and business need for the project
- Quantified project goals
- Description of the system to be developed
- Overview of the deliverables to be created
- Definition of qualitative and quantitative process goals
- Resource allocation
- Definition of responsibilities
- Management of the interfaces between the involved parties.

During the project start phase ISO/IEC 15504 poses the following requirements as base practices (BP) to project management:

- BP1: Define the scope of work
- BP2: Define the project life cycle
- BP3: Evaluate feasibility of the project
- BP4: Determine and maintain estimates for project attributes
- BP5: Define project activities and tasks
- BP6: Define needs for experience, knowledge and skills
- BP7: Define project schedule
- BP8: Identify and monitor project interfaces
- BP9: Allocate responsibilities
- BP10: Establish project plan.

The major aspects relevant for the project management of safety-related projects are the determination of the project life cycle, the definition of the project strategy and conformity with the relevant standards. Project life cycle and project strategy must be adequately established to the extent required by project size and complexity.

With the project start the respective activities at the layers of the safety life cycle and the engineering life cycle are triggered. Based upon the customer requirements the system and software requirements are derived during the requirements analysis phase of the engineering life cycle. Additionally, customer requirements together with the preliminary hazard list are considered in the Preliminary Hazard Analysis (PHA) during the Functional Hazard Assessment (FHA) Phase of the safety life cycle. The PHA is a risk analysis performed on the previously identified hazards while considering the respective system context. A risk index is assigned to each hazard and mitigating measures are identified and formulated. Next, safety requirements are derived from the mitigating measures and finally, the safety requirements are amended to the system requirements specification. All findings during the FHA phase are summarized in an FHA report and reported to project management.

The Preliminary System Safety Assessment (PSSA) Phase evaluates the inclusion of the safety requirements in the design at a high level of abstraction and, additionally, investigates the design with respect to potential hazards and risks. Methods applied for that purpose are System Hazard Analysis (SHA), Functional Hazard Analysis (FuHA), Software Hazard Analysis (SwHA) and Safety Requirements/Criteria Analysis (SRCA). With the help of those methods so-called Derived Safety Requirements on Elements (DSRoE) are developed for every component of the design. The DSRoE are included in the requirements specification and considered in the design. After the inclusion of all requirements in the design and the re-evaluation of the design, the safety milestone SM2 and the engineering milestone EM2 are reached. The provision of a PSSA report to project management and all relevant stakeholders marks the end of the project start phase.

Stage Gate SG2 forms the most important strategic milestone in the integrated life cycle because it determines the further course of the project. The developed design specification, the re-worked plans and the updated effort and cost estimates allow management to re-evaluate the project and to decide upon its future. If the decision is to continue the project, the activities of System Safety Assessment (SSA) and of system development are triggered. Those activities are monitored by project control.

2.3 The 'Solution Space'

If the project is continued after Stage Gate SG2, the operative activities start. Software component designs are created during the software construction phase and evaluated by means of a Software Safety Design Analysis (SSDA). The SSDA is part of the System Safety Assessment (SSA). The source code undergoes code reviews and critical parts of the source code are subjected to a Code Hazard Analysis (CoHA). After coding is finished, test activities start according to verification, validation and test processes. Test activities are specified in the test management plan and synchronised with the project management plan. Test reports are provided to project management and are essential for safety cases as evidence for system safety. The SSA is continued after the project close-down until decommissioning and disposal of the system. Respective activities must be considered during specification of the safety plan. Findings and modifications of the system or the system environment must be handled appropriately.

3 Conclusion

From the project management point of view the role of a project manager in the safety field is essential in order to ensure that the project conforms to all demanded standards, including the relevant engineering and safety requirements.

The project manager has to take care that an overall project life cycle is defined and properly described. The project management life cycle, engineering life cycle and safety life cycle have to be integrated into an overall project life cycle model. This life cycle has to specify the order in which the management, engineering and safety tasks are to be carried out. Involvement and commitment of the project team and relevant stakeholders is absolutely necessary.

In addition, project managers take overall responsibility for all activities within the project. They have to take care that all planning activities and alignments to the overall project plan are carried out. Apart from costs, schedule and performance, the additional aspects of safety and quality are relevant in safety related projects. A safe product or system needs to be of high quality because this forms the prerequisite for a safe product.

Following a defined life cycle in a consistent manner and staying focused on the safety related issues increases not only efficiency and effectiveness but at the same time assures quality and safety. Top level issues like work products and features have to be figured out as early as possible – at least during the project start phase. Tracking those issues through the whole life cycle of the project increases the importance of the project organization.

Safer Systems for a Safer World!

[Vienna Institute for Safety & Systems Engineering]

References

IEC (2005) IEC 61508 Functional safety of electrical/electronic/programmable electronic safety-related systems. International Electrotechnical Commission

ISO (2004) ISO/IEC 15504 Information technology – process assessment. International Organization for Standardization

ISO (2008) ISO/IEC 12207 Systems and software engineering – software life cycle processes. International Organization for Standardization

PMA (2007) pm baseline. Project Management Austria, Vienna. http://debian.p-m-a.at/docs/pm%20baseline%202.4%20dt.pdf. Accessed 6 October 2009

Patterns in Safety-Related Projects

Mike Parsons and Charles Hunter

Logica UK

Reading, UK

Abstract Within Logica UK, safety-related projects are run in a variety of ways depending on the constraints imposed and how the risks and mitigations are owned and handled. A total of eight different types of project development patterns have been identified and this paper discusses each type. A simple decision tool has been developed based on the patterns which is used as an aid in deciding how to bid a safety project, allowing tradeoffs between risk ownership, development methods and cost to be assessed.

1 Background

Logica is a leading IT and business services company, employing 40,000 people across 36 countries, providing business consulting, systems integration, and IT and business process outsourcing services. Founded in 1969, Logica now has a turnover of £3.6bn globally of which £710M is in the UK.

Logica undertakes many types of development and integration projects and IT service deliveries in a wide variety of sectors. Most are commercial, non-safety-related projects; however a significant number must manage considerable safety risks in complex and challenging environments.

1.1 Safety-Related Projects in Logica

There are currently over fifty safety-related projects and service deliveries in the UK and about forty safety-related bids active as of today. The safety-related work is across a wide range of industry sectors including:

- Defence:
    - **FC-A and FC-BISA.** Command and control, including ballistic calculations, for guns and mortars in both standalone and networked forms (Logica 2007)

C. Dale, T. Anderson (eds.), *Making Systems Safer*, DOI 10.1007/978-1-84996-086-1_6,
© Springer-Verlag London Limited 2010

- **DMICP.** Healthcare Information System for use in primary, secondary and dental healthcare, in deployed and non-deployed environments, both in peacetime and war (Logica 2008a).

- Aerospace:

  - **EGNOS CPF Check Set.** Real-time integrity checking for critical satellite navigation applications, including aviation (Ventura-Traveset et al. 2001, Logica 2001).
  - **Galileo GMS and GCS.** Development of several key ground segment elements for this GPS-like satellite navigation system including satellite constellation control (SCCF), integrity checking (IPF) and security key management (KMF) (ESA 2009a).

- Health:

  - **NHS Spine.** Provision and support of a central infrastructure and application services to support the Care Records for the National Health Service (Logica 2009a).
  - **UCLH.** Hospital Application Development Application Support, Server Support Network support, End User Support and Service Desk provision (Logica 2009a) for major London hospitals.

- Energy and Utilities:

  - **DCWW (Welsh Water).** Provision of Managed Services covering: Geographic Information Systems, Generic Services, Applications Operations, Problem Resolution and support, Applications development and support services Logica (2009b).
  - **Instant Energy.** Provides remote management of Credit and Prepayment, Electricity and Gas meters for multiple customers (potentially including remote power on/off switching) (Logica 2009c).

- Transport:

  - **BAA.** Applications Management of several hundred applications at UK airports, including operational systems for security at Heathrow and Gatwick Logica (2009d).
  - **Metronet.** Management systems for the assets used to run the London Underground network (track, signals, arrestors, bridges, control systems, power, tunnel lighting and communications, fire detection, rolling stock, etc.) (Logica 2005)

- Government:

  - **RIMNET.** Radiation monitoring system comprising 93 fixed monitoring stations around the UK that provide identification of increased levels of radiation (e.g. from Chernobyl-type release) plus a processing centre that can be used to distribute information concerning its effects to the media, official agencies and the public (Met Office 2009).

- **CRB VBS.** IT solutions to support monitoring and barring scheme that assists the Independent Safeguarding Authority in making decisions on whether to bar individuals from the children's and/or vulnerable adults' workforces (CRB 2009).

- Telecoms

  - **Airwave.** Supply of application development, support, infrastructure and consultancy services supporting the emergency services' TETRA mobile communications system (Logica 2009e).
  - **Skynet 5 Management Segment.** Provides planning and configuration of robust and secure beyond-line-of-sight communication services in a military context, primarily via satellites (Logica 2008b).

Additional safety-related work is conducted in other Logica regions, notably in the Netherlands, Malaysia and Australia.

1.2 Safety Management in Logica

Logica's overall goal when undertaking safety projects is to reduce the safety risk associated with an IT system or service to an acceptable (that is broadly acceptable or tolerable and ALARP *and* commercially prudent) level.

1.2.1 Avoiding a SLIP

Within Logica both the immediate and the wider commercial aspects of safety are considered. Four main risk criteria are assessed:

1. **Safety** – avoiding harm due to an accident.
2. **Liability** – avoiding or minimising any claims or fines which may be associated with an accident (including costs of defending claims).
3. **Investigation** – avoiding any costly or intrusive investigations or inquiries as a result of an accident.
4. **Publicity** – avoiding or minimising any bad publicity and resulting brand damage due to an accident.

Various control and monitoring mechanisms are used within Logica to identify and manage these risks, including an initial management risk briefing produced at bid time, safety management planning, safety design and engineering, safety analysis and verification activities, and both project and independent safety assurance processes.

1.2.2 Risk Management

All four SLIP risk areas are assessed and the usual approaches to addressing the risks are considered (e.g. Wikipedia 2009):

- **Avoidance** (elimination)
- **Reduction** (mitigation)
- **Transfer** (to client or other body)
- **Retention** (acceptance)

Avoidance. The ideal solution is if the safety risks can be avoided altogether – usually by removing the risk area from scope of supply or by designing the problem out of the solution completely. It is often very difficult to avoid the risks altogether in complex IT systems.

Risk Reduction. This is often the most common method of handling safety risks on IT development projects, where specific features are added to the system or special development processes used, together with corresponding verifications. Alternatively external risk reductions may be used, including business processes and procedures.

Transfer. Sometimes clients are willing to discuss explicit transfer of safety risk as a method of speeding up delivery or reducing costs, or where it is agreed that the risk is better handled outside the IT system scope. This can take the form of specific hazard transfer strategies or comprehensive legal cover (e.g. in the form of indemnities). Note that insurance is usually classed as a risk transfer mechanism as the commercial (financial) risk associated with an accident can be covered by insurance in some cases.

Retention. This is where is risk is accepted as-is and the costs and impacts are budgeted for (e.g. self-insurance). This is rarely used in Logica for any but the lowest risk developments as it could have significant commercial impact.

2 The Project Patterns

2.1 Origins

Back in 2006/7 Logica was undertaking major development activities for the ground segment of the Galileo satellite navigation programme. Several of the element development projects were undergoing externally imposed changes to their safety requirements which made their safety status unclear. There was also confusion as to whether some projects were actually safety-related in the usual sense:

they required client safety deliverables, and/or development to a formal DAL (Development Assurance Level), but apparently had no significant safety hazards.

A first attempt was made at categorizing the project developments within the Galileo programme to aid the project teams; this was subsequently extended to include other safety projects within Logica UK.

The initial aim of this categorization was to identify at an early stage the extent of the SLIP risks relevant to a project, to establish a definitive safety status, and then to establish what controls (particularly authorizations and approvals) were required.

2.2 Safety Project Patterns

What is a *Pattern* in this context? There are various definitions which seem to fit: for example, the following are taken from object-oriented software design (Appleton 2000):

> 'A pattern is a named nugget of instructive information that captures the essential structure and insight of a successful family of proven solutions to a recurring problem that arises within a certain context and system of forces.'

Or

> 'a pattern involves a general description of a recurring solution to a recurring problem replete with various goals and constraints. But a pattern does more than just identify a solution, it also explains *why the solution is needed*.'

The following section describes the safety project development patterns that have been identified at Logica[1].

There are eight basic patterns identified to date:

1. Standard Safety-Related Development
2. External Mitigations
3. Low Risk and Comprehensive Legal Cover
4. Working under Client Direction and Management
5. Specific Risks Identified and Passed to Client
6. Not Currently Safety-Related
7. Applications Framework
8. Infrastructure Hosting

---

[1] Our concept of safety project pattern is clearly related to that of Safety Case Patterns (Weaver et al. 2002), and it would be an obvious development to use GSN to structure the arguments for justifying the patterns described. In this case the top-level claim would be that the development pattern is sufficiently safe, *and* commercially prudent.

2.2.1 Standard Safety-Related Development

This is the standard method of developing software to a recognised industry safety standard at a particular level (SIL, DAL, etc.) where the mitigations required are placed in the software or system itself.

This pattern is used as sometimes the only feasible method of reducing the safety risk to acceptable levels is to make the software itself more reliable. This is typically due to real-time or severity constraints, where it is hard to detect the problem and where there is little time to recover the situation, or little margin of error to allow remedial measures to take effect. The typical way this is done is to work to an existing, industry-sector standard of which there are many. It should be noted however, that many large programmes still insist on creating a new standard or a variation on an existing one which usually increases costs and development risks (e.g. ESA 2009b).

When working to an industry standard, there are usually many detailed process requirements to follow (e.g. those contained in DO-178B (RTCA 1992), GSWS (ESA 2009b), IEC 61508 (IEC 2005)), covering the whole software development lifecycle. There are also various specialised architectures and design techniques which may be used in this pattern, e.g. Diverse Architectures, Diverse Data, Coding Language Subsets, Defensive Programming, Partitioning, Encapsulation/Isolation, etc. (Note that all of these techniques and approaches themselves could be considered as safety *design* patterns in themselves, but that is the subject of separate work.)

This approach can be expensive and time-consuming due to:

- Detailed analysis, requirements and design.
- Emphasis on extensive verification, validation and traceability.
- Large amount of PA effort and low-level testing coverage focus.
- External verification by an independent safety authority.

2.2.2 External Mitigations

This is the set of patterns where nothing special is done to the software development (i.e. not working to a standard with a SIL or DAL), because the necessary risk mitigation is external to the software or system. However, good commercial practice still prevails, and often the software has many safety features (e.g. specific data validation checks) built-in.

2.2.2.1 External Mitigations via Non-Software Means – Process and Procedures

The system or software can generate safety hazards at the system boundary (at the boundary of Logica supply) which could lead to accidents, but these are mitigated by other, external means.

This means that no particular reliance is placed on the software operation and so allows use of commercially developed software, COTS and public domain software without further justification.

This approach requires a very active safety management process to produce and maintain a hazard log which must:

- Identify hazards at the system boundary and mitigations assigned to us or client.
- Avoid having mitigations which place reliance on project development processes.
- Be realistic and subject to regular review.
- Have external mitigations which are effective and demonstrable and checked by regular site visits/audits

2.2.2.2 External Mitigations including Supplementary Commercial Software Changes

Here the system or software can generate safety hazards at the boundary which could potentially lead to accidents. These are generally mitigated by external means but derived safety requirements are created (with corresponding design changes and verifications) and applied to the commercially developed system.

Formally, no particular reliance is placed on the software operation or development process (it has not been developed to a SIL or DAL); however, the additional safety functionality in the software can be seen as aiding the external mitigations. Note that many of the mitigations introduced in the software in this way may only be partial (i.e. only reduce the risk in some situations).

This approach allows the use of commercially developed software, COTS and public domain software, while providing additional mechanisms for reducing the overall safety risk, and also reducing the operational process overhead for the external checks.

This pattern requires a very active safety management process to produce and maintain a hazard log which must:

- Identify hazards at the system boundary and mitigations assigned to us or client.
- Treat external mitigations as before.
- Identify the safety checks or barriers as safety requirements, to be implemented as part of the system, as (partial) mitigations to particular hazards.

2.2.2.3 External Mitigation due to Separate Software Development to a Recognized Standard

This is where the main system is commercially developed, but a (small) extra subsystem (e.g. barrier or checker) formally provides the necessary mitigation.

Hence the main system development follows a commercial route with risk mitigation by external mechanisms, but here the external mechanism comprises a barrier or checker which is developed to a recognised SIL or DAL

This can be used where critical protection functions can be sensibly isolated, are small and can be easily encapsulated – and this may be based on assumptions that should be verified.

The main advantage is cost savings: the bulk of the software is developed in accordance with standard quality assurance practices and allows the use of COTS or public domain software.

However, it can be complex as a full hazard management process is required, and the project must use two different development methodologies with the SIL development activities kept separate from the commercial ones.

2.2.3 Low Risk and Comprehensive Legal Cover

In this pattern, the client explicitly relieves Logica of the bulk of the safety responsibility via a legal route.

The application of this pattern in rare, especially in the commercial domain and can only be used in very low risk situations. The main advantages of this approach are that it is no longer necessary to perform detailed hazard analysis, and the use of COTS, public domain and commercially developed software is feasible.

It can be proposed as a sensible option where the safety-related status is unclear, or where the client believes the Logica scope of supply is not safety-related because of the way system is used, or due to other (unspecified) procedural mitigations performed by the client.

The legal statements forming the cover must:

- Be explicit and include indemnities.
- Cover all failures of the IT system for all circumstances.
- Be reviewed by a qualified authority.

Commercial risks of litigation can be managed in this way, but note there may still be exposure for corporate manslaughter fines, adverse publicity leading to loss of business, and also losses due to supporting time-consuming investigations. Therefore, this pattern is only acceptable for low-risk projects, and those where the probability of risk to the public or corporate reputation are very low.

2.2.4 Working Under Client Direction and Management

In this pattern, the client implicitly relieves Logica of any systems safety responsibility because the work is done under their direction, review and control.

Legally, the contract between the client and Logica would be time and materials for staff, without reference to any deliverables. In this way the deliverables are wholly the client's responsibility.

Typically, Logica staff would work on-site under direct client supervision and management. They would work to the client's Terms of Reference, Work Package Descriptions, Safety Management Plan and local procedures.

The key issue is around the suitability of the staff provided for the roles:

- Staff supplied should be appropriately competent for the expected tasks.
- Safety skills should be verified by checks on CVs, training records and assessment data.
- Monitoring is needed that establish that staff are not put under undue pressure or work outside their competence.

Audits/on-site visits may be required to check on working conditions and that the client has the capability to effectively manage the staff. Issues can arise if the expected requirement changes significantly, or the staff are not effectively managed by the client.

2.2.5 Specific Risks Identified and Passed to Client

This is where the client formally agrees to take ownership of all significant systems safety hazards.

Typically the hazard analysis would be carried out as normal during the system design and development, and maintained by Logica throughout the lifecycle. However, once identified, each specific hazard is formally passed to the client via a suitable mechanism. The hazards may be transferred individually, so Logica retains responsibility for hazard identification and initiation of the transfer.

Features of this approach are:

- Allows the system to be commercially developed.
- Significant hazards and their suggested mitigations are clearly handed over to client.
- Each handover is formalised and accepted in writing (e.g. via meeting minutes, tagging in a joint Hazard Log or use of Hazard Transfer Forms).
- Needs very active hazard identification activity.
- Needs cooperative client.

Care must be taken that no residual parts of a hazard or its mitigation remain within Logica's scope; otherwise one of the other patterns is invoked.

2.2.6 Not Currently Safety-Related

At first sight this is a rather strange category of safety project pattern. This is where the system has no significant hazards today, but potentially could have if context, usage or requirements change. This is often the case when working in an industry or sector which typically has a mix of safety and non-safety work, e.g. space or transport.

An active hazard identification process is required, which covers:

- Changes of use or operational environment (which may not be associated with changes in requirements).
- Change management.
- Bidding for further work/extensions.
- Changes in functionality due to fixes/enhancements/etc.

However it should be noted that even if the system is clearly not safety-related, sometimes the client still wants the system developed to a SIL. This can be for various reasons including the work being part of a larger safety-related programme, or to improve other related attributes such as availability, reliability or performance.

Regardless of SIL, the client may ask for other detailed safety analyses, verifications or traceability work to be supplied which would normally only be part of a safety-related development.

However, the obvious must be stated – that most clients consider working to a SIL when not required as unnecessarily expensive and time consuming.

2.2.7 Applications Framework

This pattern is applied on projects that include provision of support and enhancement for a suite of applications which were previously developed by the client or by a third party supplier. There are normally a large number of applications (typically hundreds) so that even after a due diligence process, it is often not known which, if any, applications are safety-related.

If there is little information on safety then the lowest risk approach is to take is to bid on a strictly commercial (non-safety) basis or arrange for all identified safety risks to be transferred to the client somehow as part of the contract.

It is necessary to put in place a permanent framework of processes which:

- Retains a baseline of each application as it was handed over, so responsibility can be traced.
- Initially classifies the safety status of each application as Definitely/Possibly/Probably Not for prioritisation. This also enables similar assessment of related groups of applications.
- Has a mechanism for assessing each application's risks and mitigations, in priority order.

Eventually it should be possible to arrive at one of the earlier patterns for each application or group of applications.

2.2.8 Infrastructure Hosting

In this pattern IT hosting facilities are provided, usually for a large suite of applications of which some may be safety-related. The scope of supply may include PCs, networks, servers, monitoring equipment, telecomms and helpdesk and can include complete datacentres.

In this case there is often little control over the applications, and frequently little knowledge of how they are used.

Ideally the client accepts all safety risks as part of the contract – but frequently it is not clear that some systems or supporting infrastructure are considered safety-related until later.

It is necessary to put in place a permanent framework of processes which:

- Initially classifies the safety implications of hosting each application as Definitely/Possibly/Probably Not and enables similar assessment of each piece of equipment or additional application installed.
- Has a mechanism to highlight any infrastructure failure as potentially safety-related by identifying the applications which depend on the failed component.
- Has responses, agreed with the client, for those failures which are safety-related.
- Ensures all staff are suitably experienced and trained in these responses.

It may be necessary to arrive at a specific pattern for each component supplied or supported.

2.2.9 Other Temporary Situations

There are other, usually temporary, situations where it is not clear which pattern is appropriate: for instance when bidding with limited information, or when the client will not acknowledge a safety risk or agree to work with us on mitigations.

The approach here is usually to try and obtain more information, perform more safety analyses to provide a clearer picture or undertake a programme of education and training. Eventually one or more of the earlier patterns should be adopted.

2.3 Fitting the Example Projects to the Patterns

The example projects given earlier all fit into the patterns as shown in Table 1.

Table 1. Example Projects and Their Patterns

Project	Pattern	Further Details
FC-A & FC-BISA	Standard Safety-Related Development	Software developed to SIL 2 of DEF STAN 00-55 (MoD 1997) and DEF STAN 00-56 (MoD 2007) (Hardware to IEC 61508 SIL 2).
DMICP	External Mitigations including Supplementary Commercial Software Changes	DEF STAN 00-56 (MoD 2007) is quoted in the contract but agreed as a 'non-SIL' development.
EGNOS CPF Check Set	Standard Safety-Related Development	Developed to a tailoring of DO-178B known as AD.07 (ESA 1997) at Level B.
Galileo GMS and GCS	Standard Safety-Related Development/External Mitigations including Supplementary Commercial Software Changes/Work-ing Under Client Direction & Management.	Across the various projects most of the safety project patterns have been employed in one form or another.
NHS Spine	External Mitigations including Supplementary Commercial Software Changes	The development is largely based on COTS products.
UCLH	External Mitigations including Supplementary Commercial Software Changes/Infrastructure hosting	The Logica work for UCLH spans many areas and covers many patterns.
DCWW (Welsh Water)	External Mitigations including Supplementary Commercial Software Changes	
Instant Energy	External Mitigations including Supplementary Commercial Software Changes	
BAA	Applications Framework	The applications are progressing through an assessment framework including client questionnaires to establish the hazards and necessary mitigations
Metronet	Applications Framework	
RIMNET	External Mitigations including Supplementary Commercial Software Changes.	Although non-SIL, detailed testing has been used to gain confidence in the system
CRB VBS	External Mitigations via Non-Software Means - Process and Procedures.	The system is wrapped within a comprehensive business process with additional safeguards.
Airwave	External Mitigations via Non-Software Means – Process and Procedures	Largely based on COTS products.
Skynet 5 Management Segment	Specific Risks Identified and Passed to Client.	Specific forms are used to explicitly transfer hazards to the client

3 The Decision Tool

To aid the bidding process for new work in Logica a simple decision tool based on the safety patterns work has been developed. This presents a series of questions leading through an underlying flowchart to a particular pattern. The tool has been developed in PowerPoint as a set of linked slides so as to be familiar to sales and business development staff.

The aim is to enable non-specialists to make an initial assessment of the safety risks and appropriate risk management approach.

For usability and completeness reasons the tool includes some extra sub-patterns and the patterns are encountered in a different sequence. The mapping is in Table 2.

Table 2. Mapping of Safety Pattern Number to Decision Tool Number

Pattern	Description	Tool Number
1	Standard Safety-Related Development	P5 & P8
2	External Mitigations	P6 & P7
3	Low Risk and Comprehensive Legal Cover	P2
4	Working under Client Direction and Management	P3
5	Specific Risks Identified and Passed to Client	P4
6	Not Currently Safety-Related	P0 & P1
7	Applications Framework	F1
8	Infrastructure Hosting	F2

Two screen shots from the tool are given below. Figure 1 shows one of the initial questions showing the type of questions asked and the control buttons. Figure 2 shows the index of patterns slide which is a useful summary of the end points.

4 Current Status

The patterns work has evolved over the last two years and is reaching a stable baseline. The tool is more recent and was developed over the last nine months. It has completed beta testing using several bid and project managers and is now live on the Logica intranet for general bid use. Some further evolution is expected as the bid teams use it in detail on future proposals and offerings.

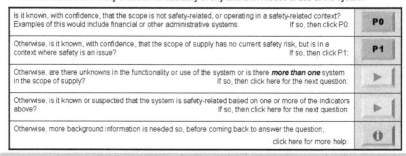

Fig. 1. First Question Slide from Decision Tool

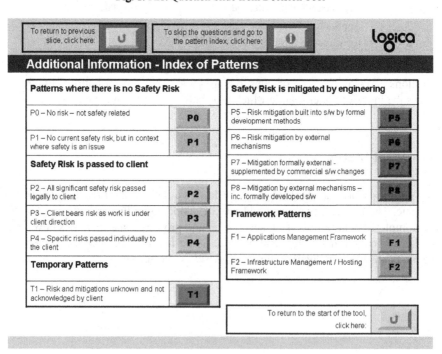

Fig. 2. Index of Patterns Slide

5 Conclusions and Further Work

The safety project patterns work brings several benefits:

- It allows focus and parameterization of many safety deliverables and project records. For example a safety management plan or safety audit report need only contain the sections relevant to that particular pattern.
- It gives more flexibility in bidding for work, as various pattern-based options can be discussed with the client.
- It allows greater use of 'template' safety arguments to assist with creating a safety case.
- The decision tool has both an evaluation and education role – both internally to Logica and also to clients – outlining what is required from the parties involved and who holds the safety risks and responsibilities.

Further work includes a more empirical approach to quantifying the additional costs involved in each pattern, utilising real project cost data.

Acknowledgments Many thanks to Rob Melville for his constructive comments and feedback.

References

Appleton B (2000) Patterns and software: essential concepts and terminology. http://www. cmcrossroads.com/bradapp/docs/patterns-intro.html. Accessed 21 September 2009

CRB (2009) Vetting and barring scheme FAQs. http://www.crb.gov.uk/faqs/vetting_and_barring _scheme.aspx. Accessed 21 September 2009

ESA (1997) EGNOS Software Qualification Requirements. European Space Agency. E-RD-CRT-E-001-ESA

ESA (2009a) http://www.esa.int/esaNA/galileo.html. Accessed 21 September 2009

ESA (2009b) Galileo SoftWare Standard (GSWS). GAL-SPE-ESA-SYST-0092. ESA

IEC (2005) IEC 61508 Functional safety of electrical/electronic/programmable electronic safety-related systems. International Electrotechnical Commission

Logica (2001) Logica secures contract to improve space aviation navigation (EGNOS). http:// www.logica.co.uk/logica+secures+contract+to+improve+space+aviation+navigation+(egnos) /400001988. Accessed 21 September 2009

Logica (2005) LogicaCMG secures £18 million IT outsourcing contract with Metronet Rail. http: //www.logica.co.uk/logicacmg+secures+%A318+million+it+outsourcing+contract+with+met ronet+rail/400002817. Accessed 21 September 2009

Logica (2007) Fire control battlefield information system application. http://www.logicaco/file/ 7814. Accessed 21 September 2009

Logica (2008a) Transforming the delivery of defence medical services. http://www.logica.com/ file/9578. Accessed 21 September 2009

Logica (2008b) Skynet 5 service provision. http://www.logica.com/file/9560. Accessed 21 September 2009

Logica (2009a) Healthcare factsheet. http://www.logica.co.uk/file/10493. Accessed 21 September 2009

Logica (2009b) Welsh Water transforms to stay on top. http://www.logica.com/file/6109. Accessed 21 September 2009

Logica (2009c) Instant energy. http://www.logica.co.uk/instant+energy/400013643. Accessed 21 September 2009

Logica (2009d) Using blended delivery to help BAA improve their applications management and reduce costs. http://www.logica.co.uk/file/15891. Accessed 21 September 2009

Logica (2009e) Operational excellence. http://www.logica.co.uk/operational+excellence/400016487. Accessed 21 September 2009

Met Office (2009) Radiation monitoring: the national radiation monitoring network and emergency response system (RIMNET), http://www.metoffice.gov.uk/publicsector/radiation.html. Accessed 9 October 2009

MoD (1997) DEF STAN 00-55 Requirements for safety related software in defence equipment. Issue 2. Ministry of Defence

MoD (2007) DEF STAN 00-56 Safety management requirements for defence systems. Issue 4. Ministry of Defence

RTCA (1992) RTCA/DO-178B Software considerations in airborne systems and equipment certification

Ventura-Traveset J, Michel P, Gauthier L (2001) Architecture, mission and signal processing aspects of the EGNOS System: the first European implementation of GNSS. http://conferences.esa.int/01C14/papers/3.3.pdf. Accessed 21 September 2009

Weaver RA, McDermid JA, Kelly TP (2002) Software safety arguments: towards a systematic categorisation of evidence. Intl Syst Safety Conf.

Wikipedia (2009) Risk management. http://en.wikipedia.org/wiki/Risk_management. Accessed 21 September 2009

Transport Safety

Applying IEC 61508 to Air Traffic Management Systems

Ron Pierce

CSE International Ltd

Scunthorpe, UK

Derek Fowler

JDF Consultancy LLP

Henley-on-Thames, UK

Abstract   IEC 61508 is often but erroneously thought of as applying only to the process industries. This paper considers how the standard can be applied to the safety management of air traffic management and control systems, examining areas where the standard is helpful and other areas where it is less useful and requires some augmentation. By considering the set of aircraft involved in controlled movements at any one time as the Equipment Under Control, a framework is provided, using the principles in IEC 61508, for deriving functional, performance and integrity requirements for the components of the overall control system.

1 Introduction

International Standard IEC 61508, Functional Safety of Electrical/Electronic/Programmable Electronic Safety Related Systems (IEC 2000), was first published in 2000 and is currently in the final stages of revision to create Version 2 of the standard. The authors have often heard the view expressed that IEC 61508 applies only to chemical and other process plant and to protection or shutdown systems. This impression has no doubt been encouraged by some of the language used in IEC 61508, which often talks about 'plant' and other similar concepts, primarily because many of the contributors to the original version of the standard (and to the revision) come from a petrochemical industry background and naturally think in these terms. The wording of IEC 61508 makes it clear however that it is intended to be a generic standard and a 'basic safety publication', which can be used as a

C. Dale, T. Anderson (eds.), *Making Systems Safer*, DOI 10.1007/978-1-84996-086-1_7,
© Springer-Verlag London Limited 2010

basis for deriving industry-specific standards. However, if no industry-specific standard has been created, it is clear that the original standard can always be used by default. The new version of IEC 61508 has been modified to some extent to remove this apparent bias towards the process industries, although it still appears in places.

This paper considers how IEC 61508 can be applied to the air traffic management industry, examining areas where IEC 61508 is helpful and other areas where it is less useful and requires some augmentation. The term air traffic management (ATM) comprises both active air traffic control (ATC) and wider aspects such as airspace design and tactical air traffic flow management.

One of the most difficult areas in ATM is quantifying risk and deriving safety integrity targets, and the paper explores how IEC 61508 may be used to provide guidance in this area.

2 The IEC 61508 Model of the World

IEC 61508 has a particular model of how a safety control system or a protection system influences the real world. The Equipment Under Control (EUC) is regarded as the hazard creating system; there is no particular implication or statement on the nature of the EUC.

The standard broadly distinguishes two kinds of systems: protection systems and control systems. With the *protection system* concept, the EUC and its control system together may create hazards, but are not regarded as safety related. A safety-related protection system is put in place to reduce the risk associated with EUC hazards to an acceptable level (IEC 61508 does not stipulate what is acceptable; this is left to local or national considerations, including legal frameworks). The protection system intervenes when it detects a possibly hazardous state developing with the EUC, and intervenes to put the EUC and its control system into a safe state. Safety integrity requirements on the protection system are stated in terms of probability of failure on demand, and the target probability will of course depend on the likelihood of the EUC and its control system creating hazards. The objective of the safety-related system (SRS) – in this case, the protection system – is *risk reduction.*

The other type of system is a safety-related control system, which controls the EUC (rather than shutting it down) such that the risk associated with EUC hazards is kept to a tolerable level. In this case the objective of the SRS is risk control. Version 2 of IEC 61508 is much clearer about the application of risk reduction to protection systems and risk control to continuously operating control systems. Of course, a given EUC could have both a safety-related control system and a protection system depending on the degree of risk presented by the EUC before the SRSs are put in place.

In both cases, IEC 61508 is quite clear that the safety functional requirements (specifying functionality and performance of the safety functions) must be completely and correctly identified before the SRS can be designed; hazard analysis of the EUC is required to determine the protection or control functions necessary – in the words of IEC 61508 to *achieve* or *maintain* a safe state. Achievement of the safe state is generally applicable to a protection or shutdown system, maintenance of a safe state to a continuous control system. Once the safety functional requirements are identified, the tolerable failure rates of the safety functions can be identified, and the Safety Integrity Level (SIL) for each function established.

3 Air Traffic as the EUC

Considering the concept of aviation in its entirety, it is clear that it is a potentially hazardous activity. There are hazards associated entirely with operation of a single aircraft (such as engine, airframe or control failure), which are outside the sphere of influence of ATM. There are however a number of other hazards which ATM has a contribution to mitigating, and some of these are listed in Table 1 below (there are others, which are omitted for the sake of brevity).

Table 1. Examples of ATM-related hazards and accidents

Hazard	Accident
Conflict between two aircraft when airborne	Mid air collision (MAC)
Conflict between aircraft and terrain or obstacle (aircraft in controllable state)	Controlled flight into terrain (CFIT)
Conflict between aircraft on the ground (including the case where one or more aircraft are landing and taking off from the runway)	Ground collision
Wake vortex turbulence	Loss of control
	Passenger injuries
Violent weather effects	Loss of control
	Passenger injuries

In this case a 'conflict' is defined as a situation where, if the trajectories of the aircraft are continued with their current horizontal velocities (speed and direction) and altitude, a collision will result.

Some of these hazards clearly apply only to cases where two or more aircraft are in the air – these can be called traffic related hazards. Others are caused by factors in the natural environment, in particular terrain and weather (but the presence of birds is also a hazard, as evidenced by the ditching of a Boeing 737 aircraft in the Hudson River in early 2009). IEC 61508 Part 1 only briefly acknowledges that the natural environment can cause EUC hazards or affect EUC risk, but it is clear that an adequate hazard analysis should identify any applicable environmental hazards.

It has been found by experience that aircraft cannot be relied upon to avoid mid-air collisions by visual means alone, even in clear weather conditions, and certainly not in cloud. The earliest recorded mid-air collision between passenger carrying aircraft occurred as long ago as 1922 when there were only a few passenger flights per day. The risk associated with civil aviation would be unacceptably high unless some form of risk control and reduction systems were put in place, and this is the origin of ATC, later extended to ATM. Similarly, a ground-based system is useful in reducing risk associated with accidents other than mid-air collision.

How is the IEC 61508 model to be applied to ATM? There is great benefit in thinking of EUC as consisting of the collection of aircraft involved in current or planned movements in controlled airspace (those actually in flight, those landing and taking off or manoeuvring on the ground, and those being prepared for flight). Admittedly this is a somewhat unusual definition of an EUC, which is most often thought of as a single fixed entity such as a piece of machinery or a process plant. It is a dynamic system, which means that the parts of the EUC (the aircraft in movement) will vary as time progresses. This EUC concept is particularly useful when a radical change to the way ATM operates is proposed, as is the case in the pan-European SESAR (Single European Skies ATM Research) Programme (Fowler et al. 2009).

There are no safe states when aircraft are airborne; thus the ATM system cannot be regarded as a protection system in the simplest sense. It must therefore be regarded as a control system although its goal is risk reduction to a level which is tolerable and As Low As Reasonably Practicable (ALARP). The ALARP principle was not traditionally applied to ATM but has become increasingly prominent in recent years and is recommended in the ICAO Safety Management Manual for ATM (ICAO 2009) and in the EUROCONTROL regulatory requirements (EUROCONTROL 2000).

Another problem is that the definition of a hazardous state which must be prevented by the ATM system is not discrete. In a railway interlocking, a signal which shows a proceed aspect (green) when it should be red is a discrete hazard which is either present or not. By contrast, aircraft could get quite close to each other without an accident resulting, so in practice it is more useful to define *separation minima* between aircraft. The separation minima for most of European airspace are five nautical miles horizontally or 1,000 feet vertically; a hazard of loss of separation is deemed to result if the applicable separation minima are infringed. These figures are not arbitrary but are determined by the speed of aircraft, the accuracy of altimeters and the accuracy of the surveillance systems used to determine the instantaneous positions of the aircraft which comprise the EUC.

One problem when applying risk tolerability criteria to ATM, and in particular to loss-of-separation hazards is that a mid-air collision will cause (in general) multiple fatalities, as will many other kinds of accident. Control of the consequences of an accident is therefore not feasible, and risk must be controlled by reducing the likelihood of accidents.

4 Deriving Safety Requirements for ATM Systems

This section of the paper concentrates on deriving safety requirements related to the control of risk from airborne collisions (loss of separation hazards) in accordance with the principles in Part 1 of IEC 61508. Similar principles can be applied to the ATM contribution to risk reduction from other hazards.

In control systems, there are two possible kinds of failure. The control system may be *ineffective*, in that a hazard which the system is designed to prevent nonetheless occurs, or the control system may operate *incorrectly*, and create a hazard where none previously existed.

A simple example of this is a car airbag. The intention of the airbag system is to reduce the severity of injuries when a collision has occurred, and therefore it is a consequence mitigation system. From this point of view, the safety function is to inflate the airbag when a collision situation is detected and to deflate immediately afterwards. There are two main hazards: ineffective operation – the airbag fails to inflate effectively when required, and spurious inflation – the airbag inflates when the car is being driven normally and is not in collision (incorrect operation). This latter hazard could cause loss of control of the car with a resulting serious or fatal accident. The safety integrity requirement associated with the first hazard is a probability of failure on demand, while for the second it will be failure rate. Part 1 of IEC 61508 makes it clear that the functionality and performance of the airbag system must be correctly specified (in terms of, for example, the deceleration threshold which will cause deployment and the time to deploy) in order to achieve the necessary risk reduction in a collision.

The case with the ATM system is similar although much more complicated – since the system is actively issuing commands to the components of the EUC (the aircraft), an incorrect command can cause a hazard such as loss of separation.

There has been a tendency for ATM safety analysis to concern itself only with hazards arising from system failures and to ignore the need to demonstrate that the functionality and performance requirements for the system are correct to achieve the necessary risk reduction (Fowler et al. 2007), in contradiction to IEC 61508.

The 'barrier model' illustrated in Figure 1 has been found useful in determining high-level ATM safety requirements. Each barrier (or layer of protection) removes a certain proportion of the conflicts between aircraft trajectories. The 'SBT hazards' represent the conflicts which would exist if airlines and other operators operated their desired flights without any consideration of conflicts. SBT stands for 'shared business trajectory' and is the SESAR term for the set of published flight trajectories (detailed flight plans) that operators would like to fly.

The Airspace Design barrier is passive (aircraft are separated, for example, by flying segregated arrival and departure routes), whereas all other barriers except Providence are active. Each active barrier is implemented by a combination of equipment and people supported by procedures (rules and methods of working).

The Demand-Capacity Balancing barrier is (currently) a euphemism for reducing the number of flights into and out of busy airports and congested airspaces to

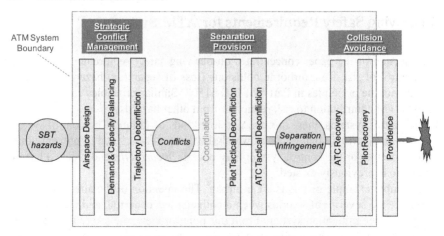

Fig. 1. Barrier model of the total ATM system

avoid overloading the ATC system – passengers perceive it when they are told by the captain that they have to wait on the ground for their 'slot time'. The Pilot Recovery barrier is the only one which has no ATC involvement, and is implemented by the TCAS airborne collision avoidance system or last-minute see and avoid actions by the flight crew.

The barrier model can be used to set safety performance objectives for conflict removal and collision avoidance, and thus contributes to the definition of the function and performance requirements for the systems which implement the barriers – for example the necessary accuracy of surveillance systems. The barrier model can also be used to set integrity targets for the incorrect operation of the barriers. This can be illustrated by the conceptual model in Figure 2, which shows the risk reduction achievable by the correct operation of each group of barriers (left-pointing arrows) and the risk increase from incorrect operation of the barriers (right-pointing arrows).

In practice, most of the ground-based ATC barriers are implemented by the same controllers and equipment items so the barriers are not independent, and methods such as Fault Tree Analysis (FTA) are needed to apportion both success and failure targets to individual subsystems within the overall ATM system.

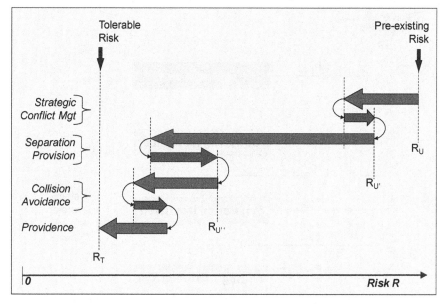

Fig. 2. Positive and negative risk reduction

An overall risk target (tolerable probability of an accident) is required for numeric modelling, and this can be derived from the Integrated Risk Picture (IRP) developed by EUROCONTROL (Perrin et al. 2007). The IRP uses historical incident data and a modified form of FTA to predict the risk associated with a number of top-level aviation hazards listed in Table 1 (weather hazards are not covered). Figure 3 shows, in a schematic manner, the top levels of a fault tree which can be used to apportion barrier success and failure targets, using an abbreviated notation for compactness. The P labels are the success probabilities for the barriers, and the F labels are the frequencies of incorrect operation of the barriers, creating conflicts where none previously existed (labelled as *system-generated* hazards).

The effectiveness of the current ATM system in European airspace can be seen from the IRP; the predicted risk of a mid-air collision in the baseline year 2005 was 0.12 collisions per annum, whereas without ATM it could at least in theory be many tens of thousands per annum. To avoid such a high accident rate, the volume of air traffic would have to be drastically reduced, which is what happens in practice after major ATM equipment failures.

Applying the barrier model can be complex, and in many cases safety integrity requirements are applied to equipment failure by a simpler means such as a risk classification scheme, as discussed in (Pierce 2005). There is no intrinsic problem with using this method provided that the function and performance requirements for the equipment in question are also shown to be correctly established and it is recognized that safety integrity requirements and function and performance requirements are interdependent (Fowler et al. 2007).

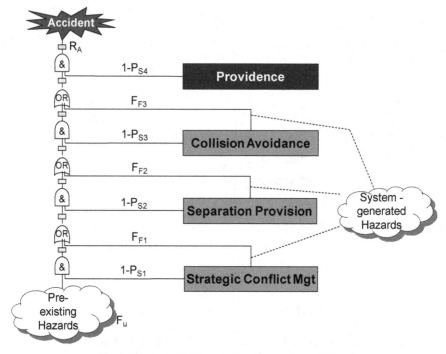

Fig. 3. Schematic fault tree for barrier success and failure

5 Unusual Aspects of ATC

In addition to the fact that the EUC consists of a dynamically varying collection of moving objects, ATC is unusual (in terms of the IEC 61508 model of safety) in that the human being (the Air Traffic Control Officer or ATCO) provides the control service, with equipment to support him or her in that task. In ATC, the sensors are electronic systems such as surveillance radar, but the actuators are people. The standard recognises that human being can be part of the SRS and that the SRS can output information for humans to act upon, but provides almost nothing in the way of normative requirements or guidance where the human being is in control. Therefore human performance is crucial to the safe functioning of the ATM system and ATCOs are subject to rigorous selection, training, licensing and in-service assessment, developed over many years of practical experience.

6 Increased Need for Automation

With the predicted continuing increase in air traffic in the medium to long term of around 5% per annum (despite the worldwide recession which started in 2008, which has caused a reduction in traffic), it has been recognised that increased automation of functions formerly performed by human beings will be required if the traffic increase is to be accommodated without an increase in the overall aviation accident risk with an ATM contribution. The risk of traffic-related hazards increase as the square of the traffic density, so to achieve the threefold increase in capacity which might be required by the 2030s, a tenfold reduction in the risk of collision per flight must be achieved. How this can be done while still leaving the human being in overall control is a major topic of the SESAR Programme (Fowler et al. 2009).

It is generally recognised that the ATC Tactical Deconfliction barrier in Figure 2 (where controllers recognise a developing conflict and give instructions to avoid it in good time) cannot be made much more effective than it is at present, and SESAR efforts are centred on strengthening the more strategic Trajectory Deconfliction barrier (although the overall SESAR Programme has many other safety improvements in mind). The aim is to remove, at an earlier stage, many more potential conflicts than is possible at present, by planning aircraft movements in detail and executing them with much greater precision. Central to this concept is the idea that the ground-based ATC systems and the flight management system on each aircraft have identical copies of the aircraft's intentions (known as RBTs or Reference Business Trajectories in SESAR) at all times. Air-ground datalink technology and advanced networking between ATC centres will ensure that any modifications to the RBTs made by either ATC or at the request of the aircraft are available to all parties within a period measured in seconds. Conflicts between RBTs can be detected by automated conflict detection and resolution systems and removed by making adjustment to the affected RBTs which can then by uplinked to the affected aircraft. Use of advanced datalink technology will also reduce the frequency of miscommunication between controllers and flight crew which is currently a major cause of hazardous failures in the ATM system (VHF voice radio communications are still the major means of communication between ATC and flight crew).

Clearly, the complexity of equipment functions will increase considerably, but the principles of IEC 61508 Part 1 – specifying safety functions and deriving integrity requirements based on risk reduction and risk control requirements – will remain directly relevant.

7 Applying Parts 2 and 3 of IEC 61508

Once the safety requirements (function, performance and integrity) for the various components of the ATM system are established as discussed in the preceding sections, Part 2 and Part 3 (safety-related software) of IEC 61508 can be applied directly to the equipment elements of the overall ATM system. Indeed, many recent ATM systems have been developed to and assessed against IEC 61508.

EUROCONTROL has not chosen to recommend the use of IEC 61508, and no ATM specific derivative of IEC 61508 has been developed. For software, EUROCONTROL has developed guidance documents ANS Software Lifecycle (EUROCONTROL 2005a) and recommendations for ANS Software (EUROCONTROL 2005b). These documents introduce the concept of the Software Assurance Level (SWAL) which is similar to the SIL concept in IEC 61508; the main difference is that the defined process for assigning a SWAL to a software system is based on the consequences of software failure modes rather than being risk-based. This is unfortunately at variance with the risk-based approach using the barrier model discussed above. The recommendations for ANS Software are similar to other standards and guidelines for software development in that they suggest an overall software development process where the rigour of the verification and validation techniques increases with higher SWALs, but the overall rigour is, in the opinion of the authors, rather less than is required by Part 3 of IEC 61508.

There is no comparable EUROCONTROL document at the overall equipment system and hardware level, and the requirements and guidance in Part 2 of IEC 61508 can be applied directly to these aspects of an ATM system.

8 Conclusions

By thinking of the EUC as the collection of aircraft involved in flight operations (including ground manoeuvring) the principles of hazard and risk assessment and definition of functional and integrity requirements in IEC 61508 Part 1 can be applied to ATM. The principles of safe equipment design set out in IEC 61508 Part 2 are equally useful, and Part 3 can be readily applied to the software in ATM systems unless one is required to follow alternative guidelines.

The standard however does not help where the human performance aspects of the ATM system are concerned, and ATM service providers must look to their own established practices and other human factors literature for help.

Acknowledgements The authors would like to acknowledge the support of M. Eric Perrin and their other colleagues within EUROCONTROL in developing some of the ideas which are expressed in this paper.

References

EUROCONTROL (2000) SRC ESARR 3 Use of safety management systems by ATM service providers, edn 1.0. EUROCONTROL

EUROCONTROL (2005a) ANS software lifecycle. EUROCONTROL document SAF.ET1. ST03.1000.REP-01-00, edn 3.0

EUROCONTROL (2005b) Recommendations for ANS software. EUROCONTROL document SAF.ET1.ST03.1000.GUI-01-00, edn 1.0

Fowler D, Le Galo G, Perrin E, Thomas S (2007) So it's reliable but is it safe? Proc 7th US/ Europe Seminar on ATM Research and Development, Barcelona

Fowler D, Perrin E, Pierce R (2009) 2020 Foresight: A systems engineering approach to assessing the safety of the SESAR operational concept. Proc Eighth USA/Europe Air Traffic Management Research and Development Seminar (ATM2009), Napa, USA

ICAO (2009) ICAO document 9859 Safety management manual, 2nd edn. International Civil Aviation Organisation, Montreal

IEC (2000) ISO/IEC 61508 Functional safety of electrical/electronic/programmable electronic safety related systems, Parts 1 to 7. International Electrotechnical Commission

Perrin E, Kirwan B, Stroup R (2007) A systemic model of ATM safety: the Integrated Risk Picture. Proc 7th US/Europe Seminar on ATM Research and Development, Barcelona

Pierce RH (2005) A survey of the EUROCONTROL approach to safety risk management. Proc International System Safety Conference, Baltimore

Phileas, a Safety Critical Trip around the World

Jean-Luc Valk, Hans Vis and Gerard Koning

APTS

Helmond, The Netherlands

Abstract Phileas, developed by Advanced Public Transportation Systems (APTS) is a new concept for comfortable high frequency passenger mass transport. Its unique safety requirements impose a serious challenge for the development of a safe electronic guidance system. In particular, the standard systems engineering methodologies applied need to be tailored in order to comply with the CENELEC railway standards EN50126, EN50128 and EN50129. From formal and traceable requirements capture to the rigorous verification and validation processes, the integrated development approach must provide not only a functional system in compliance with all stakeholder needs, but also evidence of quality and safety management in all phases of the life cycle. Once certification for Phileas is achieved, the chances for APTS to become an important player in the development of safe next generation vehicle intelligence are significantly increased.

1 Introduction

Advanced Public Transportation Systems (APTS) is developing the Phileas public transport system for the Douai Region in the North of France. Phileas is a new concept for comfortable, environmentally friendly, high frequency mass public transport which combines the advantages of rail transport with the low costs and flexibility of a bus system. Vehicles can be single- or double-articulated and have an appearance very similar to that of a normal bus (see Figure 1). They will drive with relatively high speed over a dedicated bus lane on virtual rails within the existing infrastructure. Precision docking is realized with a high degree of accuracy, moving sideways to the raised platforms, ensuring a minimum gap at the bus stops. In this way a fast passenger entry and exit is made possible, so reducing stop times and increasing the average operational speed.

Safety for such new technological concepts is a dominant consideration. The focus of this paper is on safety principles embedded in the development process, based on combining techniques from the fields of railway, aircraft and automated guided vehicles to arrive at a certifiably safe integral solution for an electronically guided Phileas vehicle for mass public transportation.

C. Dale, T. Anderson (eds.), *Making Systems Safer*, DOI 10.1007/978-1-84996-086-1_8,
© Springer-Verlag London Limited 2010

Fig. 1. The Single-Articulated Phileas Vehicle for Douai

2 Guidance System Overview

Phileas is capable of driving in manual mode, similar to a normal bus, and in guided mode, similar to a tram. In guided mode, the on-board electronic Guidance Control System (GCS) is responsible for guiding the vehicle automatically along a pre-determined trajectory. This is achieved by a navigation function that determines the vehicle position with respect to the desired trajectory based on a set of sensor inputs and a control function that influences the steering, driving and braking actuators. Automatic braking can be activated by the GCS upon detection of critical failures.

2.1 Navigation

The planar motion of the vehicle is estimated from odometric sensor data such as steer angle encoders, drive encoders and gyroscopes. This is based on a planar kinematic model, containing quantities such as sensor positions and geometries of the steering mechanisms.

Integration of the estimated planar motion results in a fairly accurate position estimate of the vehicle that can be mapped to the desired trajectory. To account for odometric errors (e.g. sensor offsets) and non-measureable quantities (e.g. side slip), which are cumulative errors on the position estimate, an absolute reference system is used. This consists of a set of magnetic rulers that can determine the position of magnets embedded in the road surface. By comparing the measured positions of the magnets with their expected positions, the estimated vehicle position can be corrected.

2.2 Control

After the estimated position of the vehicle is associated to the desired trajectory, the deviation with respect to that trajectory needs to be minimized, which is the objective of the control function. Separate controllers are applied to minimize both the longitudinal and the lateral deviation.

Although the driver is responsible for the longitudinal motion of the vehicle, i.e. accelerating or braking, the longitudinal controller has the responsibility of limiting the vehicle speed to a predefined safe maximum while complying with the comfort and safety constraints on both longitudinal and lateral acceleration and jerk. The propulsion system is a parallel hybrid system in which torque from a diesel engine is combined with the torque of two electric motors. The propulsion system is able to supply a braking torque as well, in which case the electric motors act as generators and the braking energy can be stored in a battery. In addition an electronic braking system is used with pressure modulators on each axle. A fallback braking system that monitors the braking pressure per axle is on standby to apply emergency braking when necessary.

The lateral controller is responsible for calculating the set points for the steering actuators, which are located on each axle. This means that each axle can be steered independently, thus minimizing the swept path of the vehicle in curves and maximizing the manoeuvrability. For the front axle the steering actuator is implemented with a triple redundant servo steering system. The rear axles of the vehicles use a redundant electro hydraulic system to control the steering motion.

3 Safety Engineering

To realize the Advanced Vehicle Control benefits of Phileas there are requirements to establish the procedures and methodologies for safety assessment. In particular, compliance with the CENELEC standards EN50126, EN50128 and EN50129 and derived standards for electronic railway applications is a major requirement in the development of Phileas.

Safety relies both on adequate measures to avoid or tolerate faults (as safeguards against systematic failure) and on adequate measures to control random failures. Measures against both causes of failure are balanced in order to achieve the optimum safety performance of the vehicle. To achieve this, the concept of Safety Integrity Levels (SIL) is used. Safety integrity can be viewed as a combination of quantifiable elements (generally associated with the probability of hard-ware failure, i.e. random failures) and non-quantifiable elements (generally asso-ciated with systematic failures in software, specification, documents, processes, etc.).

Based on a Preliminary Hazard Analysis (PHA) and a Fault Tree Analysis (FTA) at vehicle level, the functional and safety requirements are derived for the Phileas as shown in Figure 2. To each of these functions both a qualitative safety target and a quantitative target are assigned. The qualitative target is a Safety Inte-grity Level which covers systematic failure integrity while the quantitative target is a numerical failure rate, which covers random failure integrity.

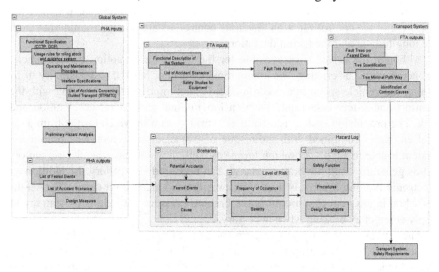

Fig. 2. Deriving Safety Requirements from Preliminary Hazard Analysis

From the hazard analysis it is immediately clear that Phileas is a safety-critical system involving several safety-critical functions, in particular the steering func-tion for lateral control of the vehicle. Compared with other related public transpor-tation systems that have mechanical guidance, for Phileas it is not trivial to bring the vehicle to a safe state. The unique top-level SIL4 requirement for the electron-ically guided Phileas vehicle implies a fail operational steering function in order to stay within the predefined safety envelop or so called clearance space. As a conse-quence APTS must demonstrate that the risk of catastrophic accidents when a Phi-leas is leaving the clearance is less than 10^{-8} per hour. This means that all the hardware and software that comprise the Guidance System must have a high and continuous availability with a hazardous failure frequency of less than once per 10,000 years. Demonstrating that the risk reduction strategy as implemented by the system design is compliant with this top-level safety requirement is compul-sory for safety certification of Phileas and approval and acceptance for driving Phileas vehicles in guided mode in Douai.

4 Development Process

The guidance function is a highly complex function with many interdependent sub-functions, which can be safety functions (SIL1-SIL4) or non-safety functions (SIL0), implemented over distributed subsystems. The integrated development approach is tailored to provide evidence of safety of the entire system through:

- Establishment of hazard log and derived safety requirements
- Justification for the traceability of the requirements flow down
- Justification for the architectural design
- Independent Verification and Validation
- Quality assurance of the development process

To this end, in accordance with the system lifecycle phases as defined in EN50126, the Phileas project distinguishes the development activities as shown in Figure 3.

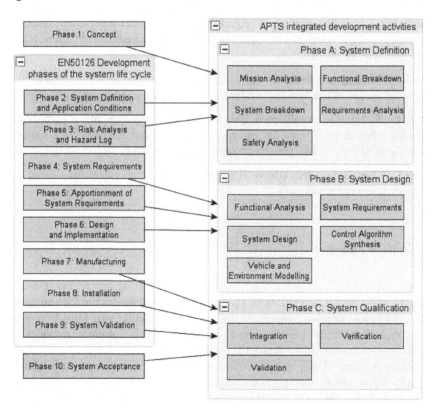

Fig. 3. EN50126 Life Cycle

4.1 System Definition

Particular attention is given to assuring completeness and correctness of the traceability from user requirements to functional and performance requirements for the vehicle system and its subsystems. This is done with the aid of dedicated tools for document and requirement management, in order to deal with the significant amount of requirements that have to be maintained throughout the development life cycle of the guidance system. The requirements are organized in a database, containing five different levels each of which represents a level of detail or characteristic.

Level 1 – Stakeholder. This specifies stakeholder requirements, including contractual and customer specific requirements, requirements extracted from applicable standards and legislation and manufacturer specific requirements (safety and non-safety related).

Level 2 – Public Transport System. This specifies public transport system requirements. This level aggregates requirements specified at level 1 and resolves any conflicts. This represents the baseline of system requirements to be developed in the scope of the project.

Level 3 – Functional Breakdown. This specifies requirements for each of the functional groups of the transport system, identified by the mission analysis.

Level 4 – Subsystem Breakdown. This specifies the requirements of each of the guidance subsystems. It also determines the required redundancy of the various components of those subsystems necessary to meet the safety requirements.

Level 5 – Component Breakdown. This specifies the requirements of each of the guidance system components.

4.2 System Design

The development of the control algorithms of the guidance system is done through a model based design process. In this process a system model is the foundation of the development process through all the phases. In addition to a formal requirements capture, a model based approach using MATLAB Simulink, provides an auxiliary specification of the desired algorithms for the Guidance Control System. A major advantage of this is that an executable specification becomes available at an early stage which can be updated continuously throughout the development process, including the implementation and test phases.

In addition to the aforementioned benefits the model based design process also provides the opportunity of automatically generating production code for the target platform when following the formal workflow as part of the overall IEC61508 software safety lifecycle. As stated by the certification entity TÜV SÜD,

MATLAB fulfils the IEC61508 normative requirements regarding tool support and automation, which reduces the number of systematic errors due to the reduction of error-prone manual activities. This workflow includes:

* Providing requirements traceability between models and formal requirements;
* Review and static analysis at the model level to guarantee compliance to modelling standards;
* Functional verification of the models by using requirements based test vectors to ensure compliance of the models with the requirements and that no unintended functionality is implemented;
* Automatic code generation with built in traceability between the source code and the models;
* Code review in order to verify compliance against coding standards and using formal methods to exclude run time errors;
* Equivalence testing of object code with the models; and
* Functional verification of object code against the formal requirements by using requirements based test vectors to ensure compliance of the models with the requirements and that no unintended functionality is implemented.

By using qualified tools within this workflow, some of these steps may be automated. When steps in the workflow are omitted or verification of the output of some steps is automated, qualification of such tools is necessary if the tool could introduce errors in the system or allow such errors to be undetected.

The whole model based design process is supported by the availability of several different development environments:

Model In the Loop. MIL consists of models for vehicle dynamics, vehicle equipment (e.g. sensors and actuators), guidance infrastructure (e.g. the road surface and the magnet grid) and the environment (e.g. wind and slippery road conditions) and runs on the same platform as the algorithms under development.

Hardware In the Loop. HIL consists of models for vehicle dynamics, vehicle equipment (e.g. sensors and actuators), guidance infrastructure (e.g. the road surface and the magnet grid) and the environment (e.g. wind and slippery road conditions) and runs on a dedicated separate platform from the algorithms under development, which run on the intended target platform.

Rapid Control Prototype. RCP consists of a dedicated hardware platform, different from the intended target platform, on which prototyped version of the control algorithms can be tested on a real vehicle.

Each of the dedicated environments has a specific purpose and role in the development cycle of the GCS, such as design optimization testing of the control algorithms, verification testing for compliance with requirements and validation testing of GCS hardware and software.

4.3 System Qualification

Independent verification and validation is achieved by using separate teams for design, verification and validation. This is in accordance with one of the organizational structures proposed by EN50126 and is intended to further reduce the incidence of safety-related human errors throughout the life-cycle, and thus minimize the residual risk of safety-related systematic faults.

Verification is an activity of confirmation by objective analysis and test that the output of each phase of the life cycle fulfils the requirements of the previous phase (are we building the product right?). This entails for each development phase assessing compliance of a (sub-)system with its requirements by test, analysis or inspection.

Validation is an activity of confirmation by objective analysis and test that the product meets in all respects its specified requirements (are we building the right product?). It entails assessing compliance of the top level requirements with all the stakeholder needs, assessing compliance of the final product with the top level requirements by analysis, test or inspection and assessing a proper conduct of the design and verification process.

5 Safety Concept

The safety concept of the Phileas guidance system corresponds with the implementation of a variety of safety protective principles and measures to reduce the likelihood and consequences of hazardous events that could result in loss of guidance. The principal causes for loss of guidance are:

- Internal technical failure of safety-relevant components or software of the guidance system; and
- External factors such as strong side winds and slippery wheel-road contacts.

Based on the high level functional view of the guidance system in Figure 4, the dominant causes of internal technical failure, which could propagate to loss of guidance, are:

- Failure of a steering actuator;
- Steering actuator receives *no* set points from the GCS; and
- Steering actuator receives *wrong* set points from the GCS.

In order to achieve fail operational behaviour of the safety critical steering function, the Guidance System is developed by defining and managing adequate risk reduction strategies in terms of mitigating measures in system design and application conditions for each safety-related hazard such as:

- redundancy and diversification against common mode failures and single points of failure;

- continuous monitoring of active safety-critical hardware components;
- automatic testing of inactive (dormant) safety-critical hardware components;
- monitoring lateral deviations of vehicle; and
- automatic braking in case of detection of any hazardous event.

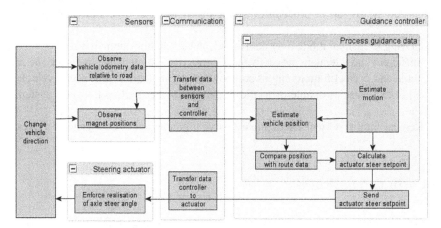

Fig. 4. High Level Functional View of the Guidance System

Examples of these measures are a triple redundant front axle steering system with hardware and software diversification, communication protocols to guarantee error free safety critical data transfer and life sign monitoring and fully redundant power supply and communication busses. The Guidance Control System is comprised of three separate guidance computers in a one-master, two-slave configuration. The actuator set points are validated through a majority voting mechanism and in case of a master-guidance computer failure both slaves will disable the master by disconnecting it from the communication busses through a dedicated cut-off device while one of the slaves will take over the master role.

Automatic braking is activated on detection of one safety-critical hazard to ensure that the guided bus is stopped quickly and safely, in principle without the need to rely on any action by the driver. Simultaneously, the propulsion of the vehicle is automatically decoupled or switched off and a warning is issued to the driver. The time at risk, i.e. the time to stop the vehicle after detection of a hazard by the guidance controller, will be between 6 and 9 seconds depending on the vehicle speed. The likelihood of loss of guidance due to the occurrence of a second safety-critical failure within this short period of time is acceptably low.

By defining a safety margin for the vehicle and monitoring lateral deviations with respect to the desired position on the route, automatic safety braking can be activated, bringing the vehicle to a safe stop before a loss of guidance could occur.

Under extreme weather conditions, with the possibility of strong side wind gusts or slippery roads, the maximum allowed speed is reduced and operation may be completely prohibited because the lateral forces exerted on the vehicle in combination with those conditions could cause the likelihood of loss of guidance to exceed the tolerable hazard rate.

The safety concept is completed with exported constraints for the operator, such as:

- Correct follow-up of procedures by the driver in case of degraded operational conditions;
- Driving in manual mode over dedicated bus lane and/or public road;
- Sufficient and adequate preventive and corrective maintenance to ensure the reliable and correct functioning of components during the life time of the vehicle;
- Limit exposure of people or traffic to dangers of the Phileas transport system; and
- Repress fatalities by efficient and effective organization of emergency services.

6 Certification Process

For certification of the Phileas Guidance System according to EN50126, EN50128 and EN50129, the overall documentary evidence APTS is required to deliver is referred to as the APTS Safety File, which consists of:

- System (or sub-system/equipment) Requirements Specification;
- Safety Requirements Specification;
- Homologation File for the Phileas vehicle equipped with the guidance system;
- APTS Safety Case; and
- Safety Assessment Report from the Independent Safety Assessor (ISA).

6.1 Safety Case

The APTS Safety Case is intended to provide evidence that the safety level of the system during the entire life cycle is ensured and to inform the organizations responsible for operation and maintenance during exploitation about the conditions under which the system can be operated safely. This is achieved by including evidence of quality management, safety management and functional and technical safety in the APTS Safety Case. EN50129 requires all these conditions to be satisfied, at equipment, subsystem and system levels, before the Phileas electronic guidance system can be qualified and accepted as adequately safe for its intended application.

6.2 Homologation

The process of bus homologation of Phileas involves the following main phased objectives:

- Phileas as a normal bus *without* electronic guidance system and steered manually by the driver on a public road must be compliant with all applicable bus legislation. The vehicle is then allowed to drive as a normal city bus on all public roads in France.
- Phileas as a normal bus *with* electronic guidance system and steered manually by the driver either on a public road or on dedicated Phileas bus lanes must be compliant with all applicable bus legislation. In this mode, the vehicle is allowed to drive on all public roads in France. For the application in the Douai region, this corresponds with a start-up mode or with a degraded mode of operation.
- Phileas as a guided bus *with* electronic guidance system and steered automatically on dedicated Phileas bus lanes must be compliant with all applicable bus legislation. This corresponds with the nominal mode of operation in the Douai region.

In phase one of the Phileas Homologation File, the Base-vehicle, which is the vehicle without any functional component of the guidance system, is certified as a normal city bus and is compliant with all applicable bus legislation. In the final Phileas Homologation File, additional certificates of new subsystems and hardware and software components of the guidance system have been added. When relevant, some of the existing certificates have been updated to account for the presence of these additional components and functionality of the vehicle equipped with the guidance system.

With the National type approval of the Phileas vehicle in France, the vehicle can be driven as a city bus on all public roads in France. Obviously, the applicable bus legislation puts constraints on the system requirement specification for Phileas driving as a guided bus using the guidance system. In cases where the Phileas safety concept for driving as a guided bus is not fully compatible with the applicable bus legislation, appropriate derogation has been requested and approved. This approach has ensured the mutual compatibility of the Homologation File and the APTS Safety Case. Together these comprise the integral part of the evidence to demonstrate that the new guidance function technology can be accepted to be adequately safe for the use in the Phileas transport system in the Douai region in France.

7 Conclusions

The approach for development and certification according to CENELEC railway standards EN50126, EN50128 and EN50129, of the Phileas Guidance System was presented. Given the complexity and the innovative character of the system it is a non-trivial exercise to fully adhere to certain development processes and standards. An added SIL4 certification requires a degree of rigor and attention to close detail that might well seem excessive to those used to development to even the most excellent commercial standards. The combination of those constraints seems to present a significant challenge. Nevertheless, the prospect of becoming a high-tech internationally oriented player in the development of safe next generation vehicle intelligence and the positive feedback within the current process regarding preliminary safety case documentation, inspires a lot of confidence for APTS to continue on the current development path.

Safety Standards

An Overview of the SoBP for Software in the Context of DS 00-56 Issue 4

Catherine Menon, Richard Hawkins, John McDermid and Tim Kelly

SSEI, University of York

Heslington, York, UK

Abstract   Defence Standard 00-56 Issue 4 is the current contractual safety standard for UK MOD projects. It requires the production of a structured argument, supported by diverse evidence, to show that a system is safe for a defined purpose within a defined environment. This paper introduces a Standard of Best Practice which has been produced by the Software Systems Engineering Initiative to provide guidance for software compliance with Defence Standard 00-56 Issue 4.

1 Introduction

Defence Standard 00-56 (DS 00-56) Issue 4 (Ministry of Defence 2007) presents a goal-based, or evidential, approach to ensuring and assuring safety. One of the major principles of DS 00-56 is the need to demonstrate system safety by means of a compelling safety argument, supported by rigorous evidence. This represents a departure from earlier prescriptive UK MOD safety standards in that DS 00-56 Issue 4 states *what* is required, but not *how* this is to be achieved.

While this approach permits the software contribution to system safety to be evaluated contextually in each situation, there is currently a lack of clear guidance on how to perform this evaluation. The absence of guidance is felt in many projects, e.g. the Chinook Mark 3, where difficulties have arisen for the Integrated Project Team (IPT) in determining safety of both the engine control software and the cockpit display software.

Consequently, the Software Systems Engineering Initiative (SSEI) has been tasked by the MOD with the production of a Standard of Best Practice (SoBP) for assessing software compliance with DS 00-56 Issue 4. The remit of this SoBP is to address all aspects of software contribution to system safety, from the integration of COTS software into safety-critical systems, to the use of civil standards such as DO-178B for military applications.

This paper introduces the first issue of the SoBP (Menon et al. 2009), which was completed in August 2009 and is currently available from the SSEI website.

C. Dale, T. Anderson (eds.), *Making Systems Safer*, DOI 10.1007/978-1-84996-086-1_9,
© Springer-Verlag London Limited 2010

This interim SoBP applies to the activities of contract assessment, software development, assurance, verification and validation and initial acceptance. It does not consider the in-service phase, nor does it consider in detail the concept and assessment phases. Nevertheless, many of the in-service issues are similar in scope to those presented here, especially considerations such as upgrading systems and the use of COTS products. It is the intent that further work will be performed to provide guidance on through-life safety considerations, including operational safety.

In Section 2 we provide a brief overview of the structure and focus of the SoBP. Section 3 addresses the managerial issues involved with assessing the contribution of software to system safety, while Section 4 describes the technical aspects of assurance. Finally, in Section 5 we conclude and discuss the planned updates to the SoBP.

2 Structure of the SoBP

The SoBP addresses two primary areas of concern for software compliance with DS 00-56: managerial and technical. This is an essential distinction, but is not always clear cut in practice. Some of the 'management' decisions identified in this document could be carried out by the prime, some by MOD, or some (more likely) by the two working together. Further, management decisions may apply at several levels in the supply chain. Consequently, the SoBP aims to be applicable independent of the particular stakeholders in any situation.

The structure of the SoBP is based around a swim-lane diagram (Figure 1 in Section 3) showing how safety-related communication should be managed throughout the project. This diagram identifies three major interested parties, or strands: 'Management', 'Assurance' and 'Ensurance'. Relevant portions of this diagram are enlarged in later sections to enhance readability.

The 'Management' strand corresponds to the activities of managerial personnel and those responsible for project management of the customer-supplier boundary. Management activities are typically concerned with overseeing safety management, facilitating customer-supplier interaction and formally assessing relevant deliverables for acceptance. Section 3 of this paper describes these managerial activities, providing guidance on project decisions which are important when producing software which can be shown to be safe with sufficient confidence. The 'Management' swim-lane of Figure 1 is the most detailed, as it is assumed that managerial input and decisions are a primary driver for any project.

By contrast, the 'Assurance' strand corresponds to the activities of those personnel responsible for demonstrating the safety of the software. Assurance activities are typically concerned with the production of a compelling safety argument, supported by rigorous evidence. Section 4 of this paper provides a primarily technical perspective on assurance activities. The swim-lane diagram of Figure 1 is intentionally simplified when representing the Assurance strand. This is because decisions about assuring the safety of the software can only be made in the context of a particular project, and consequently cannot be easily generalised.

Finally, the 'Ensurance' strand corresponds to the activities of those personnel responsible for developing the software. We have deliberately avoided providing explicit guidance for ensurance activities, as this would not be in keeping with the goal-based approach of DS 00-56. In practice, the remit of these activities may overlap. For example, performing hazard analysis and deriving safety requirements will require interactions between activities in all three strands.

2.1 Requirements of DS 00-56: Safety Cases

The purpose of the SoBP is to provide guidance for software compliance with DS 00-56. This requires an understanding of the ways in which software can contribute to system safety, and the recommendations of DS 00-56 which ensure that these contributions are acceptable. One such recommendation is the production of a *safety case*.

From Annex A of DS 00-56, a safety case is 'a structured argument, supported by a body of evidence that provides a compelling, comprehensible and valid case that a system is safe for a given application in a given operating environment' (Ministry of Defence 2007). A safety case will evolve throughout a project, and the current state of safety should be reflected via regular safety case reports. The personnel undertaking ensurance and assurance roles are responsible for producing these reports, as well as a final safety case report. The acceptability of these reports may be dependent upon input from the Independent Safety Adviser (ISA) or Safety Committee. Each software safety case report must consider all relevant aspects associated with software safety, including the following:

Requirements validity. The argument must demonstrate that all software safety requirements are complete and accurate for the purposes of mitigating the software contribution to system-level hazards.

Requirements satisfaction. The argument must comprehensively demonstrate satisfaction of all the identified software safety requirements.

Requirements traceability. The argument must demonstrate that the high-level software safety requirements are traceable to system hazards, and also down through all levels of development (detailed software requirements, software design, code etc.).

Software quality. The argument must demonstrate that the software and the development processes exhibit the basic qualities necessary to place trust in the evidence presented. For example, the software must be free from intrinsic errors (e.g. buffer overflows and divide-by-zero errors), and adequate configuration consistency and version control must be demonstrated.

All four of the aspects above must be adequately addressed within the safety case. Fundamental to this concept is the idea of the justifiable confidence in the truth of a safety claim. This is referred to as the *assurance* of that claim. A safety case should provide sufficient assurance of all claims to permit the justified use of the software in the proposed role. If sufficient assurance is not provided, we say that there is an *assurance deficit*. This is an uncertainty or lack of information which affects assurance. Assurance deficits are almost inevitable; the question is whether such deficits are *justified*. An assurance deficit can be justified if the cost of addressing the deficit (e.g. by providing additional evidence) is out of proportion to the benefit that would be gained from doing so. Section 4 provides further detail on this.

3 Managerial Issues

This section describes the key management activities and decisions, as well as the inputs that may reasonably be expected from the Ensurance and Assurance activities. The SoBP presents this material to be read in conjunction with technical guidance, which this paper discusses in Section 4.

The Management strand is concerned with the key decisions on a project level, which include issues of supplier selection (where relevant) and acceptance of the safety case. For each decision we identify:

- Inputs to the decision making activity from Ensurance, Assurance or external activities (for example safety case reports or development plans). This list of inputs is intended to be indicative of the minimum information which will be needed, and should not be considered exhaustive.
- Comparator data to allow assessment of the inputs. This data may be available from a wide range of sources.
- Criteria for making the decision (for example, the acceptability of a safety case, or the extent to which risks are shown to be reduced to an acceptable level). It is likely that for each decision, the criteria should be weighted according to their importance.
- Possible outcomes, which in each case will be one of:

    - Proceed without change to plans
    - Proceed with further safety risk management
    - Iterate selected process steps with remedial action
    - Terminate the process and end the project development

In all cases, the guidance is framed so that all reasonable ways of proceeding will have been evaluated before reaching a decision to terminate the development.

Each of these decisions may involve input from the ISA, Safety Committee or external domain experts. These roles are not distinguished and are assumed to support the Management decision-making activities. In each case, the identity of personnel involved with this decision must be recorded in relevant project documentation. Where appropriate, the documents supporting their decision must also be preserved in order to provide both traceability and accountability.

The SoBP provides detailed guidance as described above on all of the identified management decisions. In this paper we select two such decisions to discuss in detail, and refer the reader to the issued SoBP for further guidance.

3.1 Software Safety Management Phases

Software development processes can depend on the organisation, context of the project, scope of the project, and so on. This guidance identifies four major phases (Initial, Development, Containment and Acceptance) which can usefully be mapped to all software development projects. These identified phases are not intended as a software development lifecycle, but rather to identify the key decision points relevant to DS 00-56 which occur during contractual interactions. They are orthogonal to the swim-lane strands introduced in Section 2. Figure 1 shows this interaction.

3.2 Swim-lane Diagram

To reduce complexity, the diagram in Figure 1 reflects only the major input(s) for each decision. Similarly, there are a number of iterations and ongoing activities in each lane which are not explicitly shown in the diagram for reasons of clarity. While major iterations are shown (e.g. the main iteration of the development phase reflecting ongoing monitoring of safety management and safety case reports), there will be iteration and ongoing activities within each lane. A single activity – as represented in the diagram – may correspond to a number of iterations of that activity, informed by safety dialogues and checkpoints. Relevant portions of this diagram are enlarged in the following sections, which briefly describe the activities within each phase and provide detailed guidance for selected decisions.

3.2.1 Initial Phase

There are a number of activities and decisions which take place prior to establishing contractual arrangements. These include gathering requirements, establishing a project budget, writing an Invitation to Tender, assessing bids against project criteria, and negotiating with selected suppliers.

As DS 00-56 is a contractual standard, it does not strictly apply to these activities and decisions which take place at a pre-contractual stage. However, this phase is important from a safety perspective because of the importance of supplier selection. The capabilities of potential suppliers – including in-house developers where relevant – must be assessed prior to finalising a contract. Any issues identified during this assessment may then inform the contractual negotiation. Consequently, adequate assessment of suppliers and bids can enhance the likelihood of eventual delivery of software which is compliant with the requirements of DS 00-56. Full details of the decisions and activities in this phase are provided in the complete SoBP.

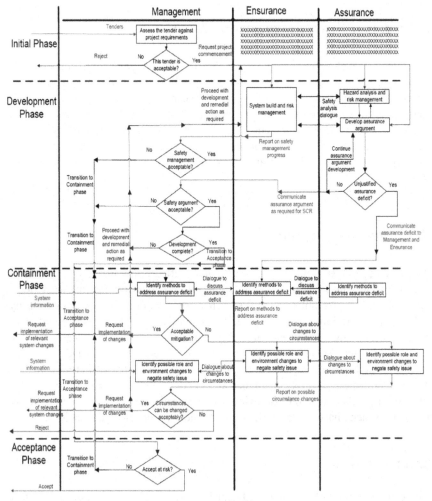

Fig. 1. Swim-Lane Diagram

3.2.2 Development Phase

The development phase is concerned more directly with achieving software safety than the Initial phase. Specifically, the managerial decisions in the development phase are intended to confirm that the software is being developed in an acceptably safe manner according to the requirements of DS 00-56. Figure 2 shows the development phase from the swim-lane diagram. There are three decisions in the phase, one of which (*Safety Argument Acceptable*) is discussed in detail here.

The development phase is iterative as shown in the swim-lane diagram, and consequently all decisions in this phase may be encountered multiple times.

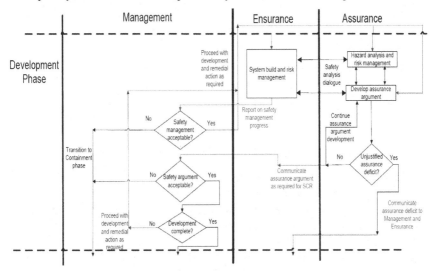

Fig. 2. Development Phase

3.2.2.1 Decision: Safety Argument Acceptable

Management decisions relating to the safety argument will typically require input from domain and safety experts. These experts (such as the ISA) can judge the technical sufficiency of the evidence presented, but the final responsibility for making the decision may be considered a managerial concern. This decision may be made multiple times throughout the software development process; for example when receiving regular safety case reports.

It is worth noting here that this decision will be encountered only where the developers undertaking assurance activities consider that all assurance deficits identified thus far are justified as far as is possible at this stage of development, or that these deficits are likely to be justified by planned future processes. If an assurance deficit is considered by developers to be unlikely to be justified given future development, the Containment phase will be entered instead, and this decision will not be encountered.

Inputs

Report on safety management progress including:

- Development of the safety argument.
- Production of evidence to support the safety argument.

Comparator data

- Safety arguments and evidence for similar projects.
- Software safety argument patterns which illustrate typical successful patterns of argumentation.

Criteria

The safety argument should satisfy the following criteria:

- It should address all four argument elements (validity, satisfaction, traceability and quality) with respect to all safety requirements.
- It should be sufficient to provide adequate assurance with respect to all safety requirements, or indicate how this assurance will be obtained.
- It should identify and justify all assurance deficits
- All assumptions should be identified and where appropriate justified, with references to supporting documentation where relevant.
- Evidence of a search for counter-evidence should be presented, and the effect of relevant counter-evidence upon the argument should be assessed.

The evidence provided to support the safety argument should satisfy the following:

- The evidence should adequately support the relevant safety requirements
- The integrity of the evidence chain should be evident, meaning that sufficient visibility into evidence-gathering procedures is provided.
- The trustworthiness and applicability of the evidence should be justified and it should be sufficiently diverse

Possible Outputs

The possible outputs for this decision are as listed below. In each case, the identity of personnel involved with this decision must be recorded in relevant project documentation. Where appropriate, the documents supporting their decision must also be preserved in order to provide both traceability and accountability.

- **Proceed with development.** This is represented as iteration in the development phase of the swim-lane diagram, and occurs when all the above criteria are met. There is no unjustified assurance deficit.
- **Proceed with development where this includes specified further safety management.** This outcome reflects that there is currently an unjustified assurance deficit, but this can be justified by means which have been identified and which will inform future safety argument development.
- **Iterate (repeat) process steps, with remedial action.** For this decision, this outcome reflects that an unjustified assurance deficit is present and can be addressed only by modifying or repeating activities in the development of the safety argument.
- **Terminate the process.** For this decision, this represents an exit to the containment phase. This occurs when there is an unjustified assurance deficit and no identified strategy for sufficiently reducing this deficit.

In practice management of information flows across contractual or organisational boundaries can be problematic. It may be the case that shortfalls in the (demonstrated) safety of the system are related to such boundaries and interfaces. Consequently, it is desirable that management explicitly consider this flow of information. It may also be the case that the flow of information down from the system level to the software is inadequate. In order to assess the potential for the software to contribute to system hazards, a degree of information is needed about the system context. In some cases, this may mean providing information to the supplier about the wider system in order to ensure that safety requirements are satisfied.

It should be noted that as shown in the swim-lane diagram, the only way to proceed to the acceptance phase is by judging the safety argument to be acceptable. This is in keeping with the requirement for an adequate safety case (Ministry of Defence 2007).

3.2.3 Acceptance Phase

While the SoBP provides guidance for assessing the completed software against the requirements of DS 00-56, assessment of the safety case is not the only activity necessary for acceptance of the software. Consequently, safety considerations must be balanced against the other acceptance criteria which are relevant for this project. If the requirements of DS 00-56 are not met (that is, if there is an issue of safety), then the containment phase is entered to attempt to remedy this problem. The issued SoBP contains further guidance on this topic.

3.2.4 Containment Phase

The containment phase is entered only on encountering a significant problem during development which cannot be remedied. Figure 3 shows the containment phase from the swim-lane diagram. Entry can be triggered in one of two ways. Firstly, personnel undertaking assurance activities may note that they are unable to adequately justify all assurance deficits, and that future development is unlikely to provide information which will justify these deficits. Secondly, management personnel may consider that significant problems are exhibited by ongoing safety management, by ongoing safety case development or by the final safety case. These problems may result in a lack of information which has the potential to affect assurance – an *assurance deficit*.

We present one of the decisions made during the containment phase in further detail here, summarising the guidance available in the SoBP.

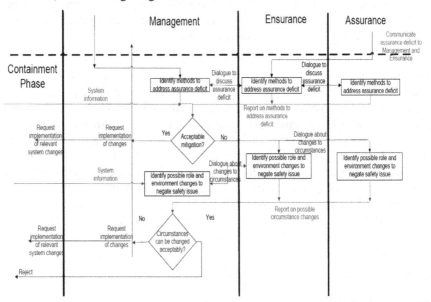

Fig. 3. Containment Phase

3.2.4.1 Decision: Acceptable Mitigation for Assurance Deficits

The decision is encountered when there is – or is likely to be – an unjustified assurance deficit, which is unlikely to be remedied within the bounds of the original safety management plan and proposed safety case structure. The (potential) presence of this assurance deficit should be communicated to Management in a timely manner. In addition to this communication, activities should be undertaken to identify possible methods of addressing the assurance deficit. These activities are undertaken across all three strands of Ensurance, Assurance and Management, and in some cases external personnel may also be involved to identify methods to address this deficit. Once these methods have been identified, Management must determine whether they represent an acceptable solution to reduce or justify the presence of this assurance deficit.

Inputs

Safety case report including:

- The safety argument
- Evidence to support the safety argument
- A report on the unjustified assurance deficit

Report on proposed methods for addressing the assurance deficit including:

- Input from Ensurance/Assurance/external personnel as relevant

Comparator data

- Safety arguments and evidence for similar projects
- Software safety argument patterns which illustrate typical successful patterns of argumentation
- Information on techniques for resolving assurance deficits

Criteria

The supplied safety argument should satisfy the following criteria, with any discrepancies addressed by the proposed methods for resolving the assurance deficit.

- It should address all four argument elements (validity, satisfaction, traceability and quality) with respect to all safety requirements.
- It should be sufficient to provide adequate assurance with respect to all safety requirements, or indicate how this assurance will be obtained.
- It should identify and justify all assurance deficits
- All assumptions should be identified and justified, with references to supporting documentation where relevant.
- Evidence of a search for counter-evidence should be presented, and the effect of relevant counter-evidence upon the argument should be assessed.

The evidence provided to support the safety argument should satisfy the following, with any discrepancies addressed by the proposed methods for resolving the assurance deficit:

- The evidence should adequately support the relevant safety requirements.

- The integrity of the evidence chain should be evident, meaning that sufficient visibility into evidence-gathering procedures is provided.
- The trustworthiness and applicability of the evidence should be justified and it should be sufficiently diverse

The assurance deficit report should provide the following information:

- An assessment of the local and system effects of this deficit, where known.

The report on methods for addressing the assurance deficit should include the following:

- Identification where possible of techniques to address this deficit, with consideration of how these may fit into the safety management plan.
- A comparison of these techniques to demonstrate how they will provide additional assurance.

Possible Outputs

The possible outputs for this decision are as listed below. In each case, the identity of personnel involved with this decision must be recorded in relevant project documentation. Where appropriate, the documents supporting their decision must also be preserved in order to provide both traceability and accountability.

- **Proceed with no change.** Not applicable.
- **Proceed with further risk management.** For this decision, this outcome is applicable in two cases. Where the identified assurance deficit can possibly be remedied with further software safety management (there are no scheduled future assurance tasks which could address this deficit, but some may be added), the identified remedial actions should inform the future development of the safety argument. Where the deficit cannot be remedied (project constraints mean that it is not feasible to add further assurance tasks to address this deficit) development may proceed provided that system-level risk management techniques are identified to justify this deficit. This latter choice will require the cooperation of external developers and approval across the entire system.
- **Iterate (repeat) process steps, with remedial action.** For this decision, this outcome reflects that further development cannot proceed until this assurance deficit is reduced. Alternative verification processes must be undertaken, as this assurance deficit could render nugatory all further development activities.
- **Terminate the process.** This outcome reflects that there is no identified strategy to reduce this assurance deficit, and the next step is to consider a possible change to the circumstances and environment of this software.

3.3 Managerial Summary

This section has summarised some of the guidance provided for managers in the SoBP. In addition to the material presented here, the full SoBP contains detailed discussions of all activities and decisions. This includes explicit listing of criteria on which decisions are made, the input which is expected for the decisions, the potential outcome of each decision, and examples to illustrate how these situations are managed on different projects. This guidance is intended to be read in conjunction with the technical guidance of the SoBP, which we summarise in the following section.

4 Technical Issues

This section provides an overview of the technically-focussed material of the SoBP. It is intended to support the managerial perspective which was discussed in Section 3 of this paper.

DS 00-56 requires the production of a safety argument which is commensurate with system risk:

'The Safety Case shall contain a structured argument demonstrating that the evidence contained therein is sufficient to show that the system is safe. The argument shall be commensurate with the potential risk posed by the system...' (Ministry of Defence 2007)

The SoBP provides guidance on how to comply with this requirement when considering the software components of systems. The aim is to provide guidance for the developers of software safety arguments (both Ensurance and Assurance personnel) on how to construct arguments which are sufficiently compelling, and how to justify the sufficiency of those arguments. In addition, the guidance should help those involved in *assessing* software safety arguments (Management personnel) to determine whether or not the arguments provided are sufficiently compelling.

A software safety argument must demonstrate that the software under consideration is acceptably safe to operate as part of the embedding system. This requires a demonstration that the potential contribution made by the software to the identified system hazards is acceptable. To be compelling, the software safety argument must provide sufficient confidence in claims which support this objective. It is inevitable for the software aspects of a system that there will exist inherent uncertainties that affect the assurance with which it is possible to demonstrate the safety of the software. The reason for this is that the amount of information potentially relevant to demonstrating the safety of the system is vast. This may be information relating to the software itself, or to the system within which the software operates. There will also be information relating to the environment and operation of the system, all of which potentially has a role in demonstrating that the software is acceptably safe.

It is simply not possible therefore to have complete knowledge about the safety of the software. This leads to uncertainty – for example, due to the presence of assumptions or known limitations in the integrity of the evidence provided. For this reason it is not normally possible to demonstrate with absolute certainty that the claims made in a software safety argument are true. For a software safety argument to be compelling it must instead establish *sufficient confidence* in the truth of the claims that are made.

It is worth noting at this point that such uncertainties in demonstrating the safety of the software are always present, but are often left implicit. Adopting a safety argument-based approach, as is required by DS 00-56, facilitates the explicit identification of such uncertainties, which makes them easier to reason about, and therefore justify. Reasoning explicitly about the extent and impact of the uncertainties in a safety argument aids in the successful acceptance of the argument as part of a safety case.

The assurance of a claim is the justifiable confidence in the truth of that claim. A useful approach to ensure that a software safety argument is sufficiently compelling is to consider assurance throughout the development of that argument. The approach defined in the SoBP is split into two main parts: a software safety argument pattern catalogue and an assurance based argument development method.

4.1 Pattern Catalogue

The software safety argument patterns introduced above are used to capture good practice for software safety arguments. These patterns can be instantiated with specific claims and evidence to create a software safety argument for any system under consideration. The SoBP provides a pattern catalogue, containing a number of patterns which have been constructed based on existing software safety argument patterns, and an understanding of current practice for software safety arguments. The following argument patterns are currently provided in the SoBP:

1. **High-level software safety argument pattern.** This pattern provides the high-level structure for a generic software safety argument. The pattern can be used to create the high level structure of a software safety argument either as a stand alone argument or as part of a system safety argument.
2. **Software contribution safety argument pattern.** This pattern provides the generic structure for an argument that the contributions made by software to system hazards are acceptably managed. This pattern is based upon a generic 'tiered' development model in order to make it generally applicable to a broad range of development processes.
3. **Software Safety Requirements identification pattern.** This pattern provides the generic structure for an argument that software safety requirements (SSRs) are adequately captured at all levels of software development.

4. **Hazardous contribution software safety argument pattern.** This pattern provides the generic structure for an argument that potentially hazardous failures that may arise at each tier are acceptably managed.

5. **Argument justification software safety argument pattern.** This pattern provides the generic structure for an argument that the software safety argument presented is sufficient.

A primary consideration during the development of these patterns was flexibility and the elimination of system-specific concerns and terminology. Consequently, these patterns can be instantiated for a wide range of systems and under a variety of circumstances. To be compelling it is necessary to be able to justify that the instantiation decisions taken in constructing the argument result in a sufficiently compelling argument for the system under consideration (such as why particular claims are chosen whilst others are not required). Guidance for justifying such decisions is provided in Section 4.2.

It is intended that the software safety argument pattern catalogue will be updated and expanded over time to ensure that it reflects current understanding of good practice.

4.2 Assurance-based Argument Development Method

As discussed earlier, there exist many potential sources of uncertainty in demonstrating the safety of the software. Any such residual uncertainty can be considered to be an *assurance deficit*.

It is possible to identify how assurance deficits may arise by explicitly considering how information may be lost at each step in the construction of the argument. As an argument is constructed, decisions are continually being made about the best way in which to proceed. Decisions are made about how goals are stated, the strategies that are going to be adopted, the context and assumptions that are going to be required, and the evidence it is necessary to provide. Each of these decisions has an influence on what is, and is not, addressed by the safety case. The things that are not sufficiently addressed are referred to as assurance deficits.

The SoBP introduces an approach for systematic consideration of how assurance deficits may be introduced at each step of software safety argument development. By identifying where potential assurance deficits may arise, this approach can be used to inform the decisions that are made on how to construct the argument. In order to produce a sufficiently compelling software safety argument, all identified assurance deficits must be satisfactorily addressed, or justification must be provided that the impact of the assurance deficit on the claimed safety of the system is acceptable. Section 4.2.2 discusses how such justifications may be made.

4.2.1 Counter Evidence

DS 00-56 states, 'Throughout the life of the system, the evidence and arguments in the Safety Case should be challenged in an attempt to refute them. Evidence that is discovered with the potential to undermine a previously accepted argument is referred to as counter-evidence.' (Ministry of Defence 2007). Since an assurance deficit corresponds to a lack of relevant information, an identified assurance deficit reveals the *potential* for counter-evidence. That is, there is the possibility that in addressing the assurance deficit (i.e. gaining the relevant information) the information gained would reveal previously unidentified counter evidence. Reasoning about assurance deficits can therefore be helpful in identifying areas in which counter evidence may exist. Conversely, where there is knowledge of existing counter evidence, this can be used to help determine the potential impact of assurance deficits. For example, if other similar projects have identified counter evidence which relates to a particular identified assurance deficit, then the observed impact of this counter evidence on the safety of the other project can be used to indicate the expected impact that such an assurance deficit may imply.

4.2.2 Addressing Assurance Deficits

The discussion above illustrates how assurance deficits may be systematically identified throughout the construction of a software safety argument. The existence of identified assurance deficits raises questions concerning the sufficiency of the argument. Therefore where an assurance deficit is identified it is necessary to demonstrate that the deficit is either acceptable, or addressed such that it becomes acceptable (for example through the generation of additional relevant evidence).

There will typically be a cost associated with obtaining the information to address an assurance deficit. In practice the benefit gained from addressing each assurance deficit does not necessarily justify the cost involved in generating the additional information. In order to assess if the required level of expenditure is warranted, the impact of that assurance deficit on the sufficiency of the argument must be determined.

To determine the impact of an assurance deficit, it is first necessary to assess the software safety argument. Such an argument will make certain claims about the hazard identification, risk estimation, and risk management of the software contribution to system hazards. Since assurance deficits have the potential to undermine the sufficiency of the argument, the impact of any assurance deficit should be assessed in terms of the impact it may have on these claims. For example, an assurance deficit may be sufficient to challenge the completeness of hazard identification, or may be sufficient to challenge the estimated residual risk.

In assessing the software safety argument, it is possible to prioritise some claims as being more important to safety than others. For example claims regarding the behaviour of an architectural component (such as a voter), which carries a greater responsibility for risk reduction than other components, are more important to the overall software safety argument. Therefore claims relating to those components would require a greater degree of assurance (more confidence must be established). This is exemplified in DS 00-56: 'An example of a way of defining the variation of the degree of rigour with potential risk is the specification of a safety integrity requirement for the system'. The document then goes on to state, 'In setting safety integrity requirements, it is therefore important to consider how much confidence is needed.' (Ministry of Defence 2007). Where safety integrity requirements have been defined, they can be used as a way of determining the importance of the software safety argument claim to which they relate.

The method introduced in the SoBP to determine the impact of an assurance deficit has two stages. In the first stage, we analyse the claim to which the identified assurance deficit relates; the importance of the truth of that claim to the overall safety argument must be determined. Secondly, we determine the extent to which the identified assurance deficit affects the confidence achieved in this particular safety claim. Not all information relevant to a claim leads to the same increase in confidence in that claim. It is therefore necessary to assess the extent to which any information provided to address the assurance deficit might increase confidence in the truth of the claim.

Knowing the importance of the truth of the claim to the safety argument, *and* the relative importance of the assurance deficit to establishing the truth of that claim, it then becomes possible to determine the overall impact of the assurance deficit. In a similar manner to risks in the ALARP approach (Railtrack 2000), the impact of the identified assurance deficits may be usefully classified into three categories. An 'intolerable' deficit is one whose potential impact on the claimed risk position is too high to be justified under any circumstances. A 'broadly acceptable' assurance deficit is one where the impact of this assurance deficit on the safety argument is considered to be negligible. In such cases no additional effort to address the assurance deficit need be sought. Finally, a potentially 'tolerable' assurance deficit is one whose impact is determined to be too high to be considered negligible, but which is also not necessarily considered to be intolerable. A potentially 'tolerable' assurance deficit may be considered acceptable only if the cost of taking measures to address that assurance deficit is out of proportion to the impact of not doing so. The greater the impact of the assurance deficit, the more system developers may be expected to spend in addressing that deficit.

Making decisions relating to the acceptability of residual assurance deficits should, where necessary, involve personnel undertaking management and ensurance activities as well as those involved in assurance. If unable to form a judgment on the acceptability of an assurance deficit, then it is advised that expert assistance should be sought.

Note that the impact of an assurance deficit can only be determined on a case-by-case basis for a specific argument relating to a particular system. The same type of assurance deficit (such as a particular assumption) whose impact is categorised as broadly acceptable when present in the software safety argument for one system, may be considered intolerable when present in the argument for a different system. This is because the impact of an assurance deficit considers its impact in terms of the overall safety of the system. It is for this reason that particular argument approaches (such as the software safety argument patterns discussed in Section 4.1) cannot be stated as sufficient for particular claims, but must be adapted on each use to be appropriate for the particular application.

Addressing an assurance deficit requires 'buying' more information or knowledge about the system relevant to the safety claims being made. There will typically be a cost associated with obtaining this information. For those assurance deficits categorised as tolerable, the value of the information in building confidence in the safety case must be considered when deciding whether to spend that money. In theory it is possible to do a formal cost-benefit analysis based on a quantitative assessment of the costs associated with the available options for addressing the assurance deficit, and the costs associated with the potential impact on the claimed risk position (such as the necessity to provide additional system level mitigations). However, in many cases a qualitative consideration of these issues will be more beneficial.

In all cases an explicit justification should be provided as to why the residual assurance deficit is acceptable and, wherever appropriate, an argument should be used to provide this justification. The software safety argument pattern catalogue (discussed in section 4.1) contains an argument pattern for constructing an argument to justify that the residual assurance deficits are appropriate.

The approach described above, although similar to ALARP, rather than considering the necessity of adopting measures to directly decrease risk, instead considers measures intended to increase the confidence that is achieved. As such the framework could be considered to help establish a claimed risk position in the software safety case that is ACARP (As Confident As Reasonably Practicable).

5 Conclusions

This paper has introduced the Standard of Best Practice (Menon et al. 2009) for software compliance with DS 00-56 Issue 4. In Section 2 we described the basic structure of the SoBP, emphasising the distinction between the managerial and technical perspectives. Section 3 then summarised the managerial guidance provided in the SoBP. Four development phases (Initial, Development, Containment and Acceptance) were identified, and information was provided about the decisions and activities of each phase. Section 4 introduced the technical guidance which is provided in the SoBP. In this section we described the software safety argument pattern catalogue, which contains patterns or 'blueprints' for constructing safety arguments. Additionally, this section described the assessment of assurance deficits to determine whether these can be justified, or whether they must be addressed by further work on the safety argument. Section 3 and 4 should be read in conjunction, as they represent different perspectives upon the same issues of software contribution to system safety.

It is anticipated that this SoBP will continue to be updated regularly. One of these planned updates will consist of an examination of the issues involved with using other standards – such as DO-178B – to comply with DS 00-56. Another planned update will further refine the technical guidance on assurance deficits by discussing the advantages and limitations of different types of software safety evidence. The SoBP is not intended to be a static document, but rather to represent current best practice. Consequently, further updates, refinements and validation of the results will be anticipated throughout the life of DS 00-56 Issue 4.

Acknowledgments The authors would like to thank the UK Ministry of Defence for their support and funding. This work is undertaken as part of the research activity within the Software Systems Engineering Initiative (SSEI), www.ssei.org.uk.

References

Menon C, Hawkins R, McDermid J (2009) Interim standard of best practice on software in the context of DS 00-56 Issue 4. Technical Report SSEI-BP-000001. Software Systems Engineering Initiative, York. https://ssei.org.uk/documents/. Accessed 5 October 2009.

Ministry of Defence (2007) Defence Standard 00-56 Issue 4: Safety management requirements for defence systems

Railtrack (2000) Engineering safety management – Yellow Book 3, volumes 1 and 2 – Fundamentals and guidance. Railtrack PLC

IEC80001 and Future Ramifications for Health Systems not currently classed as Medical Devices

Ian Harrison[1]

NHS Connecting for Health

Leeds, UK

Abstract Traditionally a medical device is viewed as a standalone hospital system with a carefully segregated private network running on specialist bespoke equipment, managed by highly skilled medical technicians. The regulations in force implementing the Medical Devices Directive support this view. The emerging reality in the modern health organisation is a patient-centric shared electronic record, networked over the organisation's local area network, with medical devices hanging as endpoints off that shared network and contributing to the central pool of patient data – all the time reliant on the shared network services. The IEC80001 standard has been developed to provide guidance on the measures that the medical devices community considers are required best practice in order to ensure that the integrity and safety of the interconnected medical device is not compromised. This in itself is both a laudable and pragmatic action. The question that it immediately prompts for those left with the new and very real task of 'compliance' with the new standards – primarily the over worked health organisation's IT department, is 'what impact does this have on me?'. A number of papers exist prepared from a health-system-supplier standpoint. This paper is principally focused on examining the ramifications of IEC80001 from a health organisation stand point. This paper seeks to identify the areas where a health organisation may expect to have their business-as-usual IT processes impacted, and offers a simple framework to address these challenges.

---

[1] This work represents solely the views and opinions of the author as a Chartered Engineer and safety professional.

C. Dale, T. Anderson (eds.), *Making Systems Safer*, DOI 10.1007/978-1-84996-086-1_10,
© Springer-Verlag London Limited 2010

1 Introduction

This paper considers the implications of the new standards paper (IEC80001) being issued by Joint Working Group 7 (of TC62a) for health informaticians working in UK health organizations (IEC 2009).

There are a considerable number of papers available which examine IEC80001 from the perspective of the supplier of medical devices and the impact that they will face. This paper will examine the standard from the view point of a health informatician, delivering interoperable e-health within a modern health organisation.

The health sector in the UK is currently in a period of massive technological change, with national infrastructure changes allowing considerable advance in interoperability of medical systems. European and UK policy and project initiatives in support of the electronic patient record have generated a step change in health informatics.

With several technical 'enablers' arriving in a similar two to three year time frame (National Clinical Records Spine, HL7 ebxml messaging standards, N3 broadband capability), the health sector is seeing a revolution in ICT systems similar to that which the mail order home shopping sector saw when domestic broadband services became readily available. However, the speed of innovation has outpaced the capability of standards makers to issue updated and relevant regulations to maintain the safety of these systems for patients. The health standards world is struggling to comprehend the needs and ramifications of new e-health systems.

The first section of the paper overviews the current legislation and its origins, looking at the Medical Devices Directive (European Parliament 2007) (currently the sole piece of EU safety legislation in respect of healthcare systems) and its UK implementation. Following on from this, the mismatches between current EU/UK safety legislation and the needs and challenges faced by the modern e-health organisation are discussed. IEC80001 grew as a response to some of these challenges, hence the background of IEC80001 and its likely anticipated impact in terms of new safety requirements.

We then look at the specific pressures faced by health organisations in complying with IEC80001 and consider how the new National Health Service (NHS) Information Standards Board (ISB) clinical safety management system standard can be used as a framework to demonstrate compliance with these emerging requirements.

The paper concludes by examining the future direction that safety standards are expected to take, and more importantly the challenges this presents for health informatics as a profession – with an emerging need for new safety engineering disciplines alongside the existing technical and clinical skills/knowledge sets.

The subjects of data security and privacy are *not* considered by this paper, although they are commonly used as part of the patient safety definition when discussing regulation in an international or European forum. In the UK our view of patient safety does not include these facets. This exclusion is justified in Section 4.4 below – where the paper considers the aspects of IEC80001 where no impact is expected for UK health organisations.

2 Current Medical Device Regulation

2.1 Origins

Understanding the origins of the Medical Devices Directive is important, it being the only piece of 'best practice' safety legislation which currently exists covering medical devices in Europe.

This section is designed to provide a short overview of the origins of current regulation in the UK. If a more detailed appreciation of the Medical Devices Directive and associated UK regulation is required, the Medicines and Healthcare Regulatory Agency website (MHRA 2009) should be visited.

In 1993 the EU issued a directive (European Parliament 2007) which became known as the Medical Devices Directive (MDD). This EU mandate was enacted into UK law in 2002 by the Medical Devices Regulations 2002. These regulations implement the provisions of the Medical Devices Directive, 93/42/EEC.

All medical devices are required to carry a CE marking unless they come within the definitions of 'custom-made devices' or 'devices intended for clinical investigation'.

The MDD has been amended by the EU a number of times, supplementing it with new guidelines as medical technology has advanced. Unfortunately, the directive still lacks clear guidance for e-health software systems. Indeed the 2007 amendment made the situation more difficult with a definition thus:

> 'It is necessary to clarify that software in its own right, when specifically intended by the manufacturer to be used for one or more of the medical purposes set out in the definition of a medical device, is a medical device. Software for general purposes when used in a healthcare setting is not a medical device.'

The four medical device regulations currently in force are:

- Statutory Instrument 2002 No 618 (Consolidated legislation);
- Statutory Instrument 2003 No 1697;
- Medical Devices Regulations 2007 No 400; and
- Medical Devices (Amendment) Regulations 2008 No 2936.

They have been issued under the Consumer Protection Act and can be found on the Office of Public Sector Information (OPSI) website (OPSI 2009).

2.2 What is a Medical Device?

According to article 1 paragraph 2(a) of the MDD the term 'medical device':

'means any instrument, apparatus, appliance, material or other article, whether used alone or in combination, including the software necessary for its proper application intended by the manufacturer to be used for human beings for the purpose of:
-    diagnosis, prevention, monitoring, treatment or alleviation of disease,
-    diagnosis, monitoring, treatment, alleviation of or compensation for an injury or handicap,
-    investigation, replacement or modification of the anatomy or of a physiological process,
-    control of conception,
and which does not achieve its principal intended action in or on the human body by pharmacological, immunological or metabolic means, but which may be assisted in its function by such means;'

The EU mandate clearly gives the national Competent Authority (MHRA) powers to define the classification of a medical device:

'For the appropriate and efficient functioning of Directive 93/42/EEC as regards regulatory advice on classification issues arising at national level, in particular on whether or not a product falls under the definition of a medical device, it is in the interest of national market surveillance and the health and safety of humans to establish a procedure for decisions on whether or not a product falls under the medical device definition.'

The directive applies different safety requirements to devices depending on the risk which they present to the patient – in a similar manner to other standards in the safety field (e.g. IEC 61508 (IEC 2000) whereby SIL level is used to determine the level and nature of safety controls required). There are four classifications:

- Class I – generally regarded as low risk
- Class IIa – generally regarded as medium risk
- Class IIb – generally regarded as medium risk
- Class III – generally regarded as high risk

Any review of the current guidance documentation issued by the MHRA clearly shows that there is currently no meaningful guidance on software classification for Patient Administration Systems or other such e-health systems (MHRA 2006). Indeed the EU Directive itself only provides the following:

-    'Multi-application equipment such as laser printers and identification cameras, which may be used in combination with medical devices, are not medical devices unless their manufacturer places them on the market with specific intended purpose as medical devices.
-    Standalone software, e.g. software which is used for image enhancement is regarded as driving or influencing the use of a device and so falls automatically into the same class. Other standalone software, which is not regarded as driving or influencing the use of a device, is classified in its own right.'

Nevertheless, in considering the precedent set by other regulatory standards, including RTCA/DO178B (RTCA 1992), Defence Standards 00-55/56 (MOD 1997 and 2007) and IEC 61508 (IEC 2000), it would appear logical that the majority of current e-health software should properly fall within the Class 1 definition of a medical device. This would appear consistent with their use as 'safety related advisory software' – as defined by (HSE 2002):

> 'safety related software is always used in an advisory way to support the activity of a human assessor. The assessment decision never depends wholly on the system output. The software assists the assessor with time consuming or error prone tasks and embodies good practise.'

At the current time however, there is very clear guidance in the UK that software of this (safety related) nature is not covered by the provisions of the medical devices directive.

This is consistent with the current guidance issued in the US by their Competent Authority. In a perverse way, this is actually quite beneficial for the e-health industry, as at least one significant EU report (see Section 8.2 below) suggests that the current MDD regulation has some significant negative effects on technical innovation.

2.3 What does the Medical Device Directive require?

Given the evidence presented in sections above – that e-health software is 'not classified', the safety requirements of the MDD are of no direct relevance to this type of system. However as tranches of systems which *are* classified (for instance X-ray equipment, pathology systems and theatre systems) are being interconnected with these unclassified systems, understanding the requirements placed on suppliers of medical devices helps us understand the ramifications of IEC80001 – given that it deals expressly with systems interoperating with medical devices.

The following extract comes from the MHRA Guidance for Manufacturers of Class 1 Medical Devices (MHRA 2006):

- 'Review the classification rules to confirm that their products fall within Class I (Annex IX of the Directive);
- Check that their products meet the Essential Requirements (Annex I of the Directive);
- prepare relevant technical documentation;
- draw up the "EC Declaration of Conformity" before applying the CE marking to their devices;
- implement and maintain corrective action and vigilance procedures;
- obtain notified body approval for sterility or metrology aspects of their devices, where applicable;
- make available relevant documentation on request for inspection by the Competent Authority;
- register with the Competent Authority;

- notify the Competent Authority, in advance, of any proposals to carry out a clinical investigation to demonstrate safety and performance of a device as required by the Regulations.'

In addition, within the guidance document, requirements are also introduced for:

- Risk (hazard) assessment and mitigation;
- Design verification; and
- Post market surveillance (safety incident reporting).

In this respect, the Medical Devices Directive requirements are little different from core safety standards which other industries use – in that a safety management system is required to ensure that the process by which a software product is manufactured ensures that the software is safe and fit-for-purpose.

3 Dilemmas in the Health Software Sector

The health informatician in a health organisation is faced with a growing list of day-to-day health system pressures and imperatives which spring from often conflicting needs:

- from the health organisation to make best and effective use of scare IT resource;
- from highly intelligent and articulate users (clinicians) whose own basic professional training highlights the operational potential of health systems in managing and delivering better and safer care (training of junior doctors now routinely includes familiarisation with ICT);
- from professional bodies who are seeking to encourage health informatics best practices within the health organisations (the Royal College of GPs issues professional guidance to doctors on the safe-use of IT systems);
- from the strategic leadership of the National Health Service – keen to harness health informatics to push the patient agenda.

This pressure is best summed up by a research extract presented on the EU's own eHealth News Portal (eHealthNews 2009b):

'Although most hospitals in Europe have some kind of information system in place, very few have a fully integrated and functional hospital information systems (HIS) solutions installed. The adoption rate of HIS solutions in 2008 in Europe varied from about 73.0 per cent in Italy and Spain to 95.0 per cent in Scandinavia. Increasing accountability pressures on the government and regulatory authorities to garner more investments into healthcare IT adoption is boosting the HIS market potential. New analysis from Frost & Sullivan, Hospital Information Systems Market in Europe, finds that market earned revenues of over $3.4 billion in 2008 and estimates this to reach $4.26 billion in 2015.'

Following on from this and in this general vein, the EU DG's 2009 Prague declaration (eHealthNews 2009b) includes a clear 'Call for action on building an eHealth area for European citizens'. Anyone reading this call for action will be left in no doubt as to the EU agenda on eHealth.

At the same time as there is this pressure to rapidly harness and deliver the benefits of eHealth systems in the health organisation, there is a realisation in the health informatics profession that we lack the formal regulatory framework that has underpinned the development of technology in medical devices per se. Traditionally the health informatician has kept the medical device world segregated from eHealth systems to insulate against this perceived 'contamination of medical devices'.

These dilemmas translate into some practical areas of concern which have been regularly voiced in professional circles such as the British Computer Society (BCS) Primary Care Special Interest Group (whose 29th July 2009 Summer Conference had papers such as 'Clinical Safety Testing of the Care Record' and 'Clinical Risk Management' on the agenda):

- How do we integrate a medical device into a health organisation's network without compromising its integrity?
- How can we safely transfer information between a medical device and the electronic patient record system?
- How do we assess the risk from unclassified components such as: software, hardware, operating systems and networks?
- How can we interact such that we reduce the risk of unforeseen ICT events to the medical device?
- How do we build this into the IT service management aspects of a health organisation?

These simple questions encapsulate where the health informatician's core concerns are at the moment. The next section will set out the nature of IEC80001, the need for which has grown from many of these shared concerns.

4 IEC 80001

4.1 Background and Development

The need for IEC80001 grew from a realization in the medical device suppliers and regulators community that the modern health IT arena was changing significantly, and 'standalone' medical devices were rapidly becoming a historical concept where the more sophisticated products (with software content) were concerned. The new generation of X-ray, pathology and theatre systems, were designed to produce output which would easily integrate with an electronic health record.

As you can see, the standard itself cites concerns very similar to the issues do-cumented in Section 3 above:

'There remain a number of potential problems associated with the incorporation of medical devices into IT-networks, including:
- lack of consideration for risk from use of IT-networks during evaluation of clinical risk;
- lack of support from manufacturers of medical devices for the incorporation of their products into IT-networks, (e.g. the unavailability or inadequacy of information provided by the manufacturer to the operator of the IT-network);
- incorrect operation or degraded performance (e.g. incompatibility or improper configuration) resulting from combining medical devices and other equipment on the same IT-network;
- incorrect operation resulting from combining medical device software and other software applications (e.g. open email systems or computer games) in the same IT-network; and
- the conflict between the need for strict change control of medical devices and the need for rapid response to an attack by malware.
When these problems manifest themselves, unintended consequences frequently follow. The incorporation of a medical device into the IT-network is to be designed, and risk management is to be used to address unintended consequences associated with the incorporation.'

The development of IEC80001 commenced in 2006 following an FDA (US Food and Drug Administration) study session on 12th December 2005, to discuss issues surrounding the lack of safety regulation when incorporating medical devices into IT networks. The standard is currently being developed by ISO/TC 215 Working Group 7 (medical devices) and Working Group 4 (security). The standard is in its final draft stages and has entered voting. UK voting completes shortly (at time of writing in August 2009).

In line with its stated intent, the standard is a *process* standard and specifies de-sign and risk management activities required of medical device suppliers, health organisations and other IT vendors when medical devices are connected to a ge-neric IT network. In order to ensure harmonisation of standards, the risk manage-ment processes described in IEC80001 mirror those expected in the Medical De-vice Directive.

In this respect the net impact of IEC80001 could be said to be – extending the Medical Devices Directive best practice to those areas where the interaction of a medical device with unclassified systems could create hazards – namely the cur-rently unregulated area of e-health systems.

The standard cites four primary goals:

- patient safety
- effectiveness (as in the enhancement of the delivery of care through safe and effective connectivity)
- data and system security, and
- interoperability.

Again, in line with the Medical Devices Directive, the risk management activity is carried out as part of a lifecycle model wherein the consideration of safety risks commences with upfront design of the elements of network integration, pre-integration, and concludes with safety considerations during decommissioning of the network at the end of its life.

This (whole lifecycle view of safety hazard assessment) is very similar in concept and practice to the lifecycle risk processes and models used in IEC61508 (the safety life cycle for which has 16 phases which can be divided into three broad lifecycle steps: phases 1-5 define safety design measures, phases 6-13 define safe control of build/test activity and phases 14-16 consider the safe operation of the system).

4.2 Overview of IEC80001 Contents

This section is a little dry, being comprised of an overview of different requirements of a standards document. The requirements have been considered in their three key sections, with an additional view of what is provided in the Annexes A-D.

The version of the standard used for this section is the Brussels Final Revision 4.

Section 3: Roles and Responsibilities. This section defines the term *Responsible Organisation*, meaning in essence the health organisation. The standard then allocates overarching responsibility for ensuring the necessary safety measures are in place when medical devices are incorporated into general IT networks, by default to the responsible organisation. Also covered in this section are senior management responsibilities to establish policies, resources and processes in support of risk management. Lesser roles are also defined for medical device manufacturers and other suppliers – mainly relating to provision of supporting information.

Section 4: Lifecycle Risk Management in Medical IT Networks. The prime focus of this section is on establishing the mechanics of risk management during the design of those elements of the IT network and associated interoperating systems, which will eventually incorporate the medical device. Key within this section is risk planning/evaluation/management/control and verification. The term *Responsibility Agreement* also surfaces herein – this being a formal (contractual) agreement raised by the health organisation covering responsibilities and products across the different suppliers making up the integration project. In the UK we would probably refer to this as *scope of supply*, and include it within respective commercial contracts. Importantly this section also described many of the documents which health organisations are required to maintain, and the 'Go-Live' gate. The section concludes with descriptions of safety event management requirements.

Section 5. Document control, and the need to have a risk management file for the medical device network, are covered in this is rather short section.

Annexes A-D. These provide guidance for implementation of IEC80001 and are not well developed. Separate guidance documents are planned including one which will be health organisation implementation focused and is termed currently 'IEC80001-2' although this is expected to change.

This is only a short overview of IEC80001; the health informatician impacted by this standard would be well advised to purchase a copy of the standard at its current draft state to allow a more informed consideration of its ramifications and impact.

4.3 Key Areas of Impact

The key focus areas within the IEC80001 standard which should sound alarm bells for the health informatician working within a UK health organisation are:

Section 3: Roles and Responsibilities

3.2 Responsible Organisation. This makes it clear that the buck stops with the health organisation using the medical device network, irrespective of what suppliers provide – hence the need for robust and detailed contractual arrangements with all contributing suppliers. This could cause some difficulty where poor legacy contracts are involved. The standard requires (in later sections) that the responsibilities agreements are effective in securing the meeting of supplier obligations.

3.3 Top Management. This requirement covers the existence of policies, resources, an organisational structure and audited procedures underpinning the risk management regime surrounding the medical device IT network. It is very unlikely that a health organisation will have these sorts of procedures within their Quality Management System. Neither will the existing clinical governance arrangements extend to the broader IT system. This requirement will need significant internal role and structure work within the IT organisation.

3.4 Medical IT Network Risk Manager. This is a new role defined by this standard that is unlikely to exist in any UK health organisation currently. In discussion with the Joint Working Group (JWG7) responsible for this standard, it was highlighted that in the UK clinical opinion and hence clinical risk is normally dealt with by trained clinicians. The clinical governance area of a health organisation is the logical home for such a person, although this area is unlikely to possess staff with the IT skills to fill this role. The role itself is a risk management coordination and overview type of role with interfaces to suppliers, IT department and clinicians alike.

3.6 Other Providers of IT. This requirement means the health organisation will need to determine what appropriate information is required from other component and software systems suppliers and secure this documentation as part of the new responsibility agreements.

Section 4: Life Cycle Risk Management

4.2 Risk Management Policy. A comprehensive top-down piece of work is required similar to the definition and documentation of a Quality Management System. The requirements here centre on the involvement of 'top management' in defining and supporting risk management processes for the medical IT network. There are also requirements in respect of ongoing monitoring of effectiveness hence internal audit will need to be considered.

4.3.2 Asset Description. Specific change management information is required in respect of all the components which are coming in contact with the medical device through the network. This will be a significant extension to the asset tracking process. The asset tracking process will also need to document which applications and components hold what items of patient data.

4.3.3 Medical IT Network Documentation. Comprehensive application and network topological information is required to satisfy this requirement. Much of this will undoubtedly exist in an IT department, however in support of satisfying this standard it is likely that a review and update exercise will be necessary – which could be substantial if the documentation has become dated.

4.3.4 Responsibility Agreement. The responsibility agreement is seen in this standard as the prime vehicle for clarifying responsibilities with suppliers for different aspects of the new medical IT network, including provision of key document deliverables. The prime area of impact that the health organisation can expect with this requirement is the 'dusting down' of old service contracts and attempting to update them to the standard required herein. There will also no doubt be issues with legacy networks and how to deal with past work.

4.3.5 Risk Management Plan. This will introduce a new document to most health organisations' project management processes. The requirement to prepare a risk management plan for the medical IT network is largely akin to the creation of a safety approach for the network. Whilst the required document is not onerous and will be useful for ensuring a safe integration, it is an area that health organisations (and project staff with no knowledge of medical device risk management) will struggle to get to grips with.

4.4.1 Change Release Management Process. This should not really be a large change, as all organisations will have existing change impacting processes. The key impact here will be the introduction of safety-impacting prior to changes to any assets involved with the medical IT network. Introduction of this 'bus-stop' will no doubt cause teething problems for some IT departments.

4.4.2 Medical IT Network Risk Management. This is the most significant new requirement, meaning that a comprehensive formal risk management process will need to be created to plan, evaluate, monitor and manage risks associated with the clinical IT network. The impact here will include the need to make IT staff more conscious of risk management and hazard logging for these types of systems – a significant training task. Clarification of the roles within the organisational structure will also be difficult, particularly establishing the key safety roles and reporting lines.

4.4.3 Decisions on when to apply Risk Management. This is linked to earlier observations on change management and will mean an extension to the process whereby changes are impacted. Particularly change permits will need to be introduced to cover elements of the medical IT network.

4.4.4 Go-live. This requirement introduces clinical risk management into the health organisation's ready-for-operations gated review. The operational readiness gate will need to be supplemented by a clinical review to establish if the new network/change is safe-for-live operation. This will clearly introduce a task to rewrite the processes surrounding this gate.

4.5 Live Network Risk Management. This requirement will mean some significant changes to the health organisation's live service procedures, particularly with respect to adding the concept of 'Safety Incidents' as a category of incident which is higher severity than the normal 'Severity 1' defect. The involvement of clinicians in the evaluation and closure on of this new safety incident category means there are links needed with the clinical on-call arrangements. Service support arrangements may also be impacted where medical IT networks require enhanced support arrangements due to clinical hours.

Section 5: Document Control

5.2 Medical IT Network Risk Management File. The need to bring all of this documentation systematically together and under some form of control will be likely to place strains on the health organisation's quality functions.

4.4 Areas where no Impact is Expected

In the Introduction to this paper, an issue was raised that the European and international definition of patient safety is somewhat wider than the UK definition, including privacy and security in its remit. Two typical working definitions used in the UK patient safety community are:

> Patient safety is 'the freedom from accidental injury due to medical care or from medical error'. (Kohn et al. 2000)

> Patient safety is 'the process by which an organisation makes patient care safer. This should involve: risk assessment, identification and management of patient related risk, reporting and analysis of incidents, and the capacity to learn from and follow up incidents and implement solutions to minimise the risk of them recurring.' (NHS 2004)

This paper does not consider privacy and security as the UK health sector is sophisticated in its handling of these considerations, splitting each area off under its own specialism.

Privacy and patient confidentiality. The Department of Health (DoH) have extensive arrangements, guidelines and regulation in place to manage patient confidentiality, details of which can be obtained via the website (DoH 2009). *The Caldicott Guardian Manual* in particular sets out the independent system of senior officers charged with protecting patient confidentiality.

Security. The NHS Connecting for Health website information governance section (NHS 2009) sets out the information governance requirements for the NHS. This website has a comprehensive set of documents supported by training, and a network of subject matter experts available to answer queries from health organisations. The website itself illustrates the level of focus placed on this subject by the Department of Health.

Hence, given that the prime objective of this paper is to consider the IT safety ramifications for e-health systems with the advent of IEC80001, these topics are best considered outside of scope. It is very unlikely that IEC80001 will introduce any new requirements in these areas that are not well covered by existing requirements.

Clearly it is worth noting that having sophisticated security and privacy requirements in place does not prevent the occasional well publicized security breach. It is outside of the remit of this paper to examine the effectiveness of security arrangements in health organisations, but it is generally held in the health informatics profession that the information governance policy, guidance and requirements are some of the best in the world.

5 Pressures created for Health Organisations

The consequences of this new standard, as set out above, are going to have some significant impacts on health organizations, and more specifically their IT operations.

Organisational Challenges. The most significant area where the pressures will be felt are in respect of the creation of a clinical risk management structure within the organisation This combined with the need for the 'top management' to support this 'risk management' with policies and procedures will amount to a significant challenge for the organisation. Key within this reorganisation will be the creation of new roles and the allocation of safety responsibilities to existing roles. There will also be a challenge integrating the new IT risk systems with clinical governance and quality management within the health organisation.

Legacy systems. Most organisations are well advanced in the integration of medical devices into the broader IT networks. Their immediate problem will be to establish a network baseline and to bring existing systems under safety-change control. Section 6.5 below contains some suggestions for an acceptable approach for dealing with existing systems, without necessarily repeating a lump of previous assurance/testing. These suggestions are based upon guidance for Class 1 medical devices and hence should be acceptable with non-classified legacy systems. Establishing a suitable asset tracking process with the medical IT network and ensuring that each asset has appropriate documentation may also throw up some difficulties where legacy systems are concerned.

Interfaces. A prime new area where IT technical assurance will need to be strengthened is in respect of those modules in unclassified systems which are identified as being directly interoperable with medical devices. This is likely to include the systems functions:

- Provision of patient identifiers/demographics;
- Transfer of referral information (or orders) to the medical device in order that tests may be conducted;
- Collection and collation of the electronic health record - where reports and other data from medical devices is directly stored and accessed; and
- Rendering, measurement or interpretation tools used to analyse the output from a medical device.

Where the health organisation identifies clinical hazards with these interoperations, it follows that the hazardous aspects of the interface be subject to more rigor and additional controls/validation than would be the case currently. In some health organisations there is no existing capacity to perform this kind of application validation and testing.

Commercial Off The Shelf Products (COTS). Where the medical device being incorporated in the network makes use of the services of network COTS products, typically security or backup/archive packages, there will be a need to examine the likely scenarios where the COTS failure would present a hazard to the correct operation of the medical device. The manner of dealing with what is described alternately in the broader safety industry as SOUP (Software of Uncertain Pedigree) is discussed in the following section.

Routine Service Upgrades. The manner in which day-to-day IT operations tasks are conducted by the health organisation is likely to be impacted in terms of the administrative impact of changes to :

- Change control procedures
- Change impact assessment
- Pre-live assurance Gates (Ready for Operations)
- Incident management

In addition to this, any patch upgrades to tools associated with the medical IT network will need careful planning and scheduling, following consultation with the medical device manufacturer. The following section contains some useful suggestions from the FDA in respect of maintenance planning for medical IT networks.

Hardware and Network Fabric. Hardware and associated network components (routers, switches, LAN fibre, gateways etc) will need consideration prior to building into a medical IT network. In this area, JWG7 discussions indicate that it will be acceptable to look at the reliability and performance metrics for network fabric and focus on the resilience of the topography at an architectural level. In other safety sectors this would be described as 'ARM' (Availability, Reliability and Maintainability) data, and there is a wealth of electrical engineering research into establishing preventative and monitoring regimes for supporting safety related applications. Asset and configuration control will also be an issue for the hardware and network fabric.

The issues highlighted above represent a considered view of the areas where a health organisation is likely to feel the most organisation pressure when gearing up to attain compliance with IEC80001. The next section will look at some simple strategies for creating a safety programme in the health organisation to address these challenges. The size of this endeavor should not be underestimated and the health organisation would be well advised to construct a well governed programme of activity with a suitably experienced and resourced project manager in charge.

6 Creating a Framework for the Challenges

6.1 Hazard Management

The most significant aspect of the changes that need to be achieved in response to IEC80001 across the Health Service is the introduction of risk management for medical IT networks.

In anticipation of the introduction of risk management requirements under IEC80001 (or in case of expansion of the scope of the Medical Devices Directive), the NHS Connecting for Health (CfH) Clinical Safety Group commenced creating and training a network of Trust based Clinical Safety Officers to assist in the safety management tasks associated with new systems deployment.

These CSOs are to be supported in 2010 by the formation of IT Clinical Safety Officers within each Strategic Health Authority (SHA).

The CfH Clinical Safety Group has in place a team of safety engineers and Regional (Northern and Southern) Clinical Safety Officers who will provide a centre of excellent for IT safety engineering in support of Trusts and SHAs. This national infrastructure will be available to health organisations to assist with compliance planning for IEC80001.

A health organisation planning to introduce risk management measures in compliance with IEC80001 should avail themselves of the training and guidance which can be obtained free of charge through this support network.

6.2 DSCN² 14/2009 and DSCN 18/2009

In parallel with the development efforts commencing on IEC80001, in 2006 CfH started work as part of a team looking at introducing a separate standard for safety related (but not medical device classified) health systems. This work generated a pair of health standards:

- TS29321 Clinical risk management for manufacturers of health systems (for health systems suppliers); and
- TR29322 Clinical risk management during the deployment and implementation of health systems (for health organisations).

These standards closely mirror the requirements of IEC80001 but require a proportionate set of controls reflecting the less critical nature of 'advisory' or 'safety related' software systems. There is *no* regulatory requirement for this class of systems. All assurance is conducted by accreditation of supplier process and subsequent inspection of safety deliverables. In this respect it was hoped to avoid the burdens of a compliance scheme such as the medical devices directive (which in its current form is felt by suppliers to be burdensome and overly bureaucratic for this category of software).

In December 2008 the CfH standards were voted down in Europe, with views expressed that the issuing of alternate safety standards to the MDD would be confusing.

CfH were supported by the NHS Information Standards Board in viewing the risks associated with unclassified domains (such as maternity, prescribing/dispensing and A&E triage) as being too important to remain unregulated.

Hence the NHS ISB agreed to adopt the supplier standard (TS29321) and the health organisation standard (TR29322) as UK health standards under the banners DSCN 14/2009 and DSCN 18/2009 respectively.

This gives the UK health sector a suitable clinical risk management regime to cover these prime clinical domains, whilst other suitable standards developments occur. This is a unique world safety standards position.

The NHS ISB standard DSCN 18/2009 is obligatory across England and Wales for health organisations, and requires the introduction of clinical risk management regimes for health software systems. A health organisation complying with DSCN 18/2009 would be broadly compliant with IEC80001 when this standard was introduced and would therefore have much less compliance work to perform.

---

[2] Data Set Change Notice, a historical term used by the NHS ISB to describe an NHS information standard.

In 2005 the Chief Medical Officer stated in his annual report (DoH 2005) that he recognised 'the importance of comprehensive and multifaceted approaches to risk management which focus on the important issues'. The risk management processes introduced in DSCN 18/2009 provide such a comprehensive approach to IT risk management.

6.3 Bringing IT Risk Management under the Health Organisation's Clinical Governance Umbrella

The existence of a health organisation clinical governance structure in most modern health organisations provides a good and independent reporting line for IT safety roles which need to be created.

A fundamental principle of safety assurance across all industries is the existence of an independent safety assessor working alongside a project. The health organisation should consider integrating risk management across its operations.

There will be a need to supplement resource in the existing clinical governance bodies, as specialist IT clinical risk expertise is not generally available in the existing clinical governance bodies. Where health organisations have had effective clinical governance teams involved in IT projects, there is anecdotal evidence that implementing the necessary risk management process has been considerably easier.

6.4 Best Practices for interfacing with Medical Devices

There are some good ideas from regulatory bodies which been successful in dealing with some of the similar challenges and pressures health organisations will face during compliance with IEC80001. These areas are set out below.

6.4.1 Legacy Applications Safety Baselining

The guidelines issued by MHRA in respect of Class 1 medical devices set out a useful precedent for dealing with legacy applications during the base lining of the medical IT network. The guidance clearly suggests that aspects of the interoperating software system (e.g. central patient records system) documentation can be derived from the past pedigree of the system in use:

'If the manufacturer can provide information showing that a safe design has been established for a number of years and that the product has been performing as intended during that time such information is likely to cover this requirement.' [in respect of design documentation]

The theme reflected here is one which IEC61508 (a respected software engineering safety standard) also echoes. In IEC61508, Annex C.2.10 also suggests that a 'proven capability' safety argument can be used (in mitigation of product revalidation) where:

- the product has been stable/unchanged for over a year;
- there have been no safety related failures; and
- performance of the system in live can be clearly established by metrics and this evidences a stable, reliable and available system.

Clearly, the health informatician needs to make professional value judgements on the level to which the 'proven capability' argument is relied upon for individual network and system components.

The whole medical IT network safety case (and indeed the health organisation safety policy) can be undermined by injudicious use of the proven capability argument where no real evidence exists to substantiate it. (This evidence would normally include past test reports, help desk problem records, operational IT metrics, user acceptance tests and other such historical IT project documentation.)

6.4.2 Dealing with Safety Related Software of Uncertain Pedigree

There are well established codes of practice for dealing with safety related systems which are reliant in some way on software (typically COTS software) which has not previously had its safety pedigree validated. This type of software is termed 'Software of Uncertain Pedigree' or SOUP.

The health informatician can gain considerable advice and assistance from widely available papers on the internet such as (HSE 2001a and 2001b) that both deal with good practice in assessing safety integrity of SOUP.

Arguably, one of the most useful pieces of these documents relates to guidance on strategies that the IT organisation can adopt to minimise the safety hazards presented by such SOUP software. Many of these strategies are good IT-common sense but are worth highlighting here :

- Standardise on a limited portfolio of SOUP components;
- Procure from known and reputable suppliers;
- Establish effective processes to rapidly track and resolve problems with these components;
- Use proven SOUP versions; and
- Deploy new SOUP upgrades in low risk pilot clinical domains prior to broader roll out.

This set of 'rules' is in effect a good set of safety controls for all generic IT activities, particularly maintenance, across the medical IT network.

6.4.3 Maintenance Planning for COTS

The FDA have given considerable thought to the use of COTS within medical devices, given that many complex devices are reliant on MS-Windows desktop clients, virus packages and so forth. One of the leading FDA figures in the development of IEC80001 proposed a very good framework (Fitzgerald 2005) for dealing with the complex issue of upgrading COTS products in the medical IT network without compromising the safety integrity of the hosted medical devices. Again, interpreting this for a health organisation, this provides a useful generic rule set for all software and system upgrades for the network:

COTS maintenance rules for a Health Organisation

- Obtain a maintenance plan for any COTS components from the *medical device supplier* prior to installation;
- Seek updates for these COTS components from the *medical device supplier* (who will have validated the release), NOT directly from the COTS vendor;
- Report issues with these embedded COTS products to the *medical device supplier* through the formal defined reporting routes; and
- Formally complain when support for the COTS product is poor or slow in coming.

Compliance with this simple rules-set will allow a health organisation to comply in turn with IEC80001 risk management principles for COTS products that are part of the medical IT network.

7 Implications for Health Informaticians

7.1 Developing an IT Safety Culture in the Profession

The Chief Medical Officer, in his annual report of 2005, stated that he recognised 'the importance of building a strong safety culture that is owned by everyone in the organisation ... the importance of oversight, monitoring and clear accountabilities for action'.

It could be argued that health informatics as a profession has been aware of clinical safety (many informaticians are indeed qualified clinicians) but not necessarily related this aspect with the need for a safety culture around the development of the ICT (non-medical devices) aspects of e-health systems.

Other professional engineering disciplines promote safer design practice as fundamental skills that new engineers should acquire and understand. Indeed postgraduate aerospace engineers are required to undertake a formal engineering training course lasting (in BAE Systems) three years, during which time the graduate is inducted into key engineering disciplines including airworthiness. The training record is examined as part of the pre-assessment before chartered status is granted.

The overriding impact of IEC80001 for the health informatics profession is likely to be the need to formally define and recognise safety engineering responsibilities (and IT clinical risk management) as part of our professional responsibilities. This is what engineers in all other safety related industries do.

Safety engineering is no longer a fringe area of health informatics populated by those strange folk who understand medical devices!

7.2 Training, Skills and Competence

The HSE (with help from the IET and BCS) has issued guidance (HSE 2007) covering the need for organisations to assure competence of staff who are designing, developing and using safety related systems.

> 'This guidance on competence applies to everyone, in all industry sectors, whose decisions and work with safety-related systems can affect health and safety. The aim is for all people within scope to be suitably qualified and experienced for their own work activities, roles and responsibilities.'

With the emergence of IEC80001 as a best practice framework for governing medical IT networks, it is vital that health organisations ensure that professionally competent people are in key health informatics roles where decisions are made in respect of compliance with this safety standard.

7.3 The Profession

Health informaticians need to take the lead in this 'competence evidencing' in order to demonstrate to our clinical colleagues that we are adhering to the same fit-to-practice principles that govern their clinical world.

The value of health informaticians as an ICT profession was recognised in the acclaimed 2006 Royal Society report on ICT ramifications for health care (Royal Society 2006):

> 'Already IT specialists in healthcare are beginning to define themselves as a new profession and are establishing their own professional associations and the beginnings of a regulatory framework, such as the UK Council for Health Informatics Professions (www.ukchip.org).'

With the increased recognition of the health informatics profession within the broader engineering and scientific community, it is important that the new profession is supported and nurtured by those benefiting from it.

Health informaticians must support the professional bodies in efforts to develop our own professional standards. Failure to do this will lead to the profession being held in poor regard by the professionals in the health care community we support.

8 What will the Future see?

As a conclusion to this paper it is worth considering the likely direction safety standards development will take within the eHealth software sector.

Firstly, in the short term IEC80001 appears to have developed a groundswell of support across the international and European standards communities, and is expected to solve many of the safety quandaries presented in real-world integration of health systems for today's complex health organisation.

JWG7 is looking for support for a number of subprojects which will provide useful guidance for health organisations faced with the compliance challenge of, say, *responsibility agreements*.

It is likely that when the new IEC80001 standard is fully published, the NHS ISB will be asked to look at superseding DSCNs 14/2009 and 18/2009 with the new standard.

In the longer term however, it is clear that there is a clamour for the Medical Devices Directive to be updated. A recent Swedish paper (MPA 2009) suggests clearly that from their national viewpoint:

'It is becoming more common that electronic patient record systems and other systems are interconnected, for instance imaging systems or laboratory systems. It is obvious that such systems should not be regarded as "purely administrative"; instead they have the characteristic features that are typical for medical devices. They sort, compile and present information on patients' treatments and should therefore be regarded as medical devices in accordance to the definition.'

Indeed, as this IEC80001 paper was completed (at the end of August 2009), Health Canada published the following national directive (Health Canada 2009):

'Patient management software fits the definition of a medical device, and must therefore be classified in accordance with the classification rules for medical devices from the Medical Devices Regulations'.

It is clear that the scope of the Medical Devices Directive is gradually evolving as national guidelines are issued.

A key concern must be whether or not the existing regulation is fit-for-purpose, and from a UK standpoint it may be that it is *not*.

By way of evidence in support of this statement we would offer a EU commissioned report (IPTS 2000) which looked at the impact of the current Medical Device Directive on innovation with eHealth products (active implantable devices). The report stated, 'although many firms have taken time to adapt to the new system of accreditation, there is still the view that the new system is overly bureaucratic and therefore time and money consuming'.

Far more worrying for the UK health sector (given it is primarily publicly funded) the report cites some of the main disadvantages as being:

- Costs;
- Time for first market entry; and
- Administrative and bureaucratic efforts (paperwork).

More recently the 'Recommendation on Innovation' issued in 2007 by TABD (a transatlantic body supported by the EU Commission and the US Department of Commerce) (TABD 2007) stated:

> 'Eliminate regulatory barriers to healthcare innovations: TABD recommends streamlining the regulatory approval process in the US and the EU for core healthcare-related technologies (including healthcare IT, molecular imaging, medical nanotechnologies), including separating market approval from pricing/reimbursement decisions in order to bring innovations to the patient more quickly.'

The UK will not derive the same equation-balancing 'patient safety' benefits as other European countries may, given that many NHS suppliers already have regimes of IT clinical risk management in place.

Hence for the UK it could be that including eHealth systems within the scope of the Medical Devices Directive gives suppliers and ultimately the NHS a costly and delaying administrative task of re-badging existing safety documentation *for no patient safety benefit*.

It could be argued that the EU (without work to address the shortfalls in current medical device regulations *before* extending their application) would in fact undermine its own e-health programmes. This is a real worry on the horizon at the moment.

References

DoH (2005) The Chief Medical Officer's Annual Report 2005, Chapter 3 'Learning to Fly'. Department of Health
DoH (2009) Department of Health website patient confidentiality section. http://www.dh.gov.uk/en/Managingyourorganisation/Informationpolicy/Patientconfidentialityandcaldicottguardians/DH_4084181. Accessed 16 September 2009
eHealthNews (2009a) eHealth 2009 conference declaration. http://www.ehealthnews.eu/content/view/1510/37/. Accessed 5 October 2009
eHealthNews (2009b) Investment by the government drives growth in the European hospital information systems market. http://www.ehealthnews.eu/content/view/1722/26/. Accessed 5 October 2009
European Parliament (2007) Medical devices directives: Directive 2007/47/EC of the EUROPEAN PARLIAMENT AND OF THE COUNCIL of 5 September 2007 amending Council Directive 90/385/EEC on the approximation of the laws of the Member States relating to active implantable medical devices, Council Directive 93/42/EEC concerning medical devices and Directive 98/8/EC concerning the placing of biocidal products on the market
Fitzgerald B (2005) FDA regulatory perspectives presented to ACCE and AAMI. Tampa
Health Canada (2009) Classification of medical devices Class I or Class II patient management software. Health Canada notice file number: 09-122095-269. http://www.hc-sc.gc.ca/dhp-mps/md-im/activit/announce-annonce/md_notice_software_im_avis_logicels-eng.php. Accessed 17 September 2009

HSE (2001a) CRR 336 Justifying the use of software of uncertain pedigree (SOUP) in safety-related applications. Health and Safety Executive Contract Research Report

HSE (2001b) CRR 337 Methods for assessing the safety integrity of safety-related software of uncertain pedigree (SOUP). Health and Safety Executive Contract Research Report

HSE (2002) CRR 419 Developing advisory software to comply with IEC61508. Health and Safety Executive Contract Research Report

HSE (2007) Managing competence for safety-related systems. Part 1: Key guidance. Health and Safety Executive. http://www.hse.gov.uk/humanfactors/comah/mancomppt1.pdf. Accessed 17 September 2009

IEC (2000) ISO/IEC 61508 Functional safety of electrical/electronic/programmable electronic safety related systems, Parts 1 to 7. International Electrotechnical Commission

IEC (2009) IEC800001 Application of risk management for IT networks incorporating medical devices. International Electrotechnical Commission

IPTS (2000) The impact of single market regulation on innovation: regulatory reform and experiences of firms in the medical device industry. Institute for Prospective Technological Studies. http://ec.europa.eu/enterprise/medical_devices/c_f_f/ipts.htm. Accessed 17 September 2009

Kohn LT, Corrigan JM, Donaldson MS (eds) (2000) To err is human: building a safer health system. Committee on Quality of Health Care in America, Institute of Medicine. National Academy Press, Washington DC

MHRA (2006) EC medical devices directives guidance notes for manufacturers of class 1 medical devices. Medicines and Healthcare Regulatory Agency

MHRA (2009) http://www.mhra.gov.uk/index.htm. Accessed 16 September 2009

MOD (1997): Defence Standard 00-55 Issue 2: Requirements for Safety Related Software in Defence Equipment. Ministry of Defence

MOD (2007) Defence Standard 00-56 Issue 4: Safety Management Requirements for Defence Systems. Ministry of Defence

MPA (2009) Proposal for guidelines regarding classification of software based information systems used in health care. Swedish Medical Products Agency Working Group on Medical Information Systems. http://www.lakemedelsverket.se/upload/foretag/medicinteknik/en/Medical-Information-Systems-Report_2009-06-18.pdf. Accessed 17 September 2009

NHS (2004) Seven steps to patient safety: the full reference guide. National Patient Safety Agency. www.npsa.nhs.uk/sevensteps. Accessed 5 October 2009

NHS (2009) NHS Connecting for Health information governance website. https://www.igt.connectingforhealth.nhs.uk/. Accessed 16 September 2009

OPSI (2009) http://www.opsi.gov.uk/index.htm. Accessed 16 September 2009

Royal Society (2006) Digital healthcare: the impact of information and communication technologies on health and healthcare. The Royal Society. http://royalsociety.org/displaypagedoc.asp?id=23835. Accessed 17 September 2009

RTCA (1992) DO-178B Software considerations in airborne systems and equipment certification. RTCA Inc.

TABD (2007) TABD Recommendation on Innovation. http://www.ehealthnews.eu/content/view/540/55/. Accessed 17 September 2009

Safety Competencies

Competence, The Why? The How? and 'A Practical Approach'

Peter Duggan

Invensys Rail (UK)

Chippenham, UK

Abstract   Competence plays an important role in ensuring functional safety. Safety-related systems rely on a complex mix of hardware, software, human factors and safety management systems. This paper takes a look at the requirements for such a Competence Management System, and gives information on a practical approach to competence implemented by Invensys Rail (UK).

1 Competence – The Why?

Throughout the 19th and 20th centuries, engineering and in particular manufacturing were the primary and core industries within the United Kingdom. Highly skilled workforces existed in many engineering sectors with complex high value manufactured goods exported all over the world.

To become a qualified and skilled craftsman required an extended training period before being trusted with the most demanding work requiring the highest level of skill.

To take the railway industry as an example, the career path for the 'footplate' started with engine cleaning, learning the trade for a number of years, followed by fireman again learning the trade for a number of years. Eventually, you might progress to be a locomotive driver. Even as a driver, you would initially start on shunting and freight duties, before eventually taking on passenger work. And every step was subject to exams and assessment!

But you would not be able to drive the 'top link' prestige express trains unless you had an unblemished record and significant experience as a driver.

With a significant workforce of highly skilled people, with an established career path and apprenticeship style of career progression, the word 'competence' did not prominently feature as a subject as we see it today. However the basic principles were always there.

Today, competence is a subject in its own right, and the focus of this paper, but why has it now risen to prominence?

C. Dale, T. Anderson (eds.), *Making Systems Safer*, DOI 10.1007/978-1-84996-086-1_11,
© Springer-Verlag London Limited 2010

As we move further in the 21st century, there has been a shift in the workforce from an engineering and manufacturing base to a 'service base'. Much of the traditional industry has moved abroad to lower cost base countries whilst the UK has held on to the 'high end' and more complex knowledge based product market. This has resulted in a breakdown of the highly skilled workforce that once featured so prominently and with it, the apprenticeship style of career progression. Whilst we have competence requirements in traditional areas of industry, for instance competence requirements placed upon welders for safety critical welding, the product technology has also changed significantly, and continues to do so.

If you take into consideration new technologies and in particular programmable electronic systems, technology has enabled these systems to function more effectively and required more sophisticated ways to make them safe. Who would have imagined 'fly by wire' 30 years ago? At the same time, the new technology has brought its own challenges – particularly increased design complexity. This has thrown the spotlight on the role of staff engaged in the design, development, maintenance and use of these safety-related systems. The achievement of sufficiently low levels of risk is critically dependent on individual and team competence.

So, in 1974, we saw for the first time, the Health and Safety at Work Act of Parliament (HSW), which places general duties on employers and the self-employed to ensure that employees and others who may be affected by the work of their undertaking are not, so far as is reasonably practicable, exposed to risks to their health and safety. Particularly important, this includes the provision of safe systems of work, supervision and training.

The Management of Health and Safety at Work Regulations (HMG 1999), the statutory instrument put in place to meet the HSW Act, require employers to undertake a suitable and sufficient assessment of the risk that their activities present to their employees and others, including contractors and the public. Measures developed from such risk assessment need to encompass training, knowledge and experience – in other words 'demonstration of competence'.

The degree of rigour in defining the competence criteria (e.g. in ensuring that the criteria directly match the work activity) should be commensurate to the risk, in other words the risks should be associated with each application. Safety integrity levels could be relevant when defining the context of an assessment.

The use of competent people and demonstration of the use of competent people was realised as a significant issue within UK industry that culminated in a publication by the Institution of Electrical Engineers (IEE), the Institution of Railway Signal Engineers (IRSE) and the British Computer Society (BCS) on the subject of competence back in 1999; this was believed to be the first major work on the subject of setting of requirements for competence for systems engineering and software developed products.

Subsequent to this publication, there have been a number of further publications enhancing and extending the concept; a few are listed below.

- Industry Competency Standards:

- Managing Competence for Safety-Related Systems – Part 1: Key Guidance (HSE 2007a)
- Managing Competence for Safety-Related Systems – Part 2: Supplementary Material (HSE 2007b)
- Competence Criteria for Safety-related System Practitioners (IET 2007).

These are complemented by further publications, taking the railway industry as an example:

- Railway Industry Competency Standards:

  - Railway Safety Principles and Guidance: Part 3 Section A. Developing and Maintaining Staff Competence (HSE 2002)
  - Measurement of Safety Culture in the Rail Industry (RSSB 2003)
  - Developing and Maintaining Staff Competence (ORR 2007)
  - IRSE Licensing Scheme (IRSE 2009).

But there is also another aspect that has to be considered. The culture within the UK has changed over the years to one of litigation should consequential loss occur. How many adverts do you watch on television, urging you to make a claim if you are involved in an accident? For industry, demonstration that any development or application has followed 'good practice' is a major defence and competence forms a part.

Should a Health and Safety Executive (HSE) investigation be required after an incident, the HSE inspectors will take into account the principles as defined in Section 2 of this paper when judging the adequacy of a duty holder's arrangements for competence management. This will also take into account additional legislation and regulatory practice where applicable.

Within the rail industry, the UK Railways and Other Guided Transport Systems (Safety) Regulations 2006 (ROGS) (HMG 2006) places a broad requirement on organisations to make a suitable and sufficient assessment of the risks to the safety of any persons to ensure the safe operation of the transport system to which it places a specific requirement on 'controllers of safety critical work' to ensure that persons carrying out safety critical activities have been assessed as being competent and fit. This requirement includes the provision for monitoring and recording the competence and fitness of individuals: a requirement for a 'Competence Management System'!

1.1 Competence – A Definition.

Chambers Dictionary. Fitness, efficiency, capacity, sufficiency, enough to live on in comfort, legal power or capacity.

Invensys Rail (UK) Definition. Collection of related abilities, commitments, knowledge and skills that enable a person (or an organisation) to act effectively in a job or situation.

The following is a more refined definition from a 'management' perspective:

Competence Management. A logical and integrated cycle of activities within an organisation that will assure and further develop competent performance at work.

2 Competence – The How

2.1 Competence Management Systems

The HSE publication Developing and Maintaining Staff Competence (as updated by the ORR) (ORR 2007) identifies the concept of a 'Competence Management System' (CMS) with five phases[1].

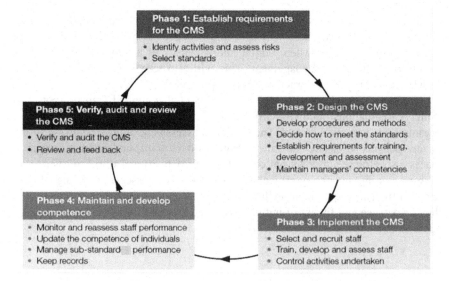

Fig. 1. The Five Phases of a Competence Management System

---

[1] (HSE 2007a) merges phases 3 and 4 under the title 'operate'. The fundamentals are the same.

2.1.1 Phase 1: Establish requirements for the CMS

The requirements for the system are established in Phase 1, starting with the identification of activities that may affect operational safety and occupational health and safety (Principle 1). The risk assessment, with control measures, identifies those activities where the competence of people to control risks is important. This leads to defining and selecting the competence standards for individuals to enable them to control risks consistently (Principle 2).

2.1.2 Phase 2: Design the CMS

The procedures, methods and work instructions for operating the system are developed to achieve consistency, and decisions are made on the storage/recording of data (Principle 3). How each competence standard is met and assessed is then established; this includes defining the level of competence required (Principle 4). The extent of the training, development and assessment requirements is established (Principle 5). The competencies and responsibilities of those managing and operating the system are established (Principle 6).

2.1.3 Phase 3: Implement the CMS

Staff and recruits are selected and recruited (Principle 7) against standards selected previously, and trained, developed and assessed (Principle 8) against the competence standards and methods already selected (Principles 2 and 4). Control processes should be established to ensure that staff and contractors only undertake work for which they are competent (Principle 9).

2.1.4 Phase 4: Maintain and develop competence

Monitoring and reassessment of the staff ensures that performance is being consistently maintained (Principle 10), and that the competence of individuals is updated (Principle 11) in response to relevant changes including changes in legislation, standards and equipment. In particular, systems are required to identify substandard performance and restore the competence of individuals (Principle 12). Records must be maintained and made available when requested (Principle 13).

2.1.5 Phase 5: Verify, audit and review the CMS

The verification and audit of the CMS (Principle 14) checks on the competence assessments and the assessment process. Company management should review the whole system and feedback, using the information from verification and audit

(Principle 15) to update the requirements for the competence management system which returns the system to phases 1 and 2, leading to changes or modifications to system design.

2.2 The IRSE Licensing Scheme

The Institution of Railway Signalling Engineers (IRSE) Licensing Scheme was introduced in 1994 and provides a means of competence certification for personnel undertaking work in the railway signalling and telecommunications industry. The scheme is accredited by UKAS to BS EN ISO/IEC17024 (Conformity Assessment – General Requirements for Bodies Operating Certification of Persons), indicating Government recognition of the scheme. The scheme continues to be developed and is that implemented within the railway industry.

3 A Practical Approach

In the Institution of Engineering and Technology (IET) safety-related systems competence criteria (IET 2007), there exists competency profiling where effectively a series of competencies and levels are set against a job title. This IET competence model includes the concept of competence levels:

- supervised practitioner
- practitioner
- expert

For your own organisation or industry, there may be different levels and different guidance for each level, to indicate the different type of evidence needed to demonstrate competence at that level.

There are a number of categories of licence available within the IRSE Licencing scheme to meet the various job roles found on the railway. These are in essence the railway industry adaptation of competency profiling. For instance if you take the activity of signalling, this is sub-divided into:

- Signalling Designer
- Signalling Installation
- Signalling Testing
- Signalling Maintenance
- Signalling Management
- Signalling Projects.

Taking as an example the role of Signalling Designer, this is further sub-divided into specific roles:

- Signalling Design Manager
- Assistant Signalling Designer
- Signalling Electronic Systems Designer
- Signalling Designer
- Signalling Principles Designer
- Signalling Principles Data Designer
- Signalling Design Verifier
- Signalling Schemes Designer

Within the IRSE Guidance Material, to gain a licence within any specific role, there exist a number of mandatory performance requirements to which evidence is required for the role.

3.1 The IRSE Licensing Scheme Implementation

Having identified the required licence category, there are two basic steps to gaining a license to which the elapsed time will depend upon the license category (Assistant Designer, Tester etc.), and it is not unusual to take between 12 and 18 months to gain a license but may have to be extended to two years in order to gain the necessary practical experience. During this period, individuals work under the mentorship of licensed engineers.

3.1.1 Workplace Assessment

Workplace assessment comprises evidence for each license category set of performance requirements, describing how each requirement is fulfilled (with references to evidence).

The individual will hold a log book which must be kept up-to-date containing work experience, training, record of formal complaints and log book audit. The work experience entries will give details of projects worked on, the size of the projects and the technology used together with the roles and responsibilities in the projects. There should be a minimum of two entries a year which could be based on work packages. Again, they are verified by the line manager or other person who can verify the work, who must be a recognised assessor (renewable every fiev years).

3.1.2 Competence Assessment

The competence assessment takes the form of a review of the log book and interview of the person to determine if the license category competence requirements have been met. Only if sufficient experience is in evidence will the assessment progress. Clearly the assessor must know the subject matter in depth to allow the person's breadth of knowledge to be fairly assessed, and again the assessor must be a recognised assessor (renewable every five years).

It should be noted however that a competence assessment must be carefully planned, rules of assessment clearly stated, means for appeal and of filing complaints identified, carefully planning and structured, and it is most important to make sure that the evidence is the work of the individual concerned. A licence is a valuable asset, not only to the company but also to the individual.

Subject to a final independent check, the application will be sent to the IRSE for acceptance and issue of the IRSE licence (credit card sized plastic card) containing the name and photo of the individual, licence categories gained and their expiry date.

Further details can be found at www.irselicences.co.uk.

3.2 The Invensys Rail (UK) CMS

The management philosophy of the Invensys Rail (UK) CMS is based on the five phases shown in Figure 1 and the specific implementation is depicted in Figure 2.

The Invensys Rail (UK) Competence Management System is primarily based on the IRSE Licensing Scheme.

Details of all people whose primary tasks require an IRSE license are held in a company database, including details of the individual, license category(ies), date of the workplace assessment and identity of the assessor, date of the competence assessment and identity of the assessor, date of issue of the license and its expiry (ten years, but subject to annual review and five yearly interim assessment).

Management reports of IRSE license capability are reported monthly within the business, with status monitoring and control of management of change to license categories and renewals. These are automatically generated with emails sent to the appropriate managers.

The selection process of people against licence category is based on the decision tree in Figure 3 using the basic principles.

Whilst a scheme of this nature is mandated upon the railway industry, it is limited in some respects to the undertaking of safety-critical work on the railway, so the likes of product development including hardware and software development for instance and more specialised elements of design do not sit within the IRSE scheme. At the same time, the categories of 'designer', 'installer' and 'tester' are quite wide-ranging in scope, so when allocating resources to projects, we have found that individuals' specialist skills are not always covered in sufficient detail.

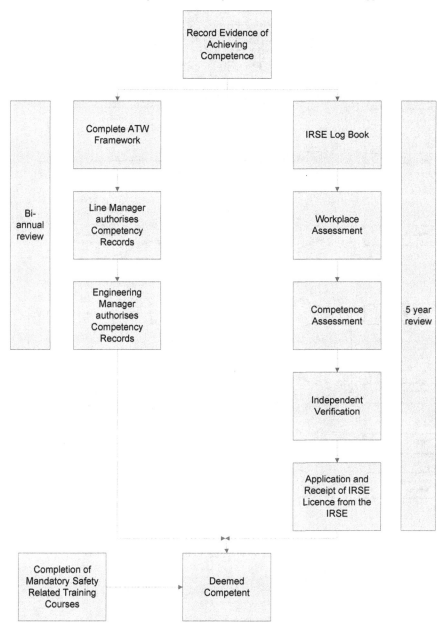

Fig. 2. The Invensys Rail (UK) CMS

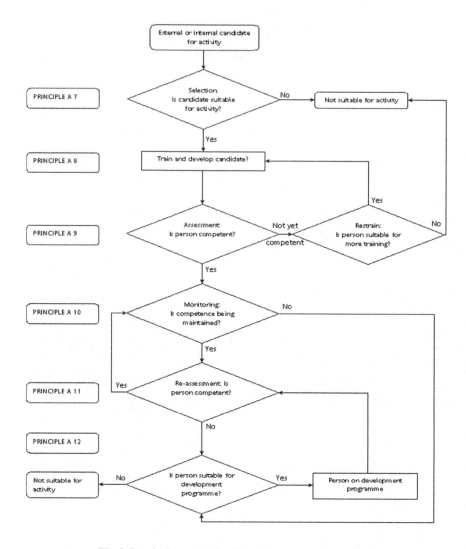

Fig. 3. Developing and Maintaining Competence of Individuals

3.3 Authority to Work

Invensys Rail (UK) have supplemented the IRSE scheme internally with an authority to work (ATW) scheme. This covers all job categories within the IRSE scheme but breaks down each specific role into a number of sub-tasks.

Whilst this means that a number of additional forms have had to be designed and produced, it does mean that when resourcing projects, it can clearly be seen where training needs are required.

An example ATW form is given in Figure 4 for a trainee design engineer.

Design Authority To Work

Name	Job Title	Location
Stan Smith	Trainee Design Engineer	London

Licence Number	Primary Licence Details	Licence Expiry Date
123456	1.1.100 Assistant Signalling Designer	01/09/2015

Quality, Environment And Safety Management

CDM Designer		Signalling Overrun Appreciation Assess.	
IOSH Managing Safely		Signal Sighting Committee Representative	
IOSH Working Safely		Signal Sighting Committee Chairperson	
Engineering Safety Management			

Application Design

Competency Description			Competency Description		
Feasibility Studies To GRIP 4			CAD Plans		
Risk Assessments			CAD Wiring		
Loc. Area Plans			Control Tables (Complex)		
TFM / Datalink Schematics			Control Tables (Simple)		
Scheme Plans			Control Tables (Axle Counter)		
TC Bonding Plans			Aspect Sequence Charts		
650 / 415V Calculations And Design			Free-Wired External (Locations / REB's)		
Cable Core Plans / Schematics					

Electronic Systems And Transmission

Competency Description			Competency Description		
TDM			TD Data Preparation		
FDM Systems			TD Hardware		
HABD					

Interlocking (Electronic)

Competency Description			Competency Description		
SSI Data Preparation			Westrace Data Preparation		
Westlock Data Preparation					

Interlocking (Relay)

Competency Description			Competency Description		
BR Spec 850			Western Region E10000		
Electro - Mechanical			Westinghouse Geographical		
GEC Geographical					

Fig. 4. Example ATW Record

Each individual is responsible for the creation of and updating of their own personal ATW competence record, with its validity subject to review by their engineering manager. The review is undertaken to ensure that the data is accurate, reflects the true capability of the individual and provides an audit trail.

Maintenance of the system is not a significant activity, with few changes occurring within each year (often driven by training updates). A bi-annual review occurs as part of the performance management review to ensure that the ATW form remains valid.

4 Conclusions

The paper has given a brief overview of the requirements for a competence management system, and an insight into the implementation of one such system by Invensys Rail (UK).

Whilst it is acknowledged that competence plays a very important role in functional safety, it must be taken in perspective. The effort expended in demonstration of conformity to the principles and guidance should be commensurate to the risk associated with inadequate competence. In general, the effort expended in competence management should be balanced with the effort required for other safety management activities, hardware, software and human factors included.

References

HMG (1999) Statutory Instrument 1999 No. 3242: The Management of Health and Safety at Work Regulations 1999. The Stationery Office

HMG (2006) Statutory Instrument 2006 No. 599: The Railways and Other Guided Transport Systems (Safety) Regulations 2006. The Stationery Office

HSE (2002) Railway Safety Principles and Guidance: Part 3 Section A. Developing and Maintaining Staff Competence. HSG197. Health and Safety Executive

HSE (2007a) Managing Competence for Safety-Related Systems – Part 1: Key Guidance. Health and Safety Executive

HSE (2007b) Managing Competence for Safety-Related Systems – Part 2: Supplementary Material. Health and Safety Executive

IEE (1999) Safety, competency and commitment: competency guidelines for safety-related system practitioners. Institute of Electrical Engineers, London

IET (2007) Competence Criteria for Safety-related System Practitioners. Institution of Engineering and Technology

IRSE (2009) IRSE Licensing Scheme. http://www.irselicences.co.uk. Accessed 8 September 2009

ISO/IEC (2003) BS EN ISO/IEC 17024:2003 Conformity Assessment – General Requirements for Bodies Operating Certification of Persons. International Organization for Standardization and International Electrotechnical Commission

ORR (2007) Developing and Maintaining Staff Competence. Railway Safety Publication 1. Office of Rail Regulation

RSSB (2003) Measurement of safety culture in the rail industry, Rail Safety & Standards Board, 2003

The new IET Guide – how to do EMC to help achieve Functional Safety

Keith Armstrong

Cherry Clough Consultants

Stafford, UK

Abstract The continuing increases in electronic complexity, and the continuing shrinking of the feature sizes in silicon integrated circuits, has made the normal testing-based approach to EMC inadequate where safety is concerned.

So the new discipline of 'EMC for Functional Safety' has had to be developed to help maintain tolerable levels of safety risks.

The IET's new Guide comprehensively describes practical and cost-effective procedures for both management and engineering, which can be used right away to help to save lives and reduce injuries, wherever electronic technologies are used in safety-implicated products, systems or installations of any type.

It includes useful checklists to aid project management, design and compliance assessment.

For a number of reasons, real financial savings can generally be expected when the Guide is correctly applied, as well as a significant reduction in financial risks.

1 Introduction to the IET's new Guide

This new Guide (IET 2008) comprehensively describes practical and cost-effective procedures for both management and engineering, to help to save lives and reduce injuries, wherever electronic technologies are used in safety-implicated products, systems or installations of any type.

It can also be used to improve reliability, although some of the 'fail-safe' design techniques it describes may not be appropriate for all such applications.

The use of ever-more sophisticated electronic technologies (including wireless, computer and solid-state power conversion) is now commonplace, and increasing in every sphere of human activity, including those where errors or malfunctions in the technology can have implications for functional safety. Activities affected include, but are not limited to:

- Commerce

C. Dale, T. Anderson (eds.), *Making Systems Safer*, DOI 10.1007/978-1-84996-086-1_12,
© Springer-Verlag London Limited 2010

- Industry
- Banking
- Government
- Security
- Medicine and healthcare
- Agriculture
- Defence
- Energy and energy efficiency
- Entertainment and leisure
- Transport (vehicles and infrastructure for road, rail, marine, air, etc.)

All electronic technologies are susceptible to suffering from errors or malfunctions caused by electromagnetic interference (EMI), and increasingly sophisticated technologies tend to be more susceptible. As well as natural sources of EMI, such as lightning, all electrical and electronic technologies are sources of EMI, and as electronic technologies become more sophisticated they tend to emit EMI at higher levels and/or higher frequencies. The consequence of all this is that without appropriate electromagnetic compatibility (EMC) engineering there will be uncontrolled consequences for people in general, plus uncontrolled financial risks for manufacturers and service providers who employ electronic technologies.

Unfortunately, over past decades the disciplines of functional safety engineering and EMC engineering have developed separately, partly because it was mandated by certain international standards committees, but also for other reasons not discussed here (Townsend et al. 1995). The result is that – in general – safety engineers do not have a detailed knowledge of EMC, and EMC engineers do not have a detailed knowledge of functional safety. Furthermore, very few engineers of any type understand the new discipline of functional safety. Also, at the time of writing in 2009, there are no published EMC standards that are appropriate for achieving functional safety, and there are no safety standards that include appropriate EMC requirements for functional safety (mostly, they have no EMC requirements at all).

The aim of this 2008 IET Guide is to provide management and technical tools that enable the use of electronic technologies in applications where they could have an impact on functional safety – controlling the risks due to EMI for customers and third-parties, and thereby reducing financial risks to manufacturers and service providers. Financial risks mostly arise due to product liability legislation, but also due to safety regulations that can cause unsafe products to be banned from large markets such as the European Union (EU) and/or undergo recall. Many companies are aware that legal claims that go against them could be very costly indeed, and could also ruin their brand reputation. For this reason, they have for decades employed legal experts to either win cases for them, or settle out of court with binding non-disclosure agreements. In this way the true cost of poor engineering has generally been hidden from the public, governments, and other companies.

It might be argued that this legal approach will also cope with inadequate EMC in the future, but the rapid growth in the use of increasingly-sophisticated electronic technologies means that at some point the costs of doing EMC engineering adequately will be less than the legal costs resulting from ignoring it. That point may already have been reached, because of the general financial improvements that are available from EMC engineering. As (Armstrong 1994) and (Armstrong 2009a) show, appropriate EMC engineering techniques have for some time been available to help reduce the costs and timescales in design and development, and reduce unit manufacturing and warranty costs, whilst also helping to maximise market share.

Although the subject of the Guide is how to do practical EMC engineering for functional safety reasons, the methods described can be used to reduce risks in high-reliability, mission-critical and legal metrology applications, as well as generally improving financial performance and market share. The Guide will also help military suppliers comply with the Annex H of the UK's Def Stan 59-411 Part 1 (MoD 2007).

The EMC for Functional Safety process described in the Guide can be applied to any electrical, electronic or programmable electronic entity that provides a function having a direct impact on safety. To avoid confusion with the many different terms used in electrical and electronic engineering (for example: device, apparatus, system, safety system, installation, etc.) a new acronym: 'EFS' has been created for the Guide.

EFS is defined as: *'Any entity employing electrical and/or electronic technologies that provides one or more functions having a direct impact on safety'* – with the intention of covering the entire range of constructional possibilities. An EFS is *never* a component, part, element, subsystem or subset of the entity that is providing the safety function. In addition to companies who call themselves 'manufacturers' there are many other types of organisations that could create an EFS, so to avoid confusion, the Guide calls all such organisations 'EFS creators'.

Figures 1a and 1b show the nine basic steps employed by the Guide, which include checklists to aid project management, design and compliance assessment. This figure is for a 'Simple EFS', but the Guide also describes an expanded process that will handle projects of any size, with any number of levels of subcontracting.

Section 2 of this paper examines the relationship between the IET's new Guide and IEC 61508 (IEC 2000). Section 3 discusses how various practitioners of functional safety and/or EMC will need to learn new tricks. Section 4 shows why it is that we can no longer rely on EMC testing alone, and Section 5 provides brief descriptions of each of the steps in the nine-step process shown in Figures 1a and 1b.

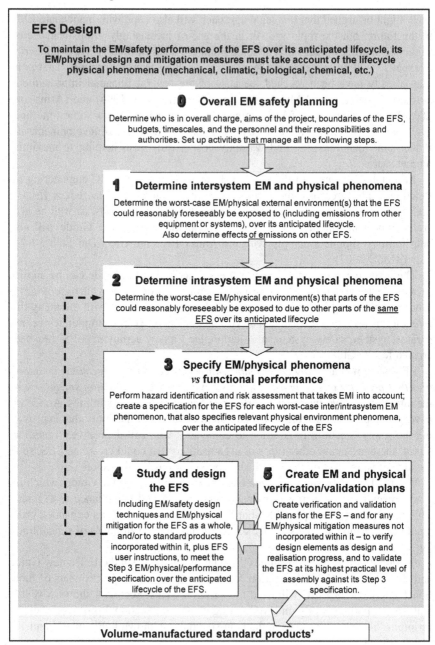

Fig. 1a. The first 5 steps in the 9-step process, applied to a 'Simple EFS'

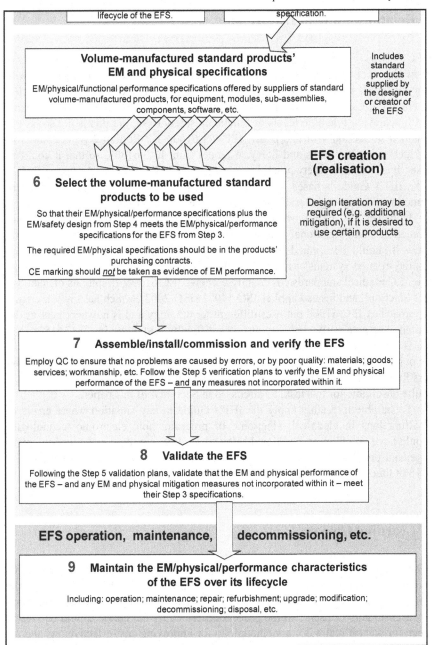

Fig. 1b. The remainder of the steps, applied to a 'Simple EFS'

2 Relationship with IEC 61508

IEC 61508 (IEC 2000) says that EMI must be taken into account, but does not say how this should be done. It is common practice to assume that compliance with the standards used for conformity to the EU's EMC Directive (European Parliament 2004, European Commission 2007) will deal with the EMI issues associated with achieving tolerable levels of functional safety risks, but this is not so, as explained in Section 4 of this paper. IEC TS 61000-1-2 Edition 2 (IEC 2008) was written using the terms and lifecycle model from IEC 61508, so that it could be used by functional safety practitioners as IEC 61508's 'missing Annex on EMC'. The IET's Guide is based upon the principles of (IEC 2008) – applying modern functional safety engineering techniques to the control of EMI.

However, IEC 61508 was written from the point of view of process control installations, and functional safety practitioners often have difficulty interpreting how it should be applied to equipment, systems and installations that are not 'safety-related systems' as defined rather narrowly in IEC 61508. For example, the IEC medical standards community eschews IEC 61508, despite its official 'pilot function', and instead applies ISO 14971 (ISO 2007), which has the same basic approach as IEC 61508 but uses different terminology and is nowhere near as detailed. The automotive industry also has difficulty with applying IEC 61508, and so is writing its own functional safety standard ISO 26262 (ISO 2009). And what about household appliances? Their basic standard IEC 60335-1 (IEC 2006a) covers functional safety, but has a simple test standards-based approach to EMI that is quite unsuitable for this task, as discussed in Section 4 of this paper.

To be able to readily apply the IET's Guide to any situation where errors or malfunctions in electrical, electronic or programmable electronic technologies could have an effect on functional safety risks, it was written as a nine-step management process, as shown in Figures 1a and 1b. The mapping between the IEC 61508 lifecycle and the IET Guide's nine-step process is shown in Figure 2.

3 Learning Curves

The approach described in the Guide will mean a significant learning curve for many EFS creators. But the alternative is a future of unacceptable levels of deaths and injuries, and unacceptable financial risks and losses by both the creators and their customers or users. So the process described by the Guide should be clearly seen for what it really is – a methodology for improving cost-effectiveness and reducing financial risks over the medium and longer term. In fact it is much more than that – it is also a methodology for ensuring customer and investor confidence. For government bodies and other non-profit organisations it provides similar benefits in their spheres of operation.

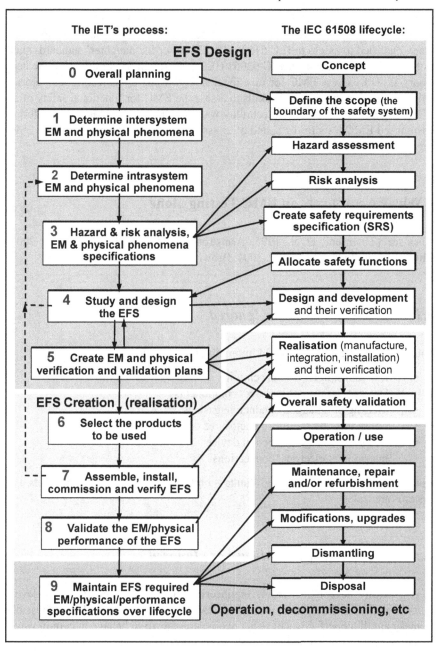

Fig. 2. Mapping between IEC 61508 lifecycle and IET Guide process

Senior corporate executives could also use it as a method for reducing their personal liability under the UK's Corporate Manslaughter Act – or similar legislation in other countries – that aims to ensure that one or more senior responsible individuals are held personally accountable when their company's actions (or inactions) cause safety accidents. In addition, functional safety assessors (e.g. those already qualified to assess to IEC 61508 (IEC 2000) or its 'daughter' standards such as IEC 61511 (IEC 2004) or IEC 62061 (IEC 2005)) will need to develop the necessary skills to assess EMC for functional safety. Some EMC testing laboratories will also develop the necessary skills to assess the EMC for functional safety of an EFS design. Some of them will certainly want to expand their markets by offering customised EMC tests for EFS, and offer assistance in developing individual EMC for Functional Safety test plans.

4 Why we can't rely on EMC Testing alone

Also see (Townsend et al. 1995, Armstrong 2004a, 2004b, 2004c and 2007, Chundru et al. 2004, Wang et al. 2004, Brown and Radasky 2004).

4.1 Foreseeable Faults are Ignored

Faults can significantly affect EM immunity, for example:

- • Dry joints, open or short circuits
- • Out-of-tolerance or incorrect components
- • Missing or damaged conductive gaskets
- • Loose/missing fixings in enclosures or cable shielding
- • Failure of a surge protection device
- • Intermittent electrical connections

But standard EMC tests ignore all faults – only perfect specimens of products and systems are tested.

4.2 Foreseeable Use and Misuse are Ignored

It is generally accepted in safety engineering that acceptable safety risk levels must be maintained despite reasonably foreseeable use or misuse. It is impossible to make anything perfectly safe – but people are known to behave in certain ways, so safety engineering should take this into account.

But standard EMC tests assume equipment is operated perfectly at all times, and is not damaged or modified.

4.3 Test Chambers are Not Realistic

Standard radiated field immunity tests specify test chambers that make tests more repeatable. Unfortunately, they are unlike all real-life EM environments experienced by equipment (e.g. an anechoic chamber most closely simulates free-space, such as a missile when it is flying through the air), so their results can differ markedly from immunity in real life. Some manufacturers 'overtest' by increasing test levels, thinking that if they test at a high enough level they will take care of the problem, but (Armstrong 2009b) shows that this is incorrect.

There are also concerns about the measurement uncertainties in the test chambers, with some EMC testing experts suggesting large and unpredictable uncertainties (Jansson and Bäckström 1999, Freyer 2003). Reverberation chambers can provide much more realistic tests (Freyer and Hatfield 1998, Freyer 2004), and for this reason are used by many manufacturers of flight-critical avionics and preferred by RTCA/DO-160F (RTCA 2007), clauses 20.4 and 20.5 of which attempt to cover the sensitivity of equipment to modulation type or frequency.

4.4 RF Modulation Types and Frequencies are Not Realistic

For ease of testing, low costs and repeatability, standard RF immunity tests use 1kHz sinewave modulation, although some vehicle manufacturers employ pulse modulation to simulate digital cellphones and radars above about 600MHz, and military standards use 1kHz squarewave.

However, real-life environments contain EM disturbances with a range of modulation types and frequencies, as pointed out by (Brewer 2007). (Wendsche and Habiger 1996) and (Vick and Habiger 1997) show that immunity can be significantly degraded (e.g. 20dB or more) when EMI modulation corresponds with frequencies or waveforms used in internal processes, or resonates with circuits, cables, transducers or loads.

The importance of modulation has been well known in military electronic warfare for many decades, but is only now just starting to be addressed by some, see (RTCA 2007) and (DaimlerChrysler 2004), Clause 7 of which attempts to address modulation type and frequency.

4.5 Simultaneous Disturbances are Not Tested

Traditional EMC testing applies a limited number of types of EM disturbance, one at a time. But in real life operation, equipment is exposed to simultaneous EM disturbances, for example: two or more RF fields at different frequencies; a radiated field plus a conducted transient or electrostatic discharge, etc. (Mardiguian 2000) shows that equipment that passes its individual immunity tests can be much more susceptible to lower levels of the same disturbances when they are applied simultaneously, as they can be in real life.

Simultaneous disturbances with different frequencies can cause EMI through intermodulation (IM), which (like demodulation) occurs naturally in non-linear devices such as semiconductors. Figure 3 shows a simple example of two RF fields at different frequencies, which can cause EMI by:

- Direct interference from each frequency independently
- Demodulation of the amplitude envelopes of either frequency, or both mixed together
- Intermodulation, in which new frequencies are created

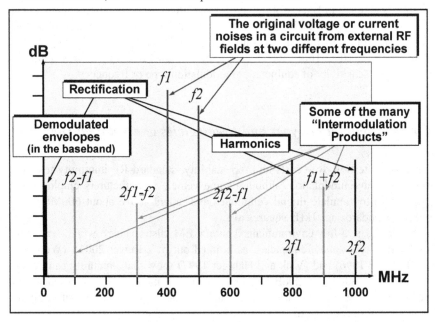

Fig. 3. Example of demodulation and intermodulation

Imagine that conventional (single frequency) testing over the frequency range 150kHz – 6GHz discovers that an equipment is too susceptible over 10-200MHz. The usual approach, carried out in dozens of test laboratories around the world on a daily basis, is to add shielding and filtering over the susceptible frequency range (10-200MHz in this case) so that the equipment now passes the test. No protection was added, for example, over the range 200MHz – 5GHz, because it was not needed to pass the test, and why add unnecessary cost? But in real life, simultaneous noises in the frequency range 200MHz – 6GHz will occur, and will enter the equipment, where they will intermodulate, with some finite probability of creating *internal* noises in the 10-200MHz range, and so causing EMI problems that the original test would never discover. In some operational environments, having two or more EM fields present at different frequencies and significant levels at the same time will be the norm, rather than the exception.

4.6 Only One Port is Tested at a Time

When an item of equipment is subjected to a radiated EM field, all of its cables pick up RF voltages, but there are phase differences between them due to their different routing, stray capacitances, etc. But traditional EMC conducted immunity tests only test one cable at a time. Experiments at Qinetiq PLC have injected RF energies into all of an equipment's conductors simultaneously, with phase shifts to match what would be expected in real life. They discovered that the immunity could be significantly worse than when one cable was tested at a time when following the standard immunity test methods. (Unpublished work at the time of writing.)

4.7 The Physical Environment is Ignored

An appropriate level of EM performance must be maintained despite the effects of the physical environment over the anticipated lifecycle of an EFS, including the following:

- Mechanical (static forces, shock, vibration, etc.)
- Climatic (temperature, humidity, air pressure, etc. – both extremes and cycling effects)
- Chemical (oxidation, galvanic corrosion, conductive dusts, condensation, drips, spray, immersion, icing, etc.)
- Biological (e.g. mould growth, etc.)
- Operational 'wear and tear' over the lifetime (friction, fretting, repetitive cleaning, grease build-up, etc.)
- Ageing

Physical effects vary from immediate (e.g. non-flat mounting opening a gap and degrading shielding), to long-term (e.g. corrosion of a shield joint or filter ground bond). MIL-STD-464 (DoD 1997) describes a number of real-life problems of this nature; (Sjögren and Bäckström 2005) and (Parker et al. 2002) are also relevant, as is the last paragraph of (Rajamäki 2004). (Beck and Sroka 1999) shows that up to 20dB degradation in filter attenuation can be caused by combinations of ambient temperature, supply voltage and load current within the filter's ratings – compared with the results of traditional immunity tests.

Some manufacturers perform a variety of highly-accelerated life tests to check that functionality is maintained over the anticipated lifecycle, but in general the resulting 'aged' units are not subsequently tested to see if their EM characteristics have been affected.

4.8 Quality of EM Design Ignored

Most manufacturers test their products using standard immunity test methods, iterating the design until it passes. But this might not reveal whether the pass was achieved by good EM design, or by something that would not be adequately controlled in serial manufacture over the production life. Standard EMC tests do not assess EM design quality, so if a product's EM design does not cope with component tolerances, semiconductor die-shrinks, variations in assembly (e.g. cable harnesses, grounding, etc.), replacement of obsolete components, firmware bug fixes, etc., they could easily degrade its EM characteristics.

The fact that one or more samples of a product passed their EMC tests means *nothing at all* for the EM characteristics of the products actually supplied, unless its design has taken care of the above variability issues.

4.9 Assembly Errors Ignored

Good safety engineering always requires testing each unit manufactured to make sure that assembly errors have not made it unsafe, but standard EMC tests do not include any requirements for manufacturers to perform routine checks on EM characteristics in serial manufacture. Test laboratories say that it is not uncommon for items of equipment that function correctly to fail EMC tests because of 'misbuild'. Although most manufacturers employ rigorous end-of-line testing, including in-circuit tests that will discover misbuilds that affect functionality, they generally do not aim to discover misbuilds that can affect EMC characteristics.

4.10 Systematic Effects Ignored

It is generally – but incorrectly – assumed that if all of the products incorporated into a system pass their immunity tests individually, then the systems created will also be immune enough.

But performance degradations that are perfectly acceptable when an equipment is EMC tested, or are not even measured during the testing, could have significant implications for the functional safety of systems that use them.

It is commonly noted that there is very poor agreement between the EMC test results on items of equipment, and on the systems that are constructed with them: see (Schrader et al. 2009).

4.11 The Maximum Test Level is Not Necessarily the Worst

All electronic devices are non-linear, and circuits/firmware can be very complex, so products can sometimes fail when tested with low-level EM disturbances – but fail in a different way – or even pass when tested with the specified levels. But some EM tests only expose equipment at the highest specified level, to save testing time and cost. Lower disturbance levels will usually be much more likely in real life, and so could be much more significant for functional safety.

4.12 Conclusion: EMC Testing can Never be Sufficient

The above has shown that EMC testing can *never be sufficient* – on its own – to demonstrate that functional safety risks are low enough, or that risk-reduction will be high enough, over the lifecycle of an EFS, taking its physical environment (including wear and ageing) into account. The number of variables is simply too large. Test plans could be drawn up which would provide the necessary design confidence, but no-one (even governments) could afford their cost, or the very long time they would take.

This is not a novel situation. In the 1990s it was realised that testing was not sufficient to demonstrate that software programmes were reliable enough for use in safety systems, resulting directly (after many hundreds of man-years of work by academia and industry) in Part 3 of IEC 61508 (IEC 2000). What is required is to adopt the approach that has been taken in every other aspect of safety engineering, including software, of employing proven good engineering techniques, and a range of verification and validation methods, including testing – that will probably need to be carefully specified for each project (rather than being a fixed set of tests). In other words, we need to apply a Risk Management methodology such as that of IEC 61508 and apply it to the discipline of EMC – and this is the approach taken by IEC 61000-1-2 (IEC 2008) and the IET's Guide that is the subject of this paper.

5 Going through the Steps in the IET's Guide

5.1 Step 0: Managing the 9-step Process

The IET's new Guide requires that an organisation with responsibility for any of the activities within the scope of the Guide's process, should appoint one or more persons to take overall responsibility for:

- The EFS, or for all relevant activities,
- Coordinating the EMC-related activities,
- The interfaces between those activities and other activities carried out by other organisations,
- Carrying out all the requirements of this Step,
- Ensuring that EMC is sufficient and demonstrated in accordance with the objectives and requirements of this document.

Responsibility for EMC-specific functional safety activities may be delegated to other persons, particularly those with relevant expertise, and different persons could be responsible for different activities and requirements. However, the responsibility for coordination, and for overall EMC for functional safety, should reside in one or a small number of persons with sufficient management authority.

As with all safety engineering undertakings, the time, effort and skill required for performing and managing an activity depends upon the level of safety risk (or risk-reductions) considered acceptable for the EFS. Lower levels of risks require greater confidence in design and verification – hence more work and more thorough documentation.

5.2 Step 1: Determine the Intersystem EM and Physical Phenomena

Step 1 of the IET's new Guide accepts that an EFS may need to maintain certain minimum levels of electromagnetic (EM) immunity despite *at least one* fault, such as the wear-out of a surge protection device by the surges it is exposed to over time. Another example is a broken filter ground connection, which could be caused by poor assembly; shock, vibration, or corrosion over the lifecycle; or wilful damage.

EFS designers need to know enough about their equipment's 'environment' (EM; physical; climatic; wear; ageing, etc. over the anticipated lifecycle) and foreseeable faults and misuse, to select appropriately-rated components, and to design circuits, software, filtering, shielding, overvoltage protection, etc. They need this information to be able to achieve the reliability required for operational functions that could have an impact on safety over the entire lifecycle.

For example, engineers need enough information to be able to design:

- EFS and its EM/physical mitigation techniques to cope with the foreseeable range of EM disturbances over the anticipated lifecycle of the EFS, including low-probability events (how low depends on the safety requirements of the EFS) and simultaneous EM disturbances.
- Feedback circuits – so that they do not become unstable due to temperature variations affecting component parameters (e.g. gain-bandwidth product, phase margin, etc.).
- Filters – so that vibration and corrosion will not cause their ground bonds to degrade; and that variations in supply voltage, load current and temperature do not degrade their attenuation too much (Beck and Sroka 1999).
- Shield joints and gaskets – so they will continue to perform as required despite twisting of the frame due to mounting on non-flat surfaces; and will withstand wear and tear, corrosion, mould growth or other lifecycle influences (Sjögren and Bäckström 2005).
- Surge protection that will withstand the foreseeable overvoltages and overcurrents for the lifecycle of the EFS, or at least for the period between maintenance activities.
- EFS and its EM/physical mitigation techniques so that their EM and physical characteristics will not be unacceptably degraded by lifecycle activities such as: maintenance; repair; refurbishment; modification; upgrade; decommissioning, etc.
- etc.

They also need this information to create a test plan for both EMC and HALT (Highly Accelerated Life Testing) that will verify/validate the design, and to design the routine EMC testing and physical stress screening required in volume manufacture.

The EM/physical environments that exist without the EFS in place are called *intersystem* environments, and are the subject of Step 1 in this EMC for functional safety process. Where the statistical distribution of an EM or physical 'threat' is not known, the 'reasonably foreseeable worst-case' value that could possibly occur during the lifecycle should be determined with sufficient accuracy, and the design based on this. Figure 4 shows some of the EM issues that should be taken into account when assessing an intrasystem EM environment.

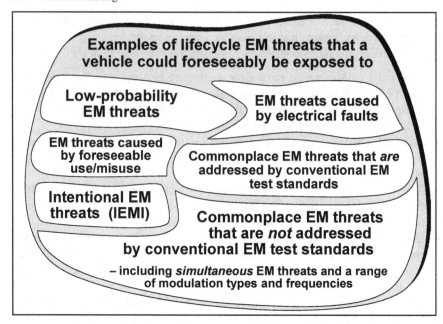

Examples of lifecycle EM threats that a
vehicle could foreseeably be exposed to

Low-probability
EM threats

EM threats caused
by electrical faults

EM threats caused
by foreseeable
use/misuse

Commonplace EM threats that *are*
addressed by conventional EM
test standards

Intentional EM
threats (IEMI)

Commonplace EM threats
that are *not* addressed
by conventional EM test standards

– including *simultaneous* EM threats and a range
of modulation types and frequencies

Fig. 4. Some of the EM environment issues to be taken into account

5.3 Step 2: Determine the Intrasystem EM and Physical Phenomena

Each item of electrical/electronic equipment creates its own EM and physical disturbances, and so has an effect on its local EM/physical environments. Where an EFS is comprised of several items of equipment, the emissions from one or more of them might interfere with one or more of the other parts of itself. This is known as *intrasystem* interference, and is the subject of this step.

Where the statistical distribution of an EM or physical 'threat' is not known, the maximum 'worst-case' value that could possibly occur during the lifecycle should be determined with sufficient accuracy, and the design based on this. The combination of the worst-case intersystem and worst-case intrasystem environments should be captured in the environmental specifications that are the output of Steps 1 and 2 to the rest of the EMC for functional safety process.

5.4 Step 3: Specify EM/Physical Phenomena vs Functional Performance

No EMC or safety standard can ever specify exactly what is required for a given EFS, because to be adopted internationally it must inevitably adopt a general approach and strike a balance between under-engineering and over-engineering, often called a technical/economic compromise. Competent engineers should therefore carefully assess each EFS with respect to its operational situations. This Step in the EMC for functional safety process creates an 'EMC safety specification' that helps a given EFS achieve tolerable levels of safety risks, or risk-reductions. It is also part of a process that helps ensure the amount of safety engineering is just right, so that under- and over-engineering is avoided.

Steps 1 and 2 assessed the worst-case EM and physical environments over the anticipated lifecycle. The outputs from these Steps are specifications for the worst-case EM and physical environments. Where appropriate, it can help to base these specifications on existing standards (such as the DEF STAN 59-411 (MoD 2007), MIL-STD-461F (DoD 2007), IEC 61000-4 (IEC 2006b) or IEC 60721 (IEC 2002) series), competently modified as necessary. Doing this can make it easier to verify and validate the design by testing, in Steps 7 and 8, because test laboratories and equipment hire companies (and many manufacturers) will already have much of the equipment and expertise necessary to apply those test methods.

This Step 3 is concerned with creating the EMC safety specification for the EFS, which will include both EM and physical specifications, and upon which Steps 4 and later steps all depend.

Where an EFS creator subcontracts part of the design, the subcontracted item requires an Item Requirement Specification (IRS) that helps to ensure that the overall EFS complies with its EMC safety specifications, see Step 6 in Section 5.7.

5.5 Step 4: Study and Design the EFS

It is important to ensure that EFS do not become unsafe as a result of EMI due to their EM environment (including EMI they create themselves). It is also important to ensure that the EM emissions from a new EFS (or part of it) do not cause safety risks by interfering with existing EFSs. Accordingly, it is the responsibility of the EFS designer (which may be a team of people) to apply appropriate EM/physical measures throughout the lifecycle of the EFS.

Where it is not within the authority of the designer to apply a certain measure (e.g. repair of an EFS after it has been sold to another company), the designer should provide appropriate and clear instructions on what should be done, and by whom, with clear warnings about the potential consequences for safety risks (or risk-reductions) of failing to follow them.

In most cases, mass-produced electrical, electronic or programmable electronic products and other devices and interconnections that are often used to assemble an EFS cannot be expected to have EM emissions and/or immunity characteristics that are adequate for all of the possible EM environments that an EFS might experience. Therefore, it is important to recognise that EM and/or physical mitigation measures, applied at the level of the equipment, system and/or installation, are often an effective way to achieve the required characteristics for the target level of safety risk.

One aim of this Step in the Guide is to provide an overview of some of the measures and techniques that are available for the achievement of functional safety with regard to EMI. It cannot specify how to design an EFS, because each EFS and its application and EM/physical environment is so different. Instead, it discusses the major design issues and some techniques by which they may be addressed.

Whilst the IET Guide describes many design techniques that can be used in Step 4, it is not comprehensive; there are other techniques that could be equally effective. They are just a list of some techniques that have been found useful in the past, and there is no obligation to use all or any of them. Some of these techniques might not be suitable for some types of EFS. How the EFS designer ensures that the desired levels of safety risks (or risk-reductions) are achieved over the anticipated lifecycle is entirely up to him or her.

Performing a risk assessment for EMC for functional safety generally requires using at least one 'bottom-up' (inductive) method, such as FMEA, Event Tree Analysis, etc., plus at least one 'top-down' (deductive) method, such as Fault Tree Analysis, plus 'brainstorming' using a wide variety of participants (not just designers), plus Task Analysis, Human Reliability Analysis, and other methods where relevant. But the normal, standardised risk assessment methods were never designed to cover EMI issues, so need competently adapting to take into account, for example:

- 'latch-up' (all integrated circuit pins held high or low simultaneously by a malfunction inside itself)
- 'common-mode' disturbances (which affect two or more subassembly 'ports' or circuit nodes simultaneously)
- EMI and intermittent contacts, which can create noises that can be mistaken for valid signals
- multiple simultaneous faults (unless their probability is shown to be low enough, over the anticipated lifecycle, to treat them one-at-a-time)
- etc.

5.6 Step 5: Create EM and Physical Verification/Validation Plans

As was shown in Section 4 of this paper, EMC testing can never be sufficient on its own to demonstrate that risks are low enough, or that risk-reduction will be high enough, over the lifecycle of an EFS, taking its physical environment (including wear and ageing) into account. Test plans could be drawn up which would provide the necessary design confidence, but no-one (even governments) could afford their cost, or the very long time they would take.

No other safety engineering discipline, including software, ever relies totally upon testing a finished product. In fact it is very well recognised in safety engineering, and especially in functional safety engineering, that testing alone is insufficient. What they employ instead, and we now need to apply to EMC, is competent design engineering, plus a variety of verification and validation techniques, which will include some carefully-targeted testing.

Different designs of EFS may employ modified or different design techniques (see Step 4 of the Guide) and/or be used in different applications – but to be time- and cost-effective we must accept that no single design methodology will be found to be suitable for *all* types of EFS.

Where EFS designs and/or applications differ, verification and validation techniques may need to be adapted – and different techniques may need to be employed. The EMC testing employed may need to be adapted, or different tests applied. No one verification/validation plan or EMC test methodology is suitable for all designs of EFS (to be time- and cost-effective).

Step 4 of the Guide's 9-step process (see Figures 1a and 1b) designed the EFS, using techniques as appropriate to its application, functions, and the EM/physical requirements of its EMC safety specification and risk assessment (from Step 3).

Step 5 now deals with planning the verification and validation of the EFS design, including its EMC testing, against the EM/physical requirements of its EMC safety specification (from Step 3). Most of the text and graphics in this Step deal with EMC testing issues, but that does not mean that testing is the most important verification and validation method of the several that must be applied. For example: Expert Review is often found to be the most powerful method for detecting design errors, and also one of the quickest and most cost-effective.

The planning of the validation and verification techniques needs to be performed by competent and knowledgeable personnel during the design phase (Step 4), because the two steps are interactive. It can be possible to avoid lengthy and expensive verification and validation programmes by doing the design in a different way, and employing certain verification and validation techniques can sometimes allow design to proceed faster, or lower-cost parts to be used.

5.7 Step 6: Selecting Standard Products and/or specifying Custom Hardware or Software Items

Step 6 applies only where the EFS designer(s) permits the EFS creator to have such freedom of choice. In some EFS designs, especially simpler ones, some EFS designer(s) will completely specify everything about the EFS, including any standard volume-manufactured or custom-engineered items of hardware or software that are to be incorporated within it. The EFS creator then has no flexibility in this regard and Step 6 does not apply to that EFS.

This Step of the process is concerned with selecting standard volume-manufactured items of hardware or software and/or specifying custom-engineered items of hardware or software, for incorporation into the EFS by the EFS creator (who may or may not be the same company as the EFS designer(s)).

The aim of this step is to ensure that – taking into account the EM/safety design of the EFS – the EM/physical/performance of any standard volume-manufactured or custom-engineered items of hardware or software incorporated into the EFS do not prevent it from meeting the EM safety specification of the EFS (from Step 3). The required EM/physical performance specifications should be in the purchasing contracts for the standard products or custom items, and 'CE marking' or Certificates of Compliance should never be taken as evidence of EM performance.

Remember: an EFS is *never* a component, part, subset, or a purchased standard product or custom-designed item that is incorporated into something else – it can *only* be the finished, complete entity that, when finally installed, is what provides the function that has a direct impact on safety risks or risk-reductions.

5.8 Step 7: Assemble, install, commission and verify the EFS

A very wide variety of assembly, installation, commissioning and verification activities are possible in this Step. Some of them might take place on the manufacturer's site (or manufacturers' sites), and some on the operational site (including fixed locations, vehicles, vessels, etc.), depending on the type of EFS and the way it is designed.

These activities all fall within the lifecycle phase known as 'Realisation' in IEC 61508 (IEC 2000), and include such 61508 concepts as 'manufacture' and 'integration'. They are all specified by the design and verification documents created during Steps 4 and 5, in order to meet the specifications created by Step 3, so that the EFS achieves the desired levels of safety risk, or risk-reduction, over its lifecycle.

5.9 Step 8: Validating the EFS

This is the Step in which the finished, fully functioning EFS is validated as complying with its Step 3 requirements for safety risks and/or risk-reductions over its lifecycle, by implementing the validation plans from Step 5.

Where the EFS is large, or is a distributed system, EMC testing of its final build stage might be impractical and/or there may be no standard test methods that are suitable. A wide variety of validation activities are available for use in this Step (see Step 5) depending on the type of EFS and the way it is designed, to support whatever testing is practical (and affordable) to achieve sufficient confidence in the safety risks or risk-reductions achieved by the EFS.

5.10 Step 9: Maintain the EM and Physical Performance Characteristics of the EFS over its Lifecycle

An EFS must maintain certain levels of safety risks and/or risk-reductions over its entire lifecycle, which of course includes operation, maintenance, repair, refurbishment, and modifications and upgrades to its mechanics, electrical and electronic hardware and software. It must also remain safe enough during dismantling and disposal. The safety of everyone who could be exposed to risks from the EFS in any of its lifecycle phases must be controlled, by appropriate design and/or management procedures. For example: where an EFS is controlling a powerful robot, during certain lifecycle activities (other than operation) it may be acceptable to remove the power to its motors and actuators, so that if the EFS suffers interference (e.g. due to the door of a shielded enclosure being opened) the robot cannot make any unintended or erroneous movements. If the robot needs to be operated whilst a shielded enclosure door is open, it may be acceptable for the person in charge of that activity to clear the area of any radio transmitters, or clear the area reachable by the robot of any personnel, both of them being precautions that are not taken during normal operation.

Different types of personnel perform the various activities during these phases of the lifecycle. For example an operator will have a different set of skills, competencies and experiences than someone performing a repair or installing an upgrade, and will generally (but not always) be exposed to safety hazards for a shorter time. For this and other reasons the levels of safety risk or risk-reduction that are necessary for the EFS during various post-manufacture activities could be different from those that are necessary during operation.

Dismantling and disposal lifecycle phases often require no safety precautions, but the issue should always be addressed because sometimes they can. For example: nuclear power plants can take a long time to dismantle and dispose of, and certain types of EFS (e.g. cooling systems, safety interlocks, radiation alarms, etc.)

need to remain operational and provide the required level of safety risks (or risk-reductions) during part or all of those phases.

6 Helpful Annexes and Checklists

The IET's new guide provides everything necessary to use it in real-life projects, and to assist those who might be unfamiliar with the topics of EMI and EMC. It includes a comprehensive glossary of terms and acronyms, a basic understanding of what EMI phenomena can occur and how they can affect equipment, and comprehensive checklists, one for each Step in the Guide's nine-step process, which may be used by project managers, and as an aid in certain types of verification and validation activities.

References

Armstrong K (1994) Profit from EMC. IEE Review, July 1994, EMC Supplement pp S-24 and S-25

Armstrong K (2004a) Why EMC immunity testing is inadequate for functional safety. IEEE Intl EMC Symp, Santa Clara pp 145-149

Armstrong K (2004b) Functional safety requires much more than EMC testing. EMC-Europe (6th Intl Symp on EMC), Eindhoven pp 348-353

Armstrong K (2004c) EMC for functional safety. IEEE Symp on Product Safety Engineering, Santa Clara

Armstrong K (2007) EMC in safety cases — why EMC testing is never enough. EMC-UK Conference, Newbury

Armstrong K (2009a) When the going gets tough – smarter design wins. The EMC Journal 81:21-24

Armstrong K (2009b) Why increasing immunity test levels is not sufficient for high-reliability and critical equipment. 2009 IEEE Intl EMC Symp, Austin

Beck F, Sroka J (1999) EMC performance of drive application under real load condition. Schaffner Application Note 11

Brewer R (2007) EMC failures happen. Evaluation Engineering. http://www.evaluationengineering.com/features/2007_december/1207_emc_test.aspx. Accessed 21 September 2009

Brown SJ, Radasky B (2004) Functional safety and EMC. IEC Advisory Committee on Safety (ACOS) Workshop VII, Frankfurt am Main

Chundru R, Pommerenke D, Wang K et al (2004) Characterization of human metal ESD reference discharge event and correlation of generator parameters to failure levels — Part I: Reference event. IEEE Trans EMC 46:498-504

DaimlerChrysler (2004) DaimlerChrysler Joint Engineering Standard DC-10614, EM performance requirements – Components

DoD (1997) MIL-STD-464 Electromagnetic environmental effects – Requirements for systems. Department of Defense Interface Standard

DoD (2007) MIL-STD-461F Requirements for the control of electromagnetic interference characteristics of subsystems and equipment. Department of Defense Interface Standard

European Commission (2007) Guide for the EMC Directive 2004/108/EC. http://ec.europa.eu/enterprise/electr_equipment/emc/directiv/dir2004_108.htm#guide. Accessed 18 September 2009

European Parliament (2004) Directive 2004/108/EC of the European parliament and of the council. http://eur-lex.europa.eu/LexUriServ/site/en/oj/2004/l_390/l_39020041231en00240037. pdf. Accessed 18 September 2009

Freyer GJ (2003) Distribution of responses for limited aspect angle EME tests of equipment with structured directional directivity. Reverberation Chamber, Anechoic Chamber and OATS Users Meeting, Austin TX, April 2003

Freyer GJ (2004) Considerations for EMC testing of systems with safety and/or reliability requirements. EMC Europe, Eindhoven, Sep 6-10 2004

Freyer GJ, Hatfield MO (1998) An introduction to reverberation chambers for radiated emission/immunity testing. The Interference Technol Eng Master (ITEM) 1998, pp 86-95

IEC (2000) ISO/IEC 61508 Functional safety of electrical/electronic/programmable electronic safety related systems, Parts 1 to 7. International Electrotechnical Commission

IEC (2002) IEC 60721 Classification of environmental conditions. International Electrotechnical Commission

IEC (2004) IEC 61511 Functional safety - Safety instrumented systems for the process industry sector. International Electrotechnical Commission

IEC (2005) IEC 62061 Safety of machinery - Functional safety of safety-related electrical, electronic and programmable electronic control systems. International Electrotechnical Commission

IEC (2006a) IEC 60335-1 Consolidated Edition 4.2 Household and similar electrical appliances - Safety - Part 1: General requirements. International Electrotechnical Commission

IEC (2006b) IEC 61000-4 Electromagnetic compatibility (EMC). International Electrotechnical Commission

IEC (2008) IEC TS 61000-1-2, Ed.2.0 Electromagnetic Compatibility (EMC) – Part 1-2: General – Methodology for the achievement of the functional safety of electrical and electronic equipment with regard to electromagnetic phenomena. International Electrotechnical Commission

IET (2008) Electromagnetic compatibility for functional safety: IET 2008 guide on EMC for functional safety. The Institution of Engineering and Technology. http://www.theiet.org/factfiles/emc/index.cfm. Accessed 17 September 2009

ISO (2007) ISO 14971, Medical Devices – Application of risk management to medical devices. International Organization for Standardization

ISO (2009) ISO/DIS 26262, Road vehicles – Functional safety. International Organization for Standardization

Jansson L, Bäckström M (1999) Directivity of equipment and its effect on testing in mode-stirred and anechoic chamber. IEEE Intl EMC Symp, Seattle

Mardiguian M (2000) Combined effects of several, simultaneous, EMI couplings. IEEE Intl EMC Symp, Washington DC pp 181-184

MoD (2007) Defence Standard 59-411 Electromagnetic Compatibility, Part 1. Ministry of Defence

Parker WH, Tustin W. Masone T (2002) The case for combining EMC and environmental testing. The Interference Technol Eng Master (ITEM) 2002, pp 54-60

Rajamäki J (2004) Correlations between EMI statistics and EMC market surveillance in Finland. IEEE Intl EMC Symp, Santa Clara pp 649-654

RTCA (2007) RTCA/DO-160F Environmental conditions and test procedures for airborne equipment, Section 20, Radio Frequency Susceptibility (Radiated and Conducted)

Schrader T et al (2009) On-site EMC testing and interference prevention. IEEE Intl EMC Symp, Austin

Sjögren L, Bäckström M (2005) Ageing of shielding joints: shielding performance and corrosion. IEEE EMC Society Newsletter, www.ieee.org/organizations/pubs/newsletters/emcs/summer05/practical.pdf. Accessed 21 September 2009

Townsend DA, Pavlasek TJF, Segal BN (1995) Breaking all the rules: challenging the engineering and regulatory precepts of electromagnetic compatibility. IEEE Int Symp on EMC, Atlanta pp 194-199

Vick R, Habiger E (1997) The dependence of the immunity of digital equipment on the hardware and software structure. Proc Int Symp EMC, Beijing pp 383-386

Wang K, Pommerenke D, Chundru R et al (2004) Characterization of human metal ESD reference discharge event and correlation of generator parameters to failure levels — Part II: Correlation of generator parameters to failure levels. IEEE Trans EMC 46:505-511

Wendsche S, Habiger E (1996) Using reinforcement learning methods for effective EMC immunity testing of computerised equipment. Proc Intl Symp EMC (ROMA'96), Rome pp 221-226

Code of Practice and Competencies for ISAs

Steve Kinnersly[1] and Ian Spalding[2]

[1]ESR Technology, Warrington, UK

[2]Praxis High Integrity Systems, Bath, UK

Abstract Independent safety assessment is widely used as a means of obtaining assurance of safety for safety related systems. Experience of both Independent Safety Assessors (ISAs) and users of ISAs, together with growing appreciation of the responsibilities and potential liabilities of ISAs, suggested that there would be safety assurance and other benefits from identifying good practice for ISAs. A voluntary Code of Practice for Independent Safety Assessors (ISAs), together with a supporting Competency Framework for ISAs, has therefore been developed by the ISA Working Group of the Institution of Engineering and Technology (IET) and the British Computer Society (BCS).

The Code of Practice consists of ten requirements and associated amplification and guidance. They address both technical and non-technical aspects of ISA work. The competence requirement is developed in the Competency Framework for ISAs. Both the Code of Practice and the Competency Framework are intended to be practical tools appropriate for wide adoption across the many technical disciplines and domains in which ISAs work. The ISA Working Group encourages their pragmatic use to help establish good practice in ISA work and discourages their use as checklists for formal compliance.

This paper describes the scope and content of the Code of Practice and Competency Framework together with examples of how they can be used by users and employers of ISAs as well as by ISAs themselves.

1 Introduction

Independent safety assessment is widely used as a means of providing confidence that a system will deliver the necessary level of safety. The role of Independent Safety Assessor (ISA) – not necessarily with that name – has become established as that of an individual who has personal responsibility for the independent assessment and the associated safety judgements. An ISA therefore carries personal and professional responsibility for the independent assessment.

C. Dale, T. Anderson (eds.), *Making Systems Safer*, DOI 10.1007/978-1-84996-086-1_13,
© Springer-Verlag London Limited 2010

As the role of ISA developed and evolved over the last decade it became clear, both to users of ISAs and to ISAs themselves, that there was a need for clarification and guidance in a number of areas. For example:

- Should an ISA be able to give advice to a client?
- What should an ISA do if they think that their assessments are being ignored?
- How can a client know that an ISA is competent to do the job?

Furthermore, the clarification and guidance should be consistent across industries and applications. The ISA Working Group of the Institution of Engineering and Technology (IET) and the British Computer Society (BCS) therefore undertook to produce a professional Code of Practice for ISAs (IET 2009a) supported by a Competency Framework for Independent Safety Assessors (ISAs) (IET 2009b). The Code of Practice was issued in December 2008. At the time of writing, the Competency Framework has just completed its public consultation period and is undergoing final revision.

Both the Code of Practice and Competency Framework are considered to be good practice and consistent with the use of independent safety assessment in safety standards such as Def Stan 00-56 and IEC 61508. Both are voluntary. However, it is hoped and intended that they will be used by ISAs and users of ISAs as a basis for ensuring that their responsibilities and reasonable expectations are met.

2 What is an ISA?

An Independent Safety Assessor (ISA) is a person, separate and independent from any system design, development or operational personnel, who is required to form a judgement in respect of the safety of the system. The ISA provides an important contribution to the safety assurance of the system in that their safety judgements are impartial and independent of any vested interest in the system.

An ISA is an individual but may be supported by a team. Typically, an ISA will assess whether the safety requirements for the system are appropriate and adequate for the planned application and that the system satisfies those safety requirements. A more limited scope may sometimes be specified, however, particularly if the assessment is a contribution to a wider scope assessment for a large, complex system.

This definition of ISA deliberately embraces a number of other terms that are used for this role. For example:

- Independent Safety Auditor as used by the UK Ministry of Defence (MoD) when their scope of work is actually that of an assessor (with audit being just one of a number of possible assessment activities).
- Functional Safety Assessor as used in the standard IEC 61508 for a person required to carry out independent assessment of safety within the scope of the standard (i.e. functional safety).

However, the definition excludes 'Independent Safety Adviser' since their advice is likely to preclude them from being sufficiently independent in respect of forming a judgement about safety.

Various degrees of independence are possible. At one end of the spectrum is a person from a separate organisation, at the other end is somebody from the same organisation but not involved in the project. Standards usually lay down the degree of independence required to comply with the standard. In general, the degree of independence required should increase with the complexity and novelty of the system and the risks that it poses.

The role of ISA is associated with a specific person, not a role or organisation. The ISA therefore carries personal responsibility for their judgements. This will, however, typically be within a contractual framework. For example, there may be both a contract between the client and the ISA's employer and the ISA's contract of employment. The legal liabilities of an individual ISA are a topic of current debate.

3 ISA Working Group

The ISA Working Group (WG) was set up in order to develop and promote the role of the ISA as a safety professional. It is affiliated to the IET and BCS and is subject to the direction of the Inter-Institutional Group on Health and Safety. Membership includes ISAs working in a wide range of industries, academics and representatives from the Health and Safety Executive (HSE), MoD, the Safety Assessment Federation (SAFed), CASS Scheme Ltd, IET and BCS.

The aims of the ISA Working Group are:

- To promote the ISA role of a safety professional as a means of providing independent safety assurance to the supplier, purchaser and user
- To promote the ISA role of a safety professional in standards
- To support safety professional development by defining minimum standards, identifying training that meets minimum standards, and supporting resources
- To provide support for professional ISA's by developing guidance and providing information that affects their role.

The activities and outputs of the ISA WG include:

- Support for professional development and conduct

  - Code of Practice
  - ISA Competency Guidelines
  - Training requirements

- Promoting good practice

  - Guidance Notes

   – Seminars

- Useful information for ISAs

   – List of standards and related documents useful to ISAs
   – ISA Frequently Asked Questions (FAQs)

- ISA input to other safety activities

   – Comments on draft standards and other relevant documents

The ISA WG maintains web pages that give information about its work and from which its documented outputs can be downloaded. The web pages are hosted by the IET at http://www.theiet.org/publicaffairs/panels/isa/index.cfm.

The ISA WG welcomes questions and comments on any matter relating to independent safety assessment, including the Code of Practice and ISA Competency Guidelines. Contact details are available via the web pages.

4 Code of Practice for ISAs

4.1 Why a Code of Practice?

The Code of Practice for ISAs was developed to address a number of issues that had arisen involving the use of ISAs. The most significant were:

- The particular professional responsibilities and potential liabilities carried by ISAs
- To assist users of ISA services in selecting an appropriate ISA
- To ensure that both ISAs and users of their services have a common understanding of the scope, responsibilities and limitations of the ISA role
- To ensure that employers understand and accept the professional responsibilities of their employees who undertake ISA work.

Codes of Practice of Professional Bodies whose members may carry out independent safety assessments provide for an appropriate level of general professional conduct. However, the particular professional responsibilities carried by ISAs were considered to warrant a Code of Practice in which these were explicitly addressed. Furthermore, the ISA WG noted that not everybody who carries out independent safety assessments is necessarily a member of a Professional Body.

4.2 Scope

The Code of Practice addresses three broad areas:

- Responsibilities in respect of safety
- Personal attributes and competence required for ISA work
- Responsibilities to the client.

The prime responsibility of an ISA is to form independent, authoritative safety judgements based on information relevant to the safety of the system. The personal attributes and competencies needed to form such judgements are clearly important. Equally important, however, are the relationship and interactions between ISA and client. An open and trusting relationship facilitates the assessment process, access to information and the mutually satisfactory resolution of any issues raised by the ISA. This triangular relationship between ISA, client and the system being assessed is shown in Figure 1.

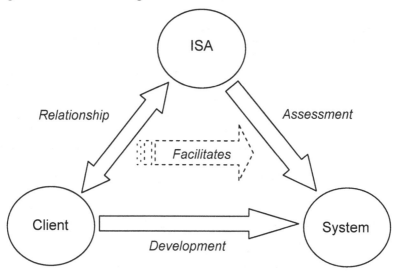

Fig. 1. The Triangular Relationship Between ISA, System and Client

4.3 Requirements and Guidance

4.3.1 Requirements

The Code of Practice includes ten requirements together with amplification and guidance to help in using the requirements. The requirements are given in Table 1 and shall always be followed.

Table 1. Requirements of the Code of Practice for ISAs

1. General professional conduct	The conduct of the ISA shall be consistent with the practices embodied in the Code of Practice of a relevant professional body.
2. Independence	The ISA shall ensure that there is nothing that might affect or call into question their ability to carry out an impartial assessment or to make impartial judgements regarding safety.
3. Competence	The ISA shall be demonstrably competent to undertake the assessment activities, to make judgements regarding safety and to communicate effectively the results of their work.
4. Communication	All formal communication regarding safety that is made by the ISA shall be clear, timely, objective and documented and shall distinguish fact and evidence from opinion and judgement.
5. Proportionality	The ISA's assessment rigour shall be in proportion to the safety risk assessed.
6. Advice	The ISA may only provide advice if it is clear that it cannot compromise their independence
7. Integrity	The ISA shall ensure that their judgements regarding safety are not influenced by inappropriate pressures or other factors.
8. Priority of Safety	The ISA shall seek to ensure that safety is given due priority.
9. Escalation	The ISA shall make best endeavours to ensure that the safety implications for the operation of the system are made known to appropriate persons or organisations that have responsibilities for its safety.
10. Management and Planning	The ISA shall ensure that the ISA work programme is planned and managed so that it delivers the required outputs when needed and minimises disruption or delay to the client project or programme.

4.3.2 Amplification and Guidance

Amplification and guidance consists of a small number of points associated with each requirement which it is expected will be followed unless there is good reason why they cannot or should not be. The amplification and guidance for a requirement addresses points that the ISA WG considered as likely to be encountered by an ISA in applying the requirement. It is neither intended nor expected to be complete. It may be modified or extended in the light of experience of using the Code of Practice; Examples of amplification and guidance (for Requirements 6 and 8) are given in Table 2.

Table 2. Examples of Amplification and Guidance

Requirement	Amplification and Guidance
6. Advice The ISA may only provide advice if it is clear that it cannot compromise their independence.	a. Customers and projects often seek advice or guidance from the ISA but this could compromise independence. b. The ISA should only offer advice or guidance that is general, not specific to the system under development and such as would be given to any broadly similar project. Examples of advice which could be given include safety management process best practice, guidance on the interpretation of standards and the consequences of specific technology choices. Examples of advice which should not be given include which design option should be taken, what technology to use and specific mitigations for hazards.
8. Priority of Safety The ISA shall seek to ensure that safety is given due priority.	a. Safety should always be the top priority for the ISA. b. When the ISA considers that safety is not being given sufficient priority or is not addressed adequately, the ISA should make best endeavours to ensure that the information is communicated to all appropriate parties, giving their reasons. c. If the ISA identifies a safety issue that is outside their remit, they should ensure that appropriate persons are notified.

4.3.3 Competence and Personal Attributes

Some of the requirements of the Code of Practice imply that an ISA needs to have certain competencies and personal attributes. They relate to the ISA being able to carry out their work effectively and providing the level of safety assurance that is the reason for them being employed in the first place.

Technical competence is obviously needed, but an ISA also needs to be able to recognise when they are not competent to make a safety assessment. The necessary technical competencies are not always clear at the start of the work and the competent/not competent boundary can be a grey area requiring careful judgement and personal integrity. An ISA also needs to be competent in planning and managing their work within the context of the overall system development activity.

Personal attributes implied by the Code of Practice include:

- Able to form sound, convincing judgements
- Communicates clearly and effectively
- Will not allow themselves to be influenced by inappropriate pressures or other factors
- Able to pursue issues to resolution while maintaining an effective working relationship with client staff at all levels.

All of these attributes are essential for an ISA but not necessarily for other safety roles, e.g. safety analyst. They are a major reason why being an ISA is not for everybody.

4.3.4 Responsibilities to the Client

The Code of Practice recognises that an ISA has important responsibilities to their client beyond simply carrying out a technically competent, independent safety assessment. Five of the ten requirements of the Code of Practice address specific responsibilities relating to the client. These are:

Communication. The client needs to understand clearly any safety concerns that the ISA may have and to be informed without undue delay. The Code of Practice requires (Requirement 4) formal communication from the ISA to be clear and timely and (Requirement 3) for the ISA to be demonstrably competent in communicating effectively the results of their work.

Advice. Clients often ask their ISA for advice. The ISA does after all have a lot of experience in safety (or they should not be an ISA!) which may benefit the client's project. The Code of Practice recognises that it is not unreasonable for a client to ask for and receive advice from an ISA. It must, however, be clear that any advice given cannot compromise the independence of the ISA (Requirement 6).

Escalation. Responsibility for safe operation of a system lies with the end user, not the ISA. An ISA might, however, have safety concerns which they believe are not reaching the relevant person or organisation. The ISA has a professional responsibility to try to ensure that the relevant person or organisation does know of and understand their concerns. This could be particularly contentious for their client. The Code of Practice recognises the ISA's responsibility for escalating safety concerns (Requirement 9) but guidance makes clear that this must be done responsibly and within the wider context of applicable Codes of Practice of relevant Professional Bodies.

Management and planning. The client's project will usually have timescales and delivery dates that must be met; failure to do so can be damaging for the client. The Code of Practice recognises the importance of project timescales and the potential for ISA work to disrupt or delay the client's project. It therefore requires ISAs to manage and plan their work so as to deliver outputs when needed and minimise disruption or delay (Requirement 10).

4.4 Status of the Code of Practice

The Code of Practice is considered by the ISA Working Group to be good practice in respect of the professional conduct of ISAs. Its use is entirely voluntary, in the absence of any scheme for ISA registration or regulation. Rather, as good practice it can be held up as a benchmark for ISA conduct as and when appropriate. Examples include:

- Development of personal attributes and skills for persons wishing to become ISAs
- Procurement of ISA services (adherence to the Code of Practice may be included in contractual requirements)
- Marketing ISA services (adherence to the Code of Practice being an indicator of the quality of the services being offered)
- Resolution of disputes (informal as well as formal) between an ISA and the client.

The Code of Practice is a stand-alone code. It does not require adherence to any other specific Code of Practice. This was considered important by the ISA Working Group as it was intended from the outset to apply to and be usable by all persons who may carry out ISA work, whether or not they belong to a relevant Professional Body. However, the Code of Practice makes clear that a standard of general professional conduct equivalent to that required by relevant Professional Bodies is necessary. The ISA Code of Practice builds on, does not replace or negate and is intended to be consistent with such conduct. An ISA who is a member of a relevant Professional Body is expected to comply with the code of practice of that body.

5 Competency Framework for ISAs

5.1 Background

One of the key requirements of the Code of Practice is that 'The ISA shall be demonstrably competent to undertake the assessment activities, to make judgements regarding safety and to communicate effectively the results of their work' (Requirement 3 'Competence'). The Code of Practice provides some basic guidance to help the ISA in determining their competence. However, this guidance is necessarily at a high level and the ISA Working Group felt that this should be expanded by means of a Competency Framework for Independent Safety Assessors to provide a set of competency criteria for ISAs and an outline process for using the criteria. It should be emphasized that this is a Framework and not an exhaustive checklist; the latter is not considered appropriate for the nature of the ISA role. It is not the intent of the ISA WG to require a bureaucratic process which adds little value.

This Competency Framework is aimed at:

- organisations who wish to procure the services of an ISA or need to know that an ISA is competent
- individuals who wish to become an ISA or develop their skills as an ISA or need to document their skills as an ISA
- regulators or those who are assessing ISAs.

At the time of writing, the Competency Framework has recently completed its public consultation period and is undergoing final revision. This paper is based on the public consultation version. However, it is not expected that there will be substantive changes in the final version.

5.2 Source Material

In order to determine the types of competency and specific competency criteria, the ISA Working Group reviewed a number of standards which included the following:

- One of the key documents defining safety related competencies is the IET/BCS 'Competence Criteria for Safety Related Practitioners' (IET 2007) (also known as the Blue Book). This contains competencies which are intended to cover the range of an organisation's safety-related activities and includes fifteen criteria specifically aimed at ISAs. The aim is that the competencies specified can be selected on a pick and mix basis to adapt to specific industry requirements and to match particular job requirements. However, whilst it was considered that the ISA competencies provided were a good starting point, ISAs are generally required to have a broader set of skills than just the fifteen provided. Therefore more guidance needed to be provided to help select both from the ISA competencies and the remaining competencies.
- The railway industry uses a set of competency requirements which Network Rail use in their accreditation of ISAs. Although these contain many competency criteria aimed specifically at assessing railway signalling, rolling stock and associated systems, they also contain many general criteria covering the safety lifecycle and conduct of the audit and assessment activities. However, the criteria are not generally available outside the rail industry, but provided a useful checklist.
- In the defence industry, the 'MoD Guidance for Integrated Project Teams for Use in Contracting for Independent Safety Auditor (ISA) Services' (MoD 2007) contains criteria covering technical, auditing and behavioural competence (noting as mentioned previously in this paper that auditing covers assessment as well). It also provides a brief outline for assessing the competence of ISAs during procurement. However, the criteria are generally phrased at a high level and it was felt more detail would be necessary.
- The IEC 61508 standard, Functional safety of electrical/electronic/programmable electronic safety-related systems (IEC 1998) lists various factors which

should be considered when assessing the competence of those who carry out functional safety assessment, but these are at a high level.

In addition, the HSE/IET/BCS guidance document 'Managing Competence for Safety-related Systems' (HSE 2007) (also known as the Red Book) and its associated supplementary material were consulted, as this defines a general framework for producing a Competency Management System and also suggests using competency categories covering technical skills, behavioural skills, knowledge and understanding.

The framework for assessing ISA competency did not want to repeat existing guidance for the development of a competency management scheme and so just refers readers to the Red Book.

5.3 Types of Competence

After analysing the competency categories in the source material, the ISA Working Group defined the following types of competence which mapped best onto the various standards:

1. Technical competence:

   a) Safety and technical skills cover the techniques and methods used to determine and analyse safety issues of importance and to make a judgement on the safety of a system, e.g. performing HAZOPs, risk assessment
   b) Understanding of the principles and concepts of safety and safety management, e.g. criteria such as ALARP for accepting risk
   c) Assessment and auditing skills, e.g. document review, process audits and independent analyses
   d) General skills, e.g. documenting findings

2. Behavioural competence covers the qualities and attributes of behaviour and character needed to perform the role of an ISA effectively, e.g. making a judgement
3. Knowledge:

   a) Safety or engineering knowledge of the domain, system, application area or technology
   b) Legal and safety regulatory framework, standards, guidelines or codes of practice
   c) Experience of other systems engineering disciplines, e.g. software, human factors

Using the above framework it was then possible to define in more detail competency categories with examples of the competencies. Table 3 is an extract from the full framework and does not include all the examples from the full framework.

Table 3. Examples of Competencies from the Competency Framework

Competency types	Sub-types	Competencies	Examples
Technical skills	Safety and technical skills	Knowledge and experience of the techniques and methods used to determine and analyse safety issues of importance and to make a judgement on the safety of a system	Examples include: • Safety Planning • Performing HAZOPs • Compiling a Safety Case
	Understanding	Understanding the principles and concepts of safety and safety management appropriate to the domain	Examples include: • Risk management, criteria for accepting risk (e.g. ALARP)
	Assessment or auditing skills	Knowledge and experience of the specific activities performed as part of a Safety Assessment and Audit (e.g. document review, process audits and independent analyses)	Examples include: • ISA Planning • Assessing safety evidence, including collecting and analysing objective evidence to support a judgement about the safety of the system • Performing Safety Audits, including formal process audits against relevant standards, plans, etc. • Specific safety assessment competencies, including Assessment of Safety Cases
	General skills	General competencies that are not particular to carrying out assessments or audits but which may be expected in carrying out a successful assessment	Examples of relevant skills: • Document findings including producing formal ISA Reports
Behavioural skills		Attributes of conduct and character needed to perform the role of ISA effectively	Examples include: • Making a judgement • Not being inappropriately influenced

Competency types	Sub-types	Competencies	Examples
Knowledge	Domain, system, application or technology	Engineering or safety engineering knowledge and experience appropriate to the application area or technology	Typically competencies that may be relevant include: • Technology areas such as embedded real-time systems • Domain specific knowledge such as Signalling Systems • Domain specific lifecycles and procedures (such as nuclear disposal, airworthiness)
	Standards	Knowledge and experience of the legal and safety regulatory framework Knowledge and experience of specific standards, guidelines or codes of practice	An example of legislation includes: • Health and Safety at Work etc Act 1974 Regulatory frameworks include: • Nuclear Installations Inspectorate – Safety Assessment Principles for Nuclear Facilities 2006 Examples of standards and guidance include: • IEC 61508 (General) • Def Stan 00-56 (Defence)
	Engineering and other functions	Experience of other systems engineering disciplines appropriate to the system	Examples of systems engineering disciplines include: • Systems • Human Factors • Software • Hardware Examples of other general disciplines include: • Assessing competency

Where additional guidance exists for the competency category then the full framework points to where this is available, i.e. the framework does not repeat existing guidance. In the majority of cases this points to the competency definitions contained in the IET/BCS Blue Book. For example:

Behavioural skills. Making a judgement points to the specific competency 'ISA7 Forming a judgement'.

Safety and technical skills. Performing HAZOPS points to the general set of competencies contained in 'HRA Safety Hazard and Risk Analysis'.

Engineering and other functions. Software points to the general set of competencies contained in 'Safety-related System Software Realisation'

From the list provided in the framework, it can therefore be seen that the competencies required of an ISA may be wider than just the specific competencies contained in the ISA section of the Blue Book and could include technical skills such as Project Safety Assurance Management, Safety Validation, and engineering disciplines such as Safety-related System Software Realisation.

5.4 Levels of Competency

It is normal to achieve different levels of competency as an individual progresses in their career. Typically these stages of increasing levels of competency are characterised by:

- Awareness of the principles and knowledge of technologies and practices
- Transfer of the knowledge to new applications and new domains
- Being able to carry out the tasks effectively in many different real world situations.

A scheme such as the Blue Book builds on the above and defines three levels of competency. The following summaries the definitions of these levels:

Supervised Practitioner. Has sufficient knowledge and understanding of best practice of the organisation or relevant industry sector to be able to work on the tasks under the supervision of a practitioner or expert.

Practitioner. Has sufficient knowledge and understanding of best practice and demonstrated experience to be able to work on the tasks without supervision; will maintain their knowledge and be aware of current developments in the context of their work.

Expert. Has sufficient understanding of why things are done, is familiar with the ways systems have failed in the past, keeps abreast of technologies, architectures, standards etc, and is able to work in novel situations.

Thus for the particular assessment or auditing skill of Performing a Safety Audit, the relevant guidance in the Blue Book is 'ISA4 Safety Auditing' and this has three levels of competence defined for Supervised Practitioner, Practitioner and Expert.

6 Putting it into Practice

6.1 The ISA Code of Practice in Procurement

6.1.1 The Procuring Organisation

The Code of Practice and the Competency Framework play complementary roles in procuring the services of an ISA. The Code of Practice helps to ensure that an ISA is chosen who will do the job right in all its aspects. An organisation seeking to procure the services of an ISA may wish to limit their use of ISAs to those who declare adherence to the Code of Practice. They can also include compliance with the Code of Practice as a condition of an ISA contract.

Two points should be noted, however, when using the Code of Practice during procurement. Firstly, the Code of Practice applies to an individual (the ISA) rather than an organization. However, it is very unlikely that an organization offering ISA services would be able to be considered a fit and proper organization for ISA services if they did not take their responsibilities as implied by the Code of Practice seriously.

Secondly, some of the requirements of the Code of Practice relate to things that the ISA can reasonably expect of the client. For instance, the client should not expect the ISA to provide advice that might compromise their independence. When an organisation is requiring an ISA to comply with the Code of Practice, they should also ensure that other relevant people involved in the project (e.g. Project Manager; Safety Manager) are aware of their implied responsibilities under the Code of Practice and adhere to them.

6.1.2 The ISA

Where adherence to the Code of Practice is required by a procuring organisation, it is clearly necessary to indicate acceptance of this in a response to the procurement request. A simple statement that the ISA will comply with the Code of Practice would be a compliant response. However, the Code of Practice deals in broad principles and the ISA should seek to show that they understand the implications of the Code of Practice for the specific project.

For instance, Requirement 5 'Proportionality' states 'The ISA's assessment rigour shall be in proportion to the safety risk assessed.' As well as making a simple statement that this will be the case, a more complete response would include an explanation of how proportionality will be applied in the specific project. In addition, where different degrees of rigour will be applied during the project, there could be an explanation of what each degree of rigour would entail.

Similarly, Requirement 10 'Management and Planning' states 'The ISA shall ensure that the ISA work programme is planned and managed so that it delivers the required outputs when needed and minimises disruption or delay to the client project or programme.' As well as noting the ISA work programme will be 'planned and managed so that it delivers…', a more complete response would include an explanation of how the planning and management will be carried out so as to deliver the required outputs when needed and minimise disruption or delay to the client project or programme. This should address the specific project, in particular taking into account the project work programme, timescales and priorities.

6.2 The Competency Framework in Procurement

6.2.1 The Procuring Organisation

There is an implied responsibility on a procuring organization to understand and define the ISA competencies required for fulfilment of the ISA's activities. Use of the Competency Framework can help to define the necessary competencies at an appropriate level. The starting point is necessarily to describe the main characteristics of the system and what has to be assessed: an ISA may, after all, be thoroughly competent in respect of one type of system but not another. For example, the system characteristics may describe aspects covering novelty, complexity, criticality, software-intensive, method of operation, and technology, and the development characteristics may cover the safety management and engineering processes, documentation to be produced, and acceptance process.

As with use of any framework, care and judgement need to be exercised to ensure that the requirements are not overly proscriptive or onerous and are proportionate to the task being undertaken. Once the system is adequately described, which may require several iterations with potential experts, the procurer may select the more detailed competency requirements using the competency categories in the Competency Framework (IET 2009b Table 1 'Competency Categories') and associated examples. The procurer needs to decide how detailed they wish to be in defining competency requirements. One possibility is to identify detailed competency requirements for the ISA. Alternatively, only high-level competencies might be identified and prospective ISAs asked to interpret the competencies in respect of the system. For procurement, it is not usual to specify competencies covering behaviour.

So, as an example, a signalling renewals project is providing processor based interlocking which will include the XXX axle counter detection system. The line side power supply system will be renewed with YYY and the telecommunications will be supplied by ZZZ. ISA services are required for the XXX axle counter application safety case and supporting documents and the scope of the safety case covers the safety engineering activities required to satisfy railway standard ABCD. The actual remit would, of course provide far more detail. The procurer would then require that the ISA shall provide competencies in the relevant areas of safety engineering (which could be listed in detail or at a high level depending on how much flexibility the procurer wanted to give the ISA in responding), signalling and control systems with a detailed knowledge of the application of XXX. The core ISA team should be supplemented by specialists in railway operation, power, telecoms, rolling stock, EMC and human factors depending on the documents to be assessed.

Once prospective ISAs have provided evidence of competency, the procurer should then analyse the responses and, if required, check any competency claims against information held in CVs, training records or qualifications. If necessary, they may audit this evidence, e.g. through interviews of ISAs.

6.2.2 The ISA

Prospective ISAs can respond using the competency table as guidance and provide evidence to demonstrate the competencies are met. This evidence should be based on training, qualifications and experience. In the above example, the ISA should ensure that all the relevant safety engineering activities have adequate competency coverage which as a minimum would probably cover safety planning, safety requirements capture, performing HAZOPS, risk assessment, safety requirements validation and compiling a safety case. Consideration would also be given to including one or more safety audits and, hence, relevant auditing competency would be appropriate.

In many cases, the Independent Safety Assessment is likely to be carried out by a team and so the team as a whole must provide the necessary level of competence. However, there should always be one individual who has overall responsibility for the conduct of the assessment, known as the Lead ISA. This person should have a higher level of competency together with a defined number of years experience in the domain area as an ISA or a relevant qualification such as Chartered Engineer.

The competency of the ISA (individual or team) should be justified in writing, for instance in an ISA Plan. Thus, the ISA should demonstrate that the overall competency is sufficient to match the ISA competency requirements for the system being assessed.

6.3 Developing ISA Competency in an Organisation

The Code of Practice and Competency framework can be used by organisations to help develop ISA services as part of their business.

The Code of Practice is a suitable starting point for:

- a policy on ISA services
- identifying persons with the necessary personal attributes for being an ISA (and equally important, who is not suited to being an ISA)
- ISA development and training.

The Code of Practice applies to individuals so an organization should encourage their ISAs to both understand and put into practice the ten requirements of the Code. This can be monitored through the organisation's normal staff development process.

Having established the Code of Practice as the basis for ISA work in an organisation, the Competency Framework can then be used to develop specific competencies for the areas in which the organization works. In particular, it needs to ensure that their competency matches the main characteristics of the systems which are the focus of its business. The organisation should be able, using the competency categories in the Competency Framework table, to select the more detailed competency requirements using the examples from column 4, adding additional categories where necessary. To these should be added competencies covering behaviour.

For example, an organisation supplying ISAs in the naval defence industry may have particular domain experience of naval maritime operations and systems, knowledge of hazards associated with naval ship operations and their consequences, and knowledge of the relevant defence standards. These should be reflected in the competency matrix.

It is also usual to define the level of competency as discussed previously. For the majority of categories, the Blue Book guidance can be used. Where levels do not exist (e.g. for particular domain knowledge not covered by the Blue Book), then the organisation will have to define its own.

Each ISA in the organisation should provide evidence to demonstrate that their required competencies are met based on training, qualifications and experience. The organisation should then review these to ensure that the documented achievements in such sources as an individual's CV, training records and qualifications can substantiate the competency claims.

Once the organisation has built up its competency matrix, it is then easier to respond to a procurer's requests. Also any gaps can be identified and addressed through organisational development or recruitment.

6.4 Individual Competency

Once an organisation has established competency requirements together with defined levels of competency, an individual ISA can ascertain how to progress from one competency level to the next, or to add new competency categories at the same level, by identifying the required experience, training or qualifications as necessary.

If an organisation does not already have an ISA competency scheme, then a good starting point would be for the individual to assess themselves against the Blue Book ISA requirements (ISA1-ISA15). Once the basic ISA skills have been determined, then additional safety and technical skills, knowledge categories (such as software or human factors) or standards can be added.

A similar process could be used for an individual wishing to become an ISA.

7 Conclusions

A voluntary Code of Practice for ISAs and a supporting Competency Framework for ISAs have been developed by the ISA Working Group of the IET and BCS. They apply to anyone who is required to form an independent judgement in respect of the safety of a system, whether or not they are called an ISA. Together, they address significant issues that have arisen in the use of independent safety assessment over the last decade or so. They cover not just the technical aspects of independent safety assessment but also – and importantly – the non-technical aspects including the relationship and mutual expectations between an ISA and the system developer.

The Code of Practice and Competency Framework are 'good practice'. They can be used by ISAs, users of ISAs, regulators and others as a basis for ensuring that independent safety assessment is carried out to an appropriately high level of professional competence. Their pragmatic use to help establish good practice in ISA work is encouraged; their use as checklists for formal compliance is discouraged. Use of the Code of Practice and Competency Framework will help to ensure that independent safety assessment delivers the degree of safety assurance that is both sought and needed from ISAs.

References

HSE (2007) Managing competencies for safety related systems, Parts 1 and 2. Health and Safety Executive

IEC (1998) IEC 61508 Functional safety of electrical/electronic/programmable electronic safety-related systems, Part 1. International Electrotechnical Commission

IET (2007) Competency criteria for safety-related system practitioners. The Institution of Engineering and Technology. http://www.theiet.org/publishing/books/policy/comp-crit.cfm. Accessed 6 October 2009

IET (2009a) Code of practice for independent safety assessors. The Institution of Engineering and Technology. http://www.theiet.org/publicaffairs/panels/isa/isa-code2008.cfm?type=pdf. Accessed 6 October 2009

IET (2009b) Competency framework for independent safety assessors. The Institution of Engineering and Technology. http://www.theiet.org/publicaffairs/panels/isa/isa-comp-frame.cfm?type=pdf. Accessed 6 October 2009

MoD (2004) Guidance for integrated project teams for use in contracting for independent safety auditor (ISA) services. STG/181/1/9/1 Version 1. Ministry of Defence

Safety Methods

Evaluation and Integration of COTS in Evidence based Assurance Frameworks

George Despotou[1], Mike Bennett[2] and Tim Kelly[1]

[1]Department of Computer Science, University of York, UK

[2]Military Air solutions, BAE Systems, UK

Abstract   COTS have increasingly been used by industrial practice as a means of maintaining low development costs of a product, whilst offering significant capability upgrades. COTS are multipurpose products driven by commonly used functionality. However, being general purpose products raises certain challenges regarding their ability to be certified. Previously used (process-based) standards stipulated a process that the product needed to adhere to. This involved production of a generic set of evidence known as the certification pack (CertPack). Being the product of a generic test process, the available (CertPack) COTS evidence may not be sufficient or suitable to support the developers' safety claims. The challenges raised by use of COTS in such assurance frameworks can have ramifications on a project both from a managerial and safety assurance perspective. The paper presents an analysis of the challenges from the use of CertPack and their impact on assurance and project management. Moreover a process is presented that assists de-risking the integration of evidence, as early as possible during system development or upgrade.

1 Introduction

Commercial Off-The-Shelf (COTS) components are multipurpose products driven by commonly used functionality. They are applied to many domains and are massively produced. Due to the latter their development costs are significantly reduced in comparison to custom built components offering an opportunity for great cost savings in a project. However, being general purpose products raises certain challenges regarding their ability to be certified. Previously used (process-based) standards stipulated a process that the product needed to adhere to. Application of the process described in the standard was considered a sufficient indicator for the safety of the COTS component. The process results in production of a generic set of evidence known as the certification pack (CertPack), prepared by the COTS developer (or an independent contractor that collaborates with the COTS devel-

C. Dale, T. Anderson (eds.), *Making Systems Safer*, DOI 10.1007/978-1-84996-086-1_14,
© Springer-Verlag London Limited 2010

oper), during the development of the COTS. The CertPack is often seen as a portfolio of evidence justifying the developer's confidence to use the component in a safety related system. Use of a CertPack provides similar benefits to use of a COTS component. The system developer does not carry the overhead of producing the evidence required; the CertPack will provide the evidence required by the assurance process of the system. Although a CertPack will provide a good degree of confidence regarding the reliable operation of the COTS component, it is less effective when justifying safety. The main reason for this is that a CertPack is not tested in the context of operation of the system that will use it, but in a generic environment. Hence it is often difficult for developers to relate the evidence to the hazards to a system in its operational context.

This problem is further exacerbated by the recent shift to goal-based standards (e.g. 00-56 (MoD 2005)), which require evidence explicitly demonstrating the safe operation of the system in the context of the hazards rising from its particular operation. Satisfactory integration of COTS should capture the contribution of the COTS to safety, establish claims about its safe operation, and identify how available evidence will support these claims. Being the product of a generic test process, the available (CertPack) COTS evidence may not be sufficient or suitable to support the developers' safety claims. Safety analysis will need to contribute to the assessment of evidence sufficiency and suitability and identify areas that may need to be augmented with further evidence generation. Insufficient evidence can result in compromising the originally required assurance, whereas generation of additional evidence may result in additional costs; both may be responsible for derailment of a project's monetary and timescale goals, which were the initial main motive for adoption of COTS.

A CertPack constitutes a potential risk for the safety assurance process of a system that needs to be evaluated as early as possible. Thus a preliminary evaluation of the COTS CertPack will be beneficial to the system developer. The system developer may not identify any shortcomings of the CertPack until well into the safety assurance process. At this stage rectifying the identified problems would involve alternative assurance strategies or contracting the COTS provider for customisation, both of which can prove to be costly. During preliminary evaluation of a COTS component the systems developer will be able to go through a number of potential issues, plan the assurance strategy and identify mitigation strategies.

2 Integration of the CertPack in the Safety Case

The CertPack of the COTS component will provide a source of evidence for the system's safety case. Figure 1 illustrates part of a proposed update to the BAE SYSTEMS Hawk T.Mk2 mission computer software safety case (Despotou et al. 2009), to incorporate COTS components. This safety case contains the arguments about the contribution of the COTS component to safety. The architecture of this modular safety case is intended to minimise the maintenance overhead during

COTS based upgrades. There are four argument modules contributing to the assurance of the COTS component:

1. The system – COTS safety argument
2. Safety integration assumptions
3. Architectural safety features
4. COTS product argument

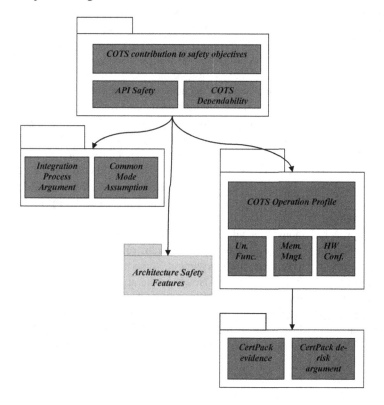

Fig. 1. Overview of the COTS related Safety Case Argument Modules

The top argument module (COTS safety argument) captures the contribution of the operation of the COTS component to the system's safety. It contains claims about the behaviour of the COTS component that was established during the safety analysis of the COTS component. These include claims that the failures identified (during safety analysis) will not affect safety. For example, that failure to call a service will be mitigated.

Such claims will then be supported by an argument about the architecture's ability to mitigate this failure (architecture safety features argument module). This depends on the assumption that the there are no common mode COTS failures of the architecture safety features, which is contained in a separate integration argument module.

The bottom right argument module assures the operation of the COTS as an independent component. This is the module assuring that the operation of the system will comply with the safety requirements. This is the argument module that will use evidence contained in the CertPack. For example, unit test evidence supporting claims about the operation of one aspect of the COTS component's functionality, such as the performance of the scheduler. This means that the argument does not contain claims relating to how it is used by the system, but claims about its behaviour, such as response time of services, and memory management, regardless of how these may affect safety, something which was established in the top argument.

Adopting a modular architecture when creating the safety case can provide advantages. Different claims in a single module can compromise the module's ability to withstand change. This happens because the argument contains both goals relating to the COTS as a standalone element, and goals relating to how the COTS is integrated and affects the safe operation of the system. Hence the argument is vulnerable to various types of change, which will require its re-evaluation and may affect how available evidence supports it. Instead, a more optimised approach would be to separate the different types of goals. This would result in an argument module about safety claims that depend on a particular context, which will rely on a COTS argument module assuring its operation, and supported by its test evidence (CertPack).

This approach demonstrates advantages when introducing a change in the design. For example a reconfiguration of the system resulting in the COTS being used differently will affect the safety argument, since the role of the component in achieving safety might have changed. However the argument assuring the operational properties of the component will remain unchanged. Similarly if the component changes the safety argument will remain unchanged. Although this is an optimised approach it does have its limitations (Despotou and Kelly 2008): depending on the degree, a change in the design will affect the validity of the safety case argument.

Figure 2 shows a more detailed view of how the argument modules are associated with each other. Each argument module contains a number of public argument elements (shaded) that can be referenced from other argument modules. Often, the rest of the reasoning contained in an argument module may not be of interest to all stakeholders. For example, the argument capturing the safety requirements for the COTS component may have been constructed by the safety analysts, whereas the argument about the COTS component's operation may be owned by the COTS integration team. This may not constitute a problem for argument modules created from different teams in the same organisation, as it is assumed easy to access another team's information. However, in the case of the COTS product argument module using CertPack evidence, the visibility of the argument may constitute a problem to assurance. This happens as, between the CertPack evidence and the COTS component's (high level) operational claims, there can be implicit or hidden reasoning. The right side of Figure 2 shows different cases of how evidence can support the COTS operation argument module.

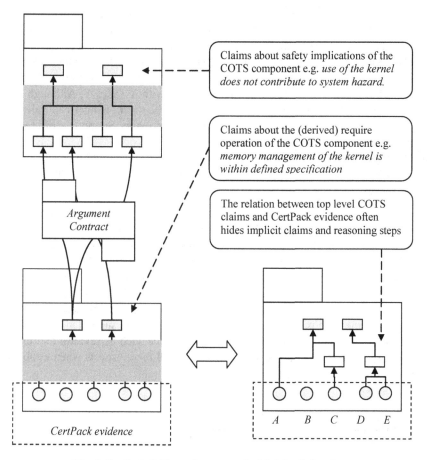

Fig. 2. CertPack Evidence Support to the Modular Safety Case

The following cases of CertPack evidence support have been identified:

1. **Direct (explicit) support (evidence A).** This includes evidence that can directly substantiate the high level claims about the COTS component.
2. **Indirect (implicit) support (evidence C).** It is unlikely that the high level claims of the COTS component are directly supported by the available evidence (evidence A). The component itself is an engineering artefact, the high level operation (e.g. the API) of which, consists of further smaller classes and modules until a level at which test cases can be applied. For example, in a COTS component the API functions consist of other internal functions which in their turn consist of individual code classes to which the majority of the available evidence corresponds. This is reflected in the argument, in which high level claims about the operation of the system are decomposed into sub-claims about the operation of the (sub-) modules, that are then supported by the available CertPack evidence.

3. **Combined support (evidence D & E).** Often, even if a piece of evidence can be directly associated with a claim (or sub-claim) it may not be able to substantiate the claims effectively on its own. For example, consider test evidence for a class covering the range value of (X, Z) (evidence D) and test evidence covering the range (Z, Y) (evidence E), supporting a claim about the correct operation of a system within range of values (X, Y), with X < Z < Y. Although both pieces of evidence are directly associated with the claim, neither can individually offer sufficient coverage to substantiate the claim. Support is offered by combining both pieces of evidence.

4. **No support (evidence B).** CertPacks are generic collections of evidence offered by the vendor. It is likely that not all evidence contained in the CertPack will be used for the argument.

Depending on how CertPack evidence is used to provide support, it may offer various degrees of assurance. Def Stan 00-56 (issue 4) (MoD 2005), provides some guidelines on what evidence is needed with relation to the required degree of assurance of a claim. For example, a claim about the operation of a system associated with a safety claim that relates to a hazard will require high assurance. Hence, in accordance to 00-56 instructions, it is expected that the claim would be supported by formal or demonstration evidence. In contrast, it can be acceptable for a claim about the quality of the development process to be supported by (what is considered in the context of 00-56) weaker evidence such as reviews and expert opinion. Integration should consider and address all these aspects when establishing system assurance using a CertPack.

3 COTS Focused Safety Analysis

Identifying the contribution of any COTS component to the system requires analysis. Figure 3 illustrates the safety analysis process that was developed during the study, designed to support the integration of software COTS components to the Hawk mission computer. The identified process consists of the following steps:

1. Identification of Component Dependencies and Operation
2. Definition of Deviations and Application of Deviation Analysis
3. Identification of Unresolved Issues and Derived Requirements
4. Examination of Suitability of Evidence
5. Modularisation of Safety Case Arguments
6. Examination of Safety Case Consistency

The first step involves identification of the dependencies between the system and the COTS component, such as functions, parameters, shared memory and shared timers and clocks. It is common for COTS to be black boxes with little visibility and access only to the interface (API) provided by the COTS developer. For this reason it was decided to perform a deviation analysis on the interfaces and the services provided by the COTS component. These two first steps result in identification of issues regarding the safety implications of the COTS component, and safety related requirements that were derived during the analysis. These requirements will eventually be expressed as claims about the COTS component in the safety case argument, and supported by the CertPack evidence. The third step involves assessment of suitability of the evidence available in the CertPack. System developers will need to identify whether the CertPack contains suitable and sufficient evidence to support these claims. *The evaluation of the CertPack described in this paper takes place in this step.* Following evaluation, the safety team of the system developer will define the skeleton of the safety case of the system aiming to create a compelling and maintainable argument (by modularising the safety case). Following specification of the envisioned safety case, the safety case will begin to be populated and the arguments developed in detail. During this process the system developer may discover that the available evidence is insufficient, in which case re-evaluation of the CertPack will be necessary.

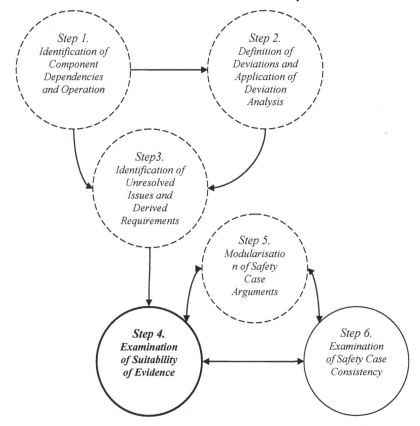

Fig. 3. Overview of the Process

The order in which the steps are applied is not strict. It has been defined having in mind the creation of a modular safety case that will enable use of COTS and reuse of evidence contained in a COTS CertPack. However, not every step will always be performed. This depends on the existence of a safety case about the system, and on whether the analysis described in certain steps has already been performed. Solid circles denote the steps that should be applied every time system stake-holders want to reuse existing evidence.

4 Evaluating CertPack Evidence

Evaluation of the CertPack should ideally take place early in a project to de-risk potential problems on assuring the final product. It may not be practicable to make a complete evaluation of the CertPack before actually purchasing it (along with the COTS component). Nevertheless, there are a number of issues that can be examined before contracting the COTS component. This process is a preliminary evaluation of the CertPack, aiming to minimise potential risks in establishing safety assurance about the system, and increase the trustworthiness of the Cert-Pack vendor. During evaluation, the system developers should understand the shortcomings of the CertPack and how these affect the assurance process. This will provide the necessary (early) input to discuss alternative assurance strategies or agree with the COTS supplier to upgrade the CertPack.

The process revolves around examination of a number of issues regarding the suitability of a CertPack. There are two categories of issues, depending on how they were derived:

1. **Immediate issues.** These are issues that were derived from attributes of assurance. For each assurance property (e.g. trustworthiness) (Weaver 2004), a number of issues (relevant to the CertPack) were identified (e.g. documentation of activities by the COTS vendor).
2. **Domain specific issues.** Domain expertise and experience is very important and can often not be replaced by theoretical frameworks. A number of issues specific to the project or the domain were described, and it was considered important for them to be addressed explicitly. An important aspect of domain specificity is the visibility of problems that other projects have encountered. This knowledge may allow developers to identify issues early during the evaluation of the CertPack that may not otherwise be considered.

Figure 4 provides an overview of the derivation and examined properties of the issues identified.

Evaluation of the CertPack involves assessment of how the issues identified may affect the assurance strategy of system developers, how the assurance process can recover from potential shortcomings, and the impact of the recovery steps on the project management. This paper focuses on discussion and presentation of the issues; managerial impact is outside the scope. Issues are specified in the form of questions that can be used during an initial interview with the CertPack vendor.

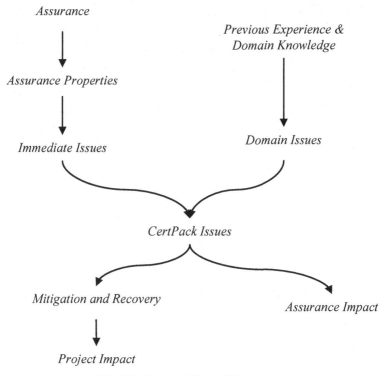

Fig. 4. Derivation of CertPack Issues

4.1 Evaluation Process

This process is intended to evaluate the CertPack, and document potential issues that may arise regarding the use of the CertPack to support the safety case. The process should be applied at the early stages of the (COTS) safety assurance process, prior to knowing the specifics of the safety case arguments. Figure 5 provides an overview of the process, the steps of which are described in subsequent sections.

4.1.1 Step 1 – Identify CertPack Issue

During this step, system analysts (or safety engineers) will examine and understand the issue on focus. Identifying its origin will assist in understanding the rationale behind examining the CertPack from that perspective. Also, the 'perform-ance' of other CertPack products with regard to this issue is identified, which will help establishing a baseline for comparing two or more different (CertPack) prod-ucts.

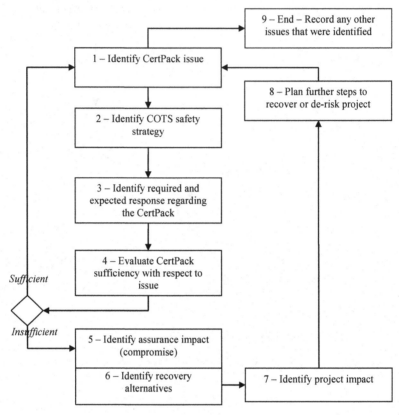

Fig. 5. Overview of the CertPack Evaluation Process

4.1.2 Step 2 – Identify COTS safety strategy

This step involves identification of the safety approach used to integrate the COTS product to the system. This will help highlight the main arguments that will be used in the safety case to assure the safety of the system. Depending on the pro-gress of the design and safety teams, the system developer's safety strategy can vary from a vision to more concrete objectives. The safety strategy for integrating the COTS component can be identified by the high level claims of the COTS safety argument module presented in Figure 1. In the case of the Hawk, in the con-text of which this study was applied, the substantiated argument claims indicate that the CertPack will need to support a number of claims about the operation and the dependability properties of the COTS component. Realising this led to the identification of the *Non Functional Requirements* issue. This included evaluation of the CertPack for sufficiency of evidence that could support certain dependability attribute claims that were identified at the early stages as being related to the COTS component (e.g. performance claims).

4.1.3 Step 3 – Identify Required and Expected Response

Based on the identified COTS safety strategy, analysts should derive requirements about how the COTS CertPack will support the COTS safety argument. One such example is performance requirements. Contrary to other types of requirements which when not met the system could provide architectural means of mitigation, achievement of performance requirements can rely entirely on the COTS. Thus there may be a need for the CertPack to encompass detailed evidence about the performance attributes of the COTS component, to support the derived (performance) requirements accordingly.

4.1.4 Step 4 – Evaluate CertPack Sufficiency with Respect to Issue

Following identification of the CertPack requirements regarding an issue, the degree to which the CertPack under analysis satisfies these requirements is evaluated. The purpose of this step is to identify aspects of the CertPack that may constitute a risk to safety assurance of the overall system. Any shortcomings of the CertPack need to be recorded and flagged. It may not always be possible to determine a degree of satisfaction of requirements accurately. The reason for this is that at his stage there can be no scale that can be used to give a metric about the CertPack. The focus should be on establishing consensus (among analysts) that the provided CertPack will not constitute a risk with regard to an issue. For example, the Non Functional Requirements issue resulted in identifying the amount of available evidence about the performance of the COTS component as potentially insufficient. At that stage a definite conclusion was not reached. It was noted that the issue should be revisited, once the COTS argument provided more concrete information about the performance related claims that need to be made.

4.1.5 Step 5 – Identify Assurance Impact (Compromise)

Once a risk has been identified, the potential impact on the communicated (by the safety case argument) assurance needs to be examined. Lack of evidence may inhibit safety analysts from adopting a safety strategy, as the argument (communicating that safety strategy) will not be supported by sufficient or suitable evidence; thus compromising system assurance. For example, the impact of not having non functional requirement evidence was considered to be substantial. The CertPack contains evidence about scheduling. However, the COTS argument identified a potential need to make specific claims about the performance of particular functions, which may not be part of the standard CertPack.

4.1.6 Step 6 – Identify Recovery Alternatives

Upon identification of the compromise a CertPack issue will have on the (effectiveness) of the safety case, analysts will need to identify recovery action. For example, in the case of non functional requirements, one recovery action could include contracting the COTS provider for further testing.

4.1.7 Step 7 – Identify Project Impact

Specifying options that will help correct the shortcomings of the CertPack will affect the cost and time required by this phase of the project. The cost and time requirements of the identified recovery alternatives need to be examined and the overhead to the entire project needs to be considered. Ideally, the alternative that will result in providing most assurance to the argument will be chosen. However, certain alternatives may be impractical or very time consuming. In such occasions a more balanced alternative may be chosen; essentially resulting in an implicit (ALARP) argument (HSE 2001) trading off assurance and cost of further assurance. This type of decision will need to be justified, clearly explaining why this is the most reasonably practicable compromise between safety assurance and cost. If not defensible, such decisions may constitute pitfalls, perceived by the regulator (or independent auditor) as weaknesses in the safety case, particularly in context of goal based standards such as 00-56.

4.1.8 Step 8 – Plan Further Steps to Recover or De-Risk Project

Selection and justification of the proper recovery alternative will be followed by planning on how it (the alternative) can be implemented. This may involve both the developers and the contractor, depending on the degree of involvement of the latter.

4.1.9 Step 9 – End – Record any other Issues that were Identified

Often, evaluating the CertPack will entail discussions that may highlight other issues about the CertPack and its suitability to support the COTS argument. These issues need to be captured for future application of the process.

4.2 CertPack Issues

A number of issues have been identified as significant to be examined during the early examination of the CertPack. These include issues identified as being pertinent to safety assurance and issues that were identified as potential risks in a previous project. The issues identified in the evaluation presented in this paper are the following:

1. Functionality scope of evidence
2. Adequacy of evidence
3. Related experience
4. Grey-box traceability
5. Failure analysis evidence
6. Evidence of absence
7. Compliance matrix
8. Traceability rationale
9. Mixed integrity evidence
10. Field evidence
11. Update process
12. Non-functional requirement
13. Tools

These are discussed in the following sections.

4.2.1 Functionality Scope of Evidence

Question. *Does the CertPack cover all functionality of the product? If so, is it all to the same level of assurance (assuming a process based standard was followed)?*

Often the CertPack consists of evidence regarding a core functionality of the COTS component. However, the COTS component may be used by the developer in a way that includes functionality outside the scope of the CertPack, such as additional functions and hardware specific drivers. For example consider a COTS operating system and I/O drivers for USB or serial, which are not included in the core of the COTS. Depending on how the COTS component is integrated to the system, this additional functionality may be a significant part of the system's safety argument. Consequently, developers will end up utilising a black box component without any evidence to support its operation.

There can be two potential alternatives that help mitigate this issue. Firstly, developers can contract the COTS provider to include in the CertPack additional evidence to cover this functionality. It should be noted that the additional evidence needs to be generated using the same rigour and processes used in the original CertPack to maintain homogeneity. Secondly, developers may opt to design and implement a wrapper layer isolating the additional functionality from the core

COTS functionality. With this approach developers can mitigate failures of the additional functionality architecturally, controlling the interfaces. However, this approach essentially results in another COTS argument (for the additional functionality), with the single assurance argument being based on architecture. Thus this will reduce the overall assurance of the system. Overall, developers should ensure that they are aware of what functionality is covered by the CertPack

Functionality scope may not always be black and white. Developers may be accessing (internal) COTS functions that are not part of the formal API. In such cases the developer should consult the COTS provider about potential implications. For example an API function may be provided using some degree of redundancy that is implemented internally. By accessing an internal (to the COTS) function, developers may bypass the provided safeguards, in the context of which the evidence is provided. In such cases new evidence will need to be generated covering the functionality scope of the developer.

4.2.2 Adequacy of Evidence

Question. *Has the adequacy of the CertPack been assessed? Has there been an independent evaluation?*

This issue examines whether the CertPack contains adequate evidence to assure the operation of the COTS component, and whether the CertPack had any evaluation previous to being released. For a CertPack developed using a process based standard, adequacy is not expected to be a risk as the evidence contained in the CertPack is stipulated by the standard. However, it should be examined whether the standard has been implemented correctly. The CertPack may not always comply with the requirements imposed by the standards.

An independent assessment of the adequacy of the CertPack evidence can provide additional assurance about the CertPack and consequently to the COTS component and the overall system. In certain cases the independent auditor may be a government organisation that will approve the use of the COTS component (e.g. FAA). This may provide opportunities to use such an organisation as the main auditor for all developers using a particular COTS component.

Alternatively, the quality team of the developer can review the CertPack. Although this will provide confidence to the developer about the adequacy of evidence, an independent auditor is more suitable for the long term assurance objectives of the system. Being part of the same company, using the quality team to audit the CertPack may undermine the final safety case of the system.

4.2.3 Related Experience

Question. Has the CertPack been used by any other customers developing a product under the same regulatory framework? If so has the COTS vendor flagged any potential risks? Were any properties singled out or it was a 'general integrity argument'.

With the introduction of goal-based standards like 00-56, developers have to focus on creating a hazard oriented argument (instead of an integrity argument), assuring the safe operation of the system. A hazard oriented argument can prove challenging as there may be cases when the available evidence cannot support a strong argument. This risk is further exacerbated when using a COTS component. Given the only recent shift to goal-based standards, any related experience the COTS providers have had can prove valuable to help identify risks at early stages of the COTS use. Moreover, even in a process-based approach there may be cases when the system developer provides additional arguments for an aspect of the COTS operation. This may happen because the developers, the regulator or the ISA identified a need for additional assurance over and above what the (process-based) standard prescribed.

4.2.4 Grey-Box Traceability

Question. Can the COTS high level requirements be traced down to individual pieces of evidence (e.g. unit test cases and results)? How easy is it to establish traceability between evidence and requirements?

An argument will eventually depend on claims about the operation (or provision of service) of the COTS components. These claims constitute the high level claims that the developer can (confidently) make about the operation of the system (e.g. scheduling claims). These are the claims ultimately supported by the evidence in the CertPack. However because the COTS component is itself a system the evidence may refer to low level components of the COTS. Hence, there may be many logical layers between the high level claims and evidence. In order to maintain confidence to the COTS components, the COTS developer should provide some sort of traceability between the high level requirements of the COTS component and the CertPack evidence. This traceability enables assessment of the degree of assurance with which the CertPack evidence supports the high level COTS behaviour.

Figure 6 illustrates an example of good traceability. The COTS component's high level requirements are decomposed to lower level requirements. The latter are eventually implemented as code classes which by collaborating provide the overall functionality. The classes are the COTS artefacts that are then tested to provide the CertPack evidence. A good CertPack should explain how the available evidence is traced to the high level requirements. This allows the system developer to understand the relationship between the evidence contained in the Cert-Pack and the high level claims that will be made about the COTS component, and evaluate the sufficiency of the available evidence.

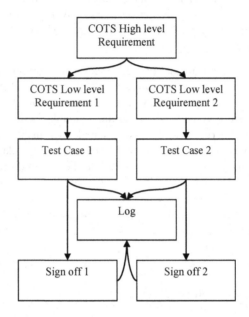

Fig. 6. Traceability between COTS Requirements and Evidence

4.2.5 Failure Analysis Evidence

Question. Is there any failure analysis evidence?

Failure analyses examine the effects of potential failures on the operation of the system. This can lead to better understanding of potential risks in the operation of the system. Moreover, it allows identification of the failures, the effect of which can propagate outside the COTS component and affect the rest of the system. A failure analysis could be used in the safety case to assure prevention or mitigation of potential failures. Given that this would happen at the COTS level it would provide additional assurance to the architectural safeguards, intended to mitigate and prevent the COTS failures.

Failure analysis evidence is not expected to be a part of the CertPack. However, during development, the COTS provider may consider a number of common issues. Ability to mitigate common exceptions will often be implemented in the COTS component. Although this is not a structured failure analysis, the widespread use of a COTS component may provide some degree of confidence that most common failures will have been identified. Nevertheless such confidence should not be misinterpreted to cover any operational context, as the system's operational context may cause unique failures. This is something anticipated as the systems that require safety assurance often operate in unique environments not covered by the majority of the COTS component's user base.

4.2.6 Evidence of Absence

Question. Is evidence all positive? Is there evidence for the absence of a negative property (e.g. failure modes?).

Usually evidence supports positive claims about the operation of the system (e.g. function X response is within 5 ms). However in safety we are also concerned with negative claims (e.g. Hazard Y does *not* occur). This question is closely related to failure analysis, as the latter is a prerequisite for the existence of evidence for the absence of a negative property. Provision of such evidence may be considered outside the responsibility of the COTS developer, particularly when a process based standard has been followed. However, DO178B in §6.4 states that: *'the second objective is to demonstrate with a high degree of confidence that errors which could lead to unacceptable failure conditions as determined by the system safety assessment have been removed'*. This may be an obscure requirement as it implicitly asks for the COTS developer to provide an argument about the operation of the component. However since explicitly capturing an argument is a practice that mostly appears in the UK, it is not expected that a COTS component will be accompanied by a document resembling a safety case. Justification of this requirement may include design rationale documents, mitigation strategies, and rationale about the coverage and the types of testing. For example, identification and handling of potential exceptions is in accordance with this clause. During CertPack evaluation, the COTS provider and the system developer should establish the amount of information (and their sources) related to this. Moreover the developer should plan for their COTS safety analysis without the assumption that a COTS component bearing a DO178B certification seal will need no further examination.

4.2.7 Documentation of Activities

Question. How are the earlier lifecycle activities (e.g. architecture) documented?

Documentation of activities is (in any project) important as it allows tracing rationale and how the CertPack evidence supports the high level COTS requirements. Good documentation is indicative of a good and well structured development process. This is expected to be a non-issue. However any unclear information about the COTS provider's documentation activities should raise serious concerns about the trustworthiness of the COTS vendor.

4.2.8 Compliance Matrix

Question. Has the existence of a compliance matrix against the standard under which the CertPack been certified?

A compliance matrix is indicative of the degree of compliance of the COTS component with a particular standard. Although in a process based standard a compliance matrix can be seen as an overview of assurance, in a goal based standard this would not make any actual contribution to assurance. Similarly to documentation of activities, this is indicative of the quality of the COTS provider's certification process.

4.2.9 Traceability Rationale

Question. Does traceability of requirements to evidence include rationale or is it just links between requirements at different abstraction levels?

Traceability of requirements allows identification of the contribution of low level evidence (provided by the CertPack) towards establishing assurance about high level requirements of the COTS component. However a mere representation of links is not the most someone can get from the documentation. Existence of rationale between links can provide significant support to the assurance team. Rationale between requirements captures the justification between design decisions. For example consider a high level performance requirement being broken to low level requirements about the scheduler and memory management. Capturing the rationale in this association will allow analysts to understand how the low level parts of the component support the high level requirement, justifying the design of the COTS component.

Design rationale is an integral part of the safety case argument as it constitutes the basis on which the argument is developed, and can help identify the assurance strategy communicated in the safety case (e.g. use of redundancy to address an availability requirement). Depending on the detail of the rationale provided, it can allow safety engineers to specify the assurance strategy of the safety case from the early stages. This can then enable the safety engineers to allocate evidence under the appropriate argument strand. Traceability rationale is not something that can definitely be expected in a CertPack: COTS vendors may not want to reveal this information. Moreover, even if they do, such information may be cryptic, encompassed in documents explaining the overall implementation strategy of the COTS component. It is preferable if the assurance team has an understanding of the safety arguments involving the COTS component, so that they can probe the

COTS vendor for specific rationale. This would require at least a basic skeleton of the safety case argument to be developed before the CertPack evaluation.

4.2.10 Mixed Integrity Evidence

Question. Does the CertPack include evidence for partition/support for mixed DAL software running alongside on the same processor?

This question probes for evidence on partitioning that will support assurance on the operation of the system running applications of different assurance (integrity in DO178B) levels. Partitioning is a common approach to overcome the problem of running applications of different integrity levels. System developers should be careful about this type of evidence and require as much clarification as possible. Even if evidence is provided, developers should enquire about the operational assumptions made when the COTS was tested. The developer's use of partitioning should comply with any assumptions made when evidence was generated.

4.2.11 Field Evidence

Question. Is there field evidence from other clients? If so, how is this knowledge communicated? Is the field evidence sufficient to create a probability argument?

Field evidence involves evidence gathered from existing and previous clients using the COTS component. This includes feedback provided to the COTS developer including errors identified by the customer, and experience using the component. Although it would be difficult for the system developer (using the COTS) to access this information directly from other clients, the COTS vendor will ideally have established processes to evaluate the feedback and improve/correct the COTS component or issue good practice guides.

Moreover a large user base would (theoretically) provide a big enough sample to probabilistically assess the operation (failure rate) of the COTS component. However there are two significant problems with this; firstly it would be very difficult to assure that the COTS clients would provide reliable and accurate data. Secondly, if the data could be recorded reliably, a probability argument would be possible. However, this argument would be of low relevance (and hence contribute little to the overall system assurance) since each client would use the COTS component in a different operational context (e.g. different configuration). It is suggested that developers do not create a field evidence argument. Nevertheless claims can be made about the trustworthiness of the COTS vendor given an extensive user base.

4.2.12 Update Process

Question. How is the CertPack updated when the product is updated or when new problems are found?

As with any system, a COTS component undergoes continuous evaluation due to the vendor's quality process and due to feedback from clients. As a result the product is updated. A safety argument about the quality of the COTS component (among others) would also appeal to the update process of the component and the effectiveness of the vendor in identifying and correcting errors, and notifying clients using the COTS. In certain cases when there are only small changes the CertPack is updated instead of being reproduced. This should happen without inconsistencies, maintaining the quality and hence the assurance contribution (to the safety argument) of the CertPack.

In case a COTS component carries the DO178B certification the Software Assurance Plan describes in detail the problem reporting and corrective action. This should include a description of the problem recording and tracking system, but also the configuration control board.

Another aspect of this issue is the classification of a problem. It is common practice for COTS vendors to assess the significance of the identified problems and suggest corrective action accordingly. For example, a problem that is considered critical will require immediate update, also changing the version of the COTS component. For a problem that is considered less critical or minor the COTS vendor may alert users about it but not correct it until the planned update of the component. However a problem that was considered minor may be critical for the operational context of the system. Hence developers will need to establish a process to assess the severity of each identified issue and request the issue to be reclassified as critical (and hence to be corrected). If this cannot be done then the issue has to be mitigated either by design (architecture) or procedures. The latter will have further impact on operations and will require full safety re-evaluation.

Finally, system developers should also enquire about the vendor's processes for alerting users when a problem is found.

4.2.13 Non-Functional Requirements

Question. Is there evidence about non-functional requirements [sic]?

Non functional requirements [sic][1] is a term given to describe requirements that usually focus on attributes such as performance, reliability and safety, as opposed to requirements that entirely on functionality. Such system properties are related to

---

[1] The term is considered by the authors as not representing all cases of requirements described by it. There can be cases when in order to achieve a non functional requirement, design and implementation of functionality is required (e.g. voting for reliability).

the high level safety requirements of a system. For example consider how the reliability of an aircraft's Head-Up Display (HUD) can affect the overall platform safety. Any evidence regarding these system properties may potentially benefit the safety case development. The term non-functional requirement is used to describe requirements regarding many system attributes such as human factors and performance. Even if such evidence is provided potential risks include completeness of such tests and their coverage (ideally they need to cover the operational context of the COTS component on the developer's system).

4.2.14 Tools

Question. Is the product accompanied by any tools? If so, are the tools qualified?

COTS products are usually accompanied by tools that help the system developers use the COTS component. However one risk with tools is that they can be Trojan horses for the system. A poor quality tool may result in errors in how the COTS component is used. This may happen despite the fact that the COTS itself is certified.

Compilers in particular are a type of tool often under scrutiny. A number of COTS components use compilers that have undergone formal analysis. Other cases may include verification and testing of the produced code but not the compiler itself. The system developer should clarify which tools are certified. An argument about the suitability of the tools used can be a part of the system safety case. Again in this case the wide user base of a component could help establish a quantitative argument about the reliability of the tools. Contrary to field evidence, such an argument would be relevant as all developers will use the tools in a very similar (if not identical) context.

5 Conclusions

Use of a COTS component can provide a number of advantages to the development process of a system. A process was adopted to integrate a COTS component. Part of this process involves evaluation of the CertPack, a portfolio of evidence assuring the reliable operation of the COTS component. It is this evidence that will ultimately be used to support the safety argument of the system's safety case. Having a defined process allows detailed work packages to be defined against which more precise estimates can be created. Use of a generic set of evidence raises a number of challenges regarding the degree of assurance that can be provided to the system safety argument. Any shortcomings of the CertPack may have significant impact on system development in terms of the assurance with which safety claims about the system can be made. This will have further ramifications to the cost and timeliness of the project. A CertPack constitutes a risk that needs to be evaluated and addressed early. Developing the process has also identified some issues constituting potential key risks for the project such as the CertPack evidence being incorrect, incomplete or insufficient, which can be incorporated in the project plan. These issues are presented as questions that can be asked to the COTS vendor during initial meetings. Probing the CertPack with these issues provided an opportunity to flag certain areas of the CertPack as potential risks. By undertaking the analysis of the Cert Pack early in the project lifecycle, these risks can be effectively managed. For example an issue that does not occur can be retired and an issue that occurs can be addressed with least impact on the critical path using contingency. Collaboration with the COTS vendor was established to address these issues before committing to the particular version of the COTS component.

References

Despotou G, Kelly T (2008). Investigating the use of argument modularity to optimise through-life system safety assurance. In Proc 3rd IET International Conference on System Safety (ICSS) 2008, Birmingham

Despotou G, Bennett M, Kelly T (2009) Supporting through life safety assurance of COTS based upgrades. In Proc peer reviewed track 27th System Safety Society (SSS) International System Safety Conference (ISSC), Huntsville AL

HSE (2001) Reducing risks protecting people. HSE Books, Norwich

MoD (2005) Safety management requirements for defence systems. Defence Standard 00-56 issue 4. Ministry of Defence

Weaver RA (2004) The safety of software – constructing and assuring argument. PhD thesis YCST-2004-01, Department of Computer Science, University of York

A Way to Successful Hazard Management

Gabriele Schedl, Werner Winkelbauer and Alexander Wendt

Frequentis AG

Vienna, Austria

Abstract The key point of every safety process is hazard identification and management. This is required by many related standards and shall be performed for every project. It's often a challenge to find all possible hazards in advance but it's possibly an even bigger challenge to manage all hazards over a wide range of products and projects.

This paper describes in brief the development and the current state of an organization wide hazard management and tracking system which allows for efficient hazard handling. The goal is to act well in advance instead of reacting to problems.

The hazard process defines the 'lifecycle' of a hazard: the phases, tasks and responsibilities from its detection to its closing. The state of each hazard is published in the organization's intranet and can be viewed by every employee, which makes the processing of hazards a transparent activity, where everyone has to participate actively or passively.

The gained knowledge about hazards is that way directly transferred to new projects where they might apply and possibly contribute to accidents. Additionally, findings about potential failure mechanisms are used for the derivation of checklists, to get another step ahead and prevent hazards from the very beginning of the development of a product.

1 Introduction

The key to system safety is the management of hazards. To effectively manage hazards, one must understand hazard theory and the identification of hazards. Hazard analysis provides the basic foundation for system safety. It is performed to identify hazards, their effects and causal factors. It is further used to determine system risk, the significance of hazards and to establish design measures that will eliminate or mitigate the identified hazards.

C. Dale, T. Anderson (eds.), *Making Systems Safer*, DOI 10.1007/978-1-84996-086-1_15,
© Springer-Verlag London Limited 2010

1.1 Hazard Definition

According to MIL-STD-882D (Department of Defense 2000), a Hazard is 'Any real or potential condition that can cause injury, illness, or death to personnel; damage to or loss of a system, equipment or property; or damage to the environment.' A less formal, but helpful definition might be: 'A Hazard is an accident, waiting to happen', for example oil on a staircase. A further, practical definition is: 'A Hazard is a physical condition at the system boundary of the regarded system which could lead to an accident'. Herein it's clearly stated that a hazard is defined at the system boundary. Figure 1 provides the connection between system functions, the possible failure modes and their causal factors within the considered system and several hazards at the system boundary, which then can lead to possible accidents.

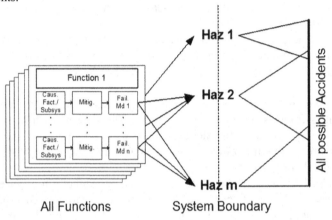

Fig. 1. Definition of Hazard

1.2 Core System Safety Process

Several standards define different safety lifecycle models, whereas the core of them is always similar. As soon as hazards are identified, their risk has to be assessed and hazard mitigation methods have to be established to mitigate the risk as low as necessary. These mitigation methods are brought into the system design via safety requirements. Hazards are continually tracked until they can be closed.

The core system safety process can therefore be reduced to: Hazard Identification -> Hazard Risk Assessment -> Hazard Risk Control -> Hazard Risk Verification-> Hazard Identification... (Ericson 2005). This is a closed-loop process where Hazards are identified and tracked until acceptable closure action is implemented and verified.

The relationship between the System Development Lifecycle and the Safety Achievement Process is illustrated in Figure 2. The first row represents a generic and simplified version of the development process. In the second row, the main phases of the safety process are shown, which start with the Safety Process Initialisation and continue with the Functional Hazard Assessment (FHA), the Preliminary System Safety Assessment (PSSA) and the System Safety Assessment (SSA). Below each main phase, the primary question to be answered during this phase is shown.

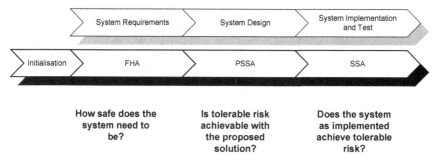

Fig. 2. System Development Lifecycle and the Safety Process

The first step in the safety process comprises identification of safety relevant functions within the domain/environment in which the system will be operated.

These functions are the basis for the Functional Hazard Assessment (FHA), for the identification of possible hazards. In workshops with experts – to combine technical, domain and safety know-how – various techniques are applied. This includes brainstorming, use of historical data and functional failure modes and effects analysis to identify possible failure modes, their operational effects and the respective severity of the worst credible outcome. Based on the safety-relevant failure modes, potential hazards are determined and respective risks are allocated according to the risk matrix. The FHA leads to derivation of top level hazards.

Derived safety requirements are defined to reduce those risks which are not in the acceptable area of the matrix and to address safety issues emerging during discussions in the workshops. These safety requirements form a mandatory part of the system requirements and have to be fulfilled and verified accordingly.

1.3 Practical Problems

It is often the case that a system safety program, and therefore hazard management, is required for a specific project.

A typical requirement is given in MIL-STD-882D: 'The contractor shall perform and document a system hazard analysis to identify hazards and assess the risk of the total system design, including software, and specifically of the subsystem interfaces.' But it would be very inefficient to perform such analyses purely on a project by project basis. If we consider each project as a stand-alone, we would miss many important results from former analyses and experience based data from similar projects.

Adequate fulfillment of such a safety process requirement is a crucial point for system safety. It is often a big challenge to find 'all' possible hazards. How can we be sure to have a complete hazard list as input for further activities? And how can we manage the different results of all performed safety analyses to have a set of hazards as an input for the next project? Detailed domain know-how is necessary to perform these tasks and to estimate the operational risk for each hazard.

A further problem is the management of hazards in already fielded systems, especially if new hazards arise after handover of the system from the supplier to the user. It is definitely a challenge to manage hazards over the whole lifecycle.

To deal with these problems we discuss in this paper the definition and implementation of a companywide 'hazard process' in our organization. This process is part of the company's internal mandatory processes, and defines the 'lifecycle' of a hazard: all the steps, responsibilities and time frames from its detection to its complete elimination. The state of each hazard is published in the organization's intranet and can be viewed by every employee, which makes the processing of hazards a transparent activity where everyone has to participate actively or passively.

2 Principles of the Organization Wide Hazard Log

The most important safety tool that was developed in the last years is the organization wide hazard tracking and logging system, where the responsibility of every single employee is emphasized.

The Hazard Log is a database containing all our systems (independent from the lifecycle phase) and all known hazards. 'Known Hazard' in this case means that this problem has already occurred, either during development or operation. We call these hazards 'Technical Hazards' to distinguish between such already emerged safety relevant technical problems and theoretical hazards, derived from safety analyses. After contract award, new projects are entered immediately into this database. Every hazard, once defined, stays in the hazard log, even if it is closed companywide, just as a project remains in it over its whole lifecycle.

2.1 Main Goal

The main goal is to act well in advance instead of reacting to problems in operation, which is both a safety benefit and a commercial one, as we all know about the cost explosion of problem solving over lifecycle time.

Hazards are therefore assigned to all projects or systems where they might possibly contribute to accidents. As soon as a new project is acquired, all known hazards of the corresponding product family are checked for applicability. All open hazards of the same product are automatically assigned.

The Hazard Log Database provides the central record of the Frequentis-wide Hazard Tracking process. It provides a means by which the resolution of safety issues is monitored. The Frequentis-wide hazard process is a continuous assessment of all projects (and respectively their delivered systems) and products, which enable the identification of potential hazards, the classification according to their severity and probability, the assessment of their tolerability and the initiation and tracking of corresponding risk resolution activities.

Defined hazards have to be taken into account at development as soon as possible to assure elimination at the next product release.

2.2 Main Input

The most important Safety input is information!

All employees are responsible for passing on any safety-related information to the safety management department. A company-wide error database, called ERRSYS, is used for error handling and as a basis for safety data. Every entry can be classified in four severity levels and as company-wide, system-specific or project-specific. The ERRSYS database is regularly checked by the safety team for any potential new hazard.

2.3 Management Responsibilities

The unique hazard performance figures, which we use as a part of a management information system, give all departmental managers quick and concise information about the safety status of our systems.

There are three main hazard performance figures:

- Performance figure 1 is related to project management and gives the number of hazards in a project not eliminated one year after finding a technical solution, divided by the total number of projects. The objective for this figure is 0.1.
- Performance figure 2 is related to the development and gives the number of hazards without released technical solution six months after classification. The objective for this figure is zero.
- Finally, performance figure 3 is a combined measure for project management and development to cover the number of hazards where actions for all affected projects are not decided within three months after finding a technical solution. The objective for this metric is zero as well.

Sometimes far-reaching system changes are necessary to eliminate a hazard. This can be, e.g. a bug fix in the operating system or a hardware redesign. The average release time of those changes is in the order of months. This can cause troubles, as special applications in projects have to be adapted again. Therefore it is important to give motivation to solve the problems as fast as possible.

Every head of a project management group signs in his annual business contract the firm intention to reach a hazard-free state of his projects according to hazard performance figure 1 as well as the heads of the development departments sign the same for performance figure 2. In addition the hazard status and all activities associated with hazards are reviewed by the Quality Manager and the Safety Manager as a condition for every delivery release. To give managers a personal incentive to keep the number of open hazards down, their bonuses depend partly on these figures.

To emphasize the importance of hazard management, a quarterly report is produced, in which the current status of the hazard log and the defined actions are reported to the executive board and the top management of the company.

3 Tools and Templates used in the Hazard Process

3.1 Hazardlog Database [HDB]

The Hazardlog Database is an SQL based database, which is accessible with a PHP user interface. Each user has his own user name and password. Two types of roles are available: administrator and user. The administrator has access to all settings in the database whereas the user role only has restricted permissions to change settings or delete projects or hazards. Only members of the Safety Management Department have the administrator or user role assigned.

The database itself consists of

- a table with all relevant project data, especially project ID data and system data
- a table with information relating to each hazard number e.g. class, responsible engineer and ERRSYS number of the parent ticket
- a table with all project specific hazards.

All tables are accessible through forms, which are adapted if required. From the project detail form it possible to open or close hazards in the current project as well as in the child projects, all available project data is shown and each hazard is linked with ERRSYS.

3.2 Error Tracking Tool ERRSYS

ERRSYS is the error, change request, open item description and administration tool (FRACAS tool), which is used throughout Frequentis. ERRSYS features the tracing and documentation of all errors – hardware, software or other errors – that occur within product development or project lifecycle, from the integration phase onward. It is accessible by every employee via the company wide intranet.

From the system integration phase onward optionally, from the start of the system tests onward mandatorily, all functional deviations, without exception, have to be logged in ERRSYS. The employee encountering the deviation adds the new ERRSYS report. Once an error has been detected, it is permanently stored. Its status can be retrieved at any time.

3.3 Hazards Checklist

The purpose of the hazards checklist is to prevent hazards in a new project that are similar to hazards already known in other systems. Checklist questions are derived from existing hazards, asking for the root cause mechanisms of those hazards. For every product family the applicability of the checklist questions is decided. All applicable questions have to be answered prior to a product release to increase the awareness of the developers of the possible problems and to avoid their implementation.

4 Hazard Processing

Figure 3 provides an overview of the Hazard Process according to the internal process management.

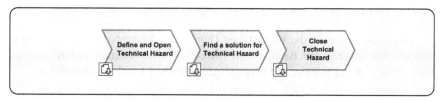

Fig. 3. Simplified Hazard Process

4.1 Hazard Definition Phase

Everybody, including the customer, is responsible for considering safety implications and identifying possible hazards. The central contact point for collecting and processing this information is the Safety Management Department.

Supplementary activities for this phase are:

- Regular reviews of Frequentis's internal project progress reports to the Project Management Board
- Project-specific hazard analysis activities in accordance with the associated Statements of Work

As soon as a new hazard has been identified and reported to the Safety Management Department, the hazard is to be entered in the Hazard Log. This recording action is mandatory, independent of the risk class associated with the hazard.

The Hazard Log is continuously maintained. All relevant changes in the status of actions and hazards are immediately entered in the current version of the log. All changes to the entries will be recorded in a way so that it is transparent why the changes were made.

4.1.1 System/Hazard Cross Reference Analysis

For each new hazard, a system/hazard cross reference analysis is carried out. With this task, the applicability of a new hazard is investigated for each system under the supervision of the hazard log. This analysis results in the adaptations of the primary hazard entries, and initiates the respective project specific actions.

4.1.2 Hazard Reporting

Newly identified hazards are distributed after their definition as hazard according to the hazard process to the management boards and to all possible affected employees.

The current status of the Hazard Log Database is presented in the Frequentis intranet. All hazards can be found in ERRSYS in the internal hazard project. There, every hazard number and every project specific hazard is administered.

4.1.3 Hazard Classification

For our internal Hazard Log we have defined an appropriate risk matrix, shown in Table 3. For products, hazards have to be eliminated at all subsequent releases. In projects, the matrix enables hazard elimination according to the ALARP principle. The categories are defined in Table 1, derived and adapted from MIL-STD-882D, extended with specific definitions for our application. The severity definitions differ according to the domain-specific needs. Table 2 shows the probability definitions.

The combination of the hazard severity and the hazard probability defines the hazard risk classes. These classes are listed in Table 4 with different levels of tolerability: Class A forms the intolerable area of the risk matrix, Class B and C the tolerable area and class D means acceptable risk.

Table 1. Hazard Severity Levels

Category	Definition
CATASTROPHIC	General: A failure, which may cause death, system loss, or severe property or environmental damage. Specific ATC: The mission of the system is unavailable for an unacceptable period of time. There are no back-up facilities to compensate the absence of the mission. Examples ATC Applications: Total loss of the Core Switch for more than one minute. Specific Voice Recording: The mission of the system is unavailable for an unacceptable period of time. There are no back-up facilities to compensate the absence of the mission. Specific Maritime: The mission of the system is unavailable for an unacceptable period of time. There are no back-up facilities to compensate the absence of the mission. Specific Public Safety: The mission of the system is unavailable for an unacceptable period of time. There are no back-up facilities to compensate the absence of the mission. Examples: 1) If an emergency call is no group call and is lost without notification, then the mission of the system is not fulfilled. Specific Public Transport: The mission of the system is unavailable for more than three minutes. There are no back-up facilities to compensate the absence of the mission. Examples: Total loss of the Ground Switching Centre (GSC), detraction of the GSC in a way that no operational service is possible for more than three minutes.

Category	Definition

General: A failure, which may cause severe injury, major system, property or environmental damage.

Specific: The mission can be re-established within an acceptable period of time, either by reconfiguration of the system or by use of back-up facilities. The use of these alternatives leads to physical distress or higher workload such that the personnel operating the system cannot be relied on to perform their tasks accurately or completely.

Examples ATC Applications: Loss of a specific number of controller positions, loss of roles, total loss of the Core Switch for less than one minute.

Specific Voice Recording: The mission can be re-established within an acceptable period of time, either by reconfiguration of the system or by use of back-up facilities (e.g.: 50% of channels lost, no replay possible, loss of data, etc.).

Specific Maritime: The mission can be re-established within an acceptable period of time, either by reconfiguration of the system or by use of back-up facilities. The use of these alternatives leads to physical distress or higher workload such that the personnel operating the system cannot be relied on to perform their tasks accurately or completely.

Specific Public Safety: The mission can be re-established within an acceptable period of time, either by reconfiguration of the system or by use of back-up facilities. The use of these alternatives leads to physical distress or higher workload such that the personnel operating the system cannot be relied on to perform their tasks accurately or completely.

Examples PS:

1) If an emergency call is a group call and is lost or not noticeable on an Operator Position (OP), but can be handled by another OP.

Specific Public Transport: The mission can be re-established within three minutes, either by reconfiguration of the system or by use of back-up facilities. The use of these alternatives leads to physical distress or higher workload such that the personnel operating the system cannot be relied on to perform their tasks accurately or completely.

Examples: Decrease of important functions of the GSC and/or deactivation or reduction of important functions of the GSM-R Application Server e.g. breakdown of the routing server (fallback to default routing).

CRITICAL

Category	Definition
MARGINAL	General: A failure, which may cause marginal injury, marginal system, property or environmental damage. Specific: The failure will result in reduction of system capability/performance or mission degradation. The users can maintain the mission of the system by other means. Examples ATC Applications: Loss of a communication path, e.g.: loss of one radio interface or one controller working position. Specific Voice Recording: The failure will result in reduction of system capability/performance or mission degradation up to a defined critical level (e.g.: loss of single IF, monitoring system, housekeeping jobs, archiving, instant replay, etc.). Specific Maritime: The failure will result in reduction of system capability/performance or mission degradation. The users can maintain the mission of the system by other means. Specific Public Safety: The failure will result in reduction of system capability/performance or mission degradation. The users can maintain the mission of the system by other means. Specific Public Transport: The failure will result in reduction of system capability/performance or mission degradation. The users can maintain the mission of the system by other means. Examples: Deactivation or reduction of medium or lower level system functions, faulty GSM-R Dispatcher.
NEGLIGIBLE	General: A failure, which does not cause injury, system, property or environmental damage. Specific: The failure will result in unscheduled maintenance or repair. The failure has no effect to a required operational or mission function. Examples ATC Applications: Loss of redundant system components. Specific Voice Recording: The failure will result in unscheduled maintenance or repair. The failure has no effect to a required operational or mission function. (e.g. loss of redundant system component) Specific Maritime: The failure will result in unscheduled maintenance or repair. The failure has no effect to a required operational or mission function. Specific Public Safety: The failure will result in unscheduled maintenance or repair. The failure has no effect to a required operational or mission function. Specific Public Transport: The failure will result in unscheduled maintenance or repair. The failure has no effect to a required operational or mission function. Examples: Loss of redundant system components.

Table 2. Hazard Probability Levels

Level	Id.	Probability per h	Definition
Frequent	a	$P \geq 10^{-3}$	may occur several times a month or more often
Probable	b	$10^{-3} > P \geq 10^{-4}$	likely to occur once a year
Occasional	c	$10^{-4} > P \geq 10^{-5}$	likely to occur once in the life of the system
Remote	d	$10^{-5} > P \geq 10^{-6}$	unlikely but possible to occur in the life of the system
Improbable	e	$10^{-6} > P \geq 10^{-7}$	very unlikely to occur
Incredible	f	$10^{-7} > P$	extremely unlikely, if not inconceivable to occur

4.1.4 Decide an Initial Hazard Probability

The hazard probability always refers to a system. If a project has more sites, each site is considered as a system. The hazard probability for a project is given by the site with the highest hazard occurrence probability. Often bigger sites have a higher hazard probability than smaller sites.

In the classification in the hazard description and in the Hazardlog Database, the worst case probability of all affected projects is defined. Therefore, each system shall be individually analysed, in order to estimate the correct probability.

Table 3. Risk Matrix

	Hazard Severity			
Hazard Probability	CATASTROPHIC	CRITICAL	MARGINAL	NEGLIGIBLE
Frequent	A	A	B	B
Probable	A	B	B	C
Occasional	B	B	C	C
Remote	B	C	C	D
Improbable	C	C	D	D
Incredible	C	D	D	D

Table 4. Risk Class Interpretation

Risk Class	Interpretation
A	Intolerable
B	Undesirable and shall only be accepted when risk reduction is impracticable
C	Tolerable with the endorsement of either the Project Manager together with the internal ordering party or the Safety Director
D	Acceptable with the endorsement of the normal project reviews

4.1.6 Hazard Decision

A problem is decided to become a Technical Hazard within the companywide hazard tracking system if the following criteria are fulfilled:

- The problem is safety relevant.
- The problem is present in more than one project.
- The problem risk class is A, B or C. Class D is considered as acceptable.

Then the data collection starts to complete problem reports regularly:

- Original cause – from Hazard Owner
- Complete failure description with technical effect

- All affected systems and affected range of known file versions
- All identified affected projects.

Original cause, complete failure description and affected systems are often provided by the hazard owner. This is usually a member of the development team, who has the technical knowledge for the specific problem.

4.2 Solution Finding Phase

4.2.1 Usage of ERRSYS for Hazard Management

In order to improve the efficiency and transparency of the hazard processing, changes in the handling of hazards have been introduced to enable hazard processing for a high number of fielded systems. All hazards open in the Hazard Log will be tracked through ERRSYS.

There are some advantages for Project Managers from using the ERRSYS records for hazard tracking:

- A hazard can be treated like an error, which means that the handling, update and closing can be done in a familiar environment.
- It is possible to get an overview of which projects have a certain hazard assigned or closed, in order to check how the problem was solved by other projects.
- The due dates of the hazards in the projects can be easily extracted.
- Through filtering, it is possible to extract a list of all hazards that fulfil certain criteria, e.g. all hazards, which are assigned to a certain Project Manager.
- If a Project Manager changes project, he can transfer the hazard to the new Project Manager and Safety will be notified.
- By the transfer of a project to the maintenance department, the ERRSYS number could be used as a hazard identifier, with its complete event history. This means no information loss.
- Easy access to hazard status information and which actions can be taken, in order to close the hazard.

But there are also some advantages for the Safety Management Department:

- The hazard history, actions taken and the current status are preserved in ERRSYS, which makes the tracking easier even after several years.
- No hazards are forgotten, because the due dates help safety management to monitor the hazards of the projects and to focus on projects with past due dates.

- If the hazard transfer between Project Managers is made correctly, the project lists can easily be kept up to date and the correct Project Manager is contacted regarding hazard issues.

4.2.2 Basic Structure

For each hazard number, a superior ERRSYS entry will be opened. This record contains the current hazard status and shows where to get detailed information about the hazard and its subordinated ERRSYS records in projects. This ERRSYS ticket is called the parent record for a hazard.

For each open hazard in any project, a child record is opened and linked to the parent record. This project specific record will be assigned to the responsible Project Manager. The due date of the record will be defined by the Project Manager or be set to the default value (see below). The child record contains information about how to close the hazard, its status and history.

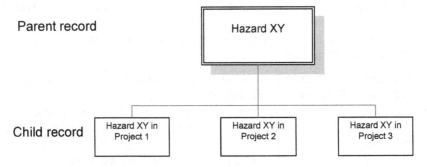

Fig. 4. The connection between parent (hazard number) and child (project) hazards

4.2.3 Project Structure in the Hazard Log

Projects are also categorized in parent projects and child projects. A parent project is an active or closed project, which is representing one or more real systems at certain locations. A product may also be a parent project, as it represents a complete system. A child project is a project derived from a parent project. This can be either if the project does not represent a whole standalone system (e.g. repair, expansions) or if a project is obsolete and replaced by a newer one (e.g. projects, which are transferred to maintenance).

In order to manage over 1,000 projects by Frequentis, projects are grouped under a parent project. The responsible Project Manager for the parent project is responsible for its child projects, too. If a hazard is opened in a child project, it is shown in the parent project as well.

4.2.4 Procedure for Projects

After definition of a new hazard all affected projects have to be opened in the Hazardlog Database, in order to open a project specific hazard in ERRSYS as the ERRSYS record is linked with the ERRSYS record in the Hazardlog Database. A parent record is created and the project specific ERRSYS record is opened by Safety. Detailed information, such as due date, operator, references, and related tickets, is added. In addition the Hazards Checklist is sent to the projects, and the respective project managers are responsible for delivering the related information in detail. All open items from the previous release or project are listed. Then the project team has to answer if the open item has been closed or not.

After finishing the action items for the project, the Project Manager reports the solution in the solution field of the ERRSYS record. It shall be detailed why the hazard is no longer opened or why the hazard can be waived (e.g. customer accepts the risk). The Project Manager sets the hazard status to 'close' and the Safety Engineer has to confirm that the solution is implemented and the argumentation is sufficient. Only the Safety Engineer is allowed to set the status of the child record to 'closed'.

The hazard is closed in the Hazard Log Database referring to the solution in the ERRSYS record.

4.2.5 Hazard Controls

In order to reduce the risk associated with a hazard As Low As Reasonably Practicable (ALARP), the appropriate measures have to be taken. These should involve considering in order of preference:

- re-specification or re-design of the system parts or functions in which the problem originates
- incorporation of safety features, which include extra functions or sub-functions to reduce the probability of occurrence of the event; these features may include redundancy, etc
- where it is not readily possible to apply one of the above methods, warning devices may be included but when calculating the revised predicted probabilities, human error should be carefully considered and analysed
- operating and training procedures to reduce workload by increasing manning levels, by increasing skill level and the degree of knowledge or by reallocating functions; analysis of the effects of operating and training procedures should be carried out and should be referenced in the risk reduction records (e.g. warnings in supporting documentation incorporated)
- attaching warning notices and signs to equipment to warn users of the hazards.

4.2.6 Communication of Hazards

Internally, Frequentis uses the Hazard Log to communicate hazards to all affected persons or groups.

In case hazards or necessary controls are identified which are outside the scope of the system, these will be communicated to the customer immediately via the regular project progress reports. All identified hazards, assumptions, and necessary controls will also be explicitly listed in the Equipment Safety Case.

4.2.7 Link to Safety Requirements

All products have to go through the various phases of the safety process shown in Figure 2. One outcome of the FHA-phase is the definition of system safety functions and related failure modes. The failure modes are categorised according to the severity of their worst case end-effect. Hazards are then defined based on each safety related failure mode and assigned the worst of the related failure mode severities. Any mitigation means defined by the development team, composed of experts of all relevant groups at Frequentis, form the basis for the definition of safety requirements imposed on the product and its development.

The same team, together with the safety management department, has also defined a set of safety requirements based on past experience, product application and results of safety analysis of previous development. All these, together with the derived safety requirements have been stored in the requirements database and are input to the development process and used to define safety recommendations for the customer.

The content of the Hazards Checklist serves as an important basis for the derived safety requirements.

4.3 Hazard Closing Phase

The hazard analysis is closed if the following criteria are met:

- Problem report is completed.
- All projects are assigned in the Hazardlog Database.
- All solutions have been defined and released.

After the hazard analysis is finished, a question based on the hazard root cause failure mechanism is created and added to the hazard checklist. The Independent Verification and Validation Group (IV&V) generates a respective test case. These test cases are collected in a Hazard Test Procedure Book.

All hazards in the projects are monitored in the Hazardlog Database and in ERRSYS until the hazards are solved, waived or the system is taken out of operation.

Finally, only if all open project specific hazards are closed, the hazard itself can be closed in the database.

5 Conclusion

It has been a long way of process development to reach our current state of hazard management and there are still enough possibilities for improvement. Hazard management as well as safety management in general are qualities that cannot be implemented in a company within a few days. They have to be built up with care, with commitment from the very top of the company and with much enthusiasm and especially endurance of the involved departments. We are convinced, though, that it is worth the effort!

References

Department of Defense (2000) MIL-STD-882D, Standard Practice for System Safety
Ericson, Clifton A. (2005) Hazard Analysis Techniques for System Safety. Wiley Interscience